Contents

Trawling for Minnows

European Competition Policy and Agreements Between Firms

Damien Neven, Penelope Papandropoulos and Paul Seabright

Centre for Economic Policy Research

90–98 Goswell Road
London
EC1V 7DB
UK

Tel: (44 171) 878 2900
Fax: (44 171) 878 2999
Email: cepr@cepr.org

© Centre for Economic Policy Research, 1998

British Library Cataloguing in Publication Data
A catalogue record for this book is available from the British Library

ISBN 1 8981 28 34 0

Printed in Great Britain

QM LIBRARY
(MILE END)

List of Tables

List of Figures

Figures

Boxes

Acknowledgements

This study originated from a suggestion by David Deacon and has been made possible thanks to the financial support offered by the Centre for Economic Policy Research (CEPR) and the Office of Fair Trading in London. Paul Seabright would also like to thank the Economic and Social Research Council for financial support under its research programme on the Single European Market. Claus-Dieter Ehlermann kindly promised us the cooperation of the staff of DG-IV, of which he was then Director General. We were particularly grateful for the help and advice of Panagiotis Alevantis, Information Officer of DG-IV and editor of its admirable *Competition Policy Newsletter*. The publication of the study was carried out by the staff of the Centre for Economic Policy Research. We should like to thank Richard Portes, CEPR's Director, for his support, and Kate Millward, Tessa Ogden, Constanze Picking and Sue Chapman for consistent advice, help and encouragement.

The organization of the survey on Competition Policy carried out for two chapters in this book proved to be long and difficult, but was an exciting and challenging exercise nonetheless. The organization of the mailing was made possible by the efficient help of Michele Cincera, Patrizia Cincera, Vincenzo Ferrara, Isabel Glorieux, and Pascale Legrand.

We should like to acknowledge with particular gratitude the advice and help of William Comanor, Mathias Dewatripont, Eleanor Fox and Bruce Lyons, each of whom provided detailed comments on an entire draft of this book. Susie Currie gave us essential editorial help in Cambridge. Others whose suggestions and comments have been valuable include Lucy Crampin, Claus-Dieter Ehlermann, John Fingleton, Peter Freeman, Alberto Heimler, Bernard Hoekman, Martin Howe, Kelley Kirklin, Kai-Uwe Kühn, Stephen Martin, Patrick Rey, Fabio Sdogati, Thomas von

Ungern-Sternberg, Vincent Verouden, Ralph Winter, Bruno van Pottelsberghe de la Potterie as well as participants at a CEPR conference on European Competition Policy in Florence, at the 1997 Enter Jamboree at Tilburg University and at a Doctoral seminar in Economics jointly organised by CEME, ECARE and ULB at the Free University of Brussels. None of the above bears any responsibility for any errors of facts or opinions expressed in this book.

Foreword

The basic principles for a competition policy to create a competitive economic environment in the European Union were set out 40 years ago, in Articles 85 and 86 of the Treaty of Rome. The European Commission's Annual Reports on Competition Policy display, however, a broad, even bewildering, set of objectives, and their priorities have shifted considerably over the period. This book examines how far modern economic analysis can clarify the aims of public intervention in the process of competition among firms and analyses the various means of achieving those aims.

The authors' style is lively, but their coverage is broad and deep. They examine what the academic literature says about the effects on competition of agreements between firms. They then analyse the Commission's procedures and decisions over the past decade. Finally, they assess the effectiveness of these procedures in implementing the policies to which the Commission is, in principle, committed. The authors then offer their own clear, often controversial, recommendations for reform. They have produced a book that is unique in its scope and depth. It is analytically sound, informative, and very practical in its conclusions.

The authors understand well the legal and the economic context of the issues. The resulting text will be valuable to practitioners, academics and analysts alike. It is especially rewarding for us to have the opportunity again to publish work arising from collaboration between Damien Neven and Paul Seabright. Their two previous titles published by CEPR: *Competition Policy and the Transformation of Central Europe* (Fingleton, Fox, Neven and Seabright, 1996) and *Merger in Daylight: The Economics and Politics of European Merger Control* (Neven, Nuttall and Seabright, 1993) were very well received and highly influential. I have every expectation that this book will continue that success.

The idea for this volume originated from a suggestion by David Deacon, to whom the authors are indebted, though he is not in any way responsible for their analysis or conclusions. For financial support, we are grateful to the Foreign and Commonwealth Office; the Office of Fair Trading; and the Economic and Social Research Council. For the timely, efficient publication of this title, I am grateful to all CEPR staff, particularly Sue Chapman, Kate Millward and Justine Supple.

Richard Portes
President
Centre for Economic Policy Research

May 1998

Executive Summary

This book examines the policy of the European Union towards agreements between firms from three perspectives. First, it considers what the literature in industrial economics has to say about the effects of such agreements on competition, and about the consequent rationale for public intervention. Second, it examines the legal framework and the decisions of the European Commission and the European Court, asking to what extent these are consistent with the recommendations that emerge from the economic literature. Third, it looks at the procedures of the Commission and the way it undertakes investigations and reaches decisions, in order to see to what extent these procedures represent an appropriate means of implementing a defensible policy.

Chapter 1 introduces the book and looks at the goals of European competition policy as articulated in statutes and the policy documents of the European Commission. Chapter 2 considers vertical agreements – that is, those between firms that produce complementary products. It emphasizes the importance of a clear and predictable policy that does not give unnecessary discretion to public officials, and recommends a three-stage decision procedure, in which relevant markets are first defined, then market power is assessed, and finally the impact of agreements on third parties is evaluated. It compares this with the actual decisions of the Commission, which it finds to be deficient in many important respects. In particular, the Commission uses a very narrow definition of what constitutes a restriction of competition, fails to distinguish between intra- and inter-brand competition and ends up catching many harmless agreements. The chapter concludes that the reforms aired in the recent Green Paper issued by the Commission go nowhere near far enough, and that present practice is a very long way from what realistic reforms might produce.

Chapter 3 considers explicit or implicit 'cartel' agreements that are concealed by the firms. It observes that the Commission's practice has a great deal to recommend it. In particular, the Commission and the Court seem, rightly, to look with tolerance on implicit agreements between firms which do not involve explicit coordination. Nevertheless, a particular concern arises because of the requirements imposed by the Court on the material evidence required to convict firms. Such requirements appear excessive in light of the small cost that wrongful conviction may entail in this area, and also explain the apparent lack of deterrent effect that the current policy has on cartels. A number of detailed proposals are also formulated which may help improve the Commission's analysis.

Chapter 4 focuses on horizontal agreements involving the creation of a joint venture (which account for a large proportion of horizontal cases). We suggest that it is useful to begin by comparing the joint venture with the benchmark case of full integration between the activities of the parents. If a merger of these activities would be allowed, then a joint venture should also be allowed. Conversely, if a merger would not be allowed, then there should be a presumption that the joint venture also involves serious restrictions of competition. In those circumstances, it should be deemed illegal unless it can be shown that the parents are unlikely to be able to use the joint venture as a coordination mechanism. We suggest that two conditions will be essential for this assessment: namely the extent to which the joint venture can appropriate the benefits from the pricing decisions of the parents, and the extent to which the parents will be able to capture the average profit made by the joint venture. Turning to the case law, we find that the Commission and the Court apply a very narrow and formal approach in assessing restrictions of competition and that there are many instances where agreements have been declared unlawful even though they have had negligible effects on third parties.

Chapter 4 also considers the evaluation of efficiency benefits under Article 85§3 and suggest that the Commission should focus on the benefits that are specific to joint ventures. These benefits arise from the various strategic commitment mechanisms that joint ventures can implement, regarding the management of specific assets and outputs from the joint venture. By contrast, the exemptions granted in the case law follow a rigid legal structure and often fail to consider efficiency benefits in any depth. The range of efficiency benefits that are referred to is also very wide, and some of them have only a remote link with economic efficiency.

Chapter 5 examines the procedures of the Commission, on the basis of a survey of firms that have undergone Commission investigation. It finds that in many crucial areas the Commission enjoys high levels of discretion with very little transparency. In addition the procedures are slow and cumbersome; unfortunately, however, many of the reforms that have sought to speed up the procedures have done so at the expense of even such little transparency as already exists (notably by increasing the proportion of cases settled under purely informal procedures).

Chapter 6 conducts a more careful econometric analysis of the determinants of lobbying behaviour by firms. We find that firms are more likely to lobby senior Commission officials for cases that appear 'difficult' or involve high technology; firm characteristics also determine lobbying behaviour, with significant differences between nationalities in this respect. Lobbying is also significantly more intense in cases in the transport sector.

The study concludes by recommending reforms in the decision-making criteria that would drastically reduce the number of cases needing to be examined by the Commission. This would mean that the Commission could examine the reduced number of remaining cases in a more transparent manner. These changes could be implemented without changing the Treaty but would require changes in secondary legislation and more than marginal changes in the Commission's approach. Such a sharp change in policy could be communicated through a set of published guidelines which clearly laid out the principles of the Commission's intended new practice, and recognised officially a degree of departure from some of the earlier case law. These guidelines would both increase the degree of consistency between cases, and ensure that firms were better able to foresee whether their agreements were in breach of the law.

1

Introduction

1.1   The Purpose of this Book

This book examines the competition policy of the European Commission
in the field of agreements between undertakings from three distinct perspectives. It discusses the academic literature on the effects of such
agreements, and therefore the justification for and nature of public intervention to constrain the agreements firms may freely make. It also
examines the decisions that have been made by the European
Commission in the period since 1989, considering to what extent these
decisions have been consistent with what the academic literature would
recommend. Finally, it looks at the procedures of the Commission in this
area, considering how effectively these procedures have operated to implement the policy to which the Commission is in theory committed.

The idea that the state should intervene to limit the agreements that
firms in a capitalist economy may make between themselves illustrates a
central paradox in the idea of economic competition. Freedom of contract is central to a competitive economy, and the recent history of central
planning has shown how damaging can be the consequences of excessive
or capricious state intervention in agreements between consenting adults
in private, even when these adults are corporate rather than individual
persons. However, agreements can often limit the freedom of the contracting parties to make subsequent agreements with third parties,
whether these are partners in a marriage who thereby become unable to
marry others while the original marriage remains in force, or suppliers in
an exclusive distribution agreement who are prevented thereby from supplying to other distributors within the same specified territory. Normally

it seems reasonable to apply a modified form of the presumption of freedom of contract: contracting parties are presumed to be able to foresee the restrictions imposed on their subsequent behaviour by the contract in question. Allowing them to make such contracts as they see fit is the best way on balance to assure both liberty and efficiency (even if they make mistakes on occasion it is unlikely that systematic state intervention can improve matters). Likewise, choosing one contractual partner implies excluding others, and to see this exclusion as an intrinsic restriction of competition would be absurd. However, even in the face of this presumption, there may be a number of circumstances where freedom of contract for the contracting parties has adverse implications for the wider economy and for society that are sufficiently severe to warrant public action. Competition policy is essentially an effort to identify and rectify these admittedly somewhat special circumstances.

The book is organized as follows. The remainder of this chapter provides a short background to European competition policy in the field of undertakings between firms. It discusses the legal basis for this policy, the goals which that policy has been understood to be pursuing, as revealed both by statements made by the Commission in such documents as the annual reports on competition policy, and by landmark decisions of the Commission and the European Court of Justice. Chapters 2, 3 and 4 discuss the contribution of economic analysis to understanding the nature of agreements between firms and the circumstances in which they can distort competition; they also examine recent decisions of the Commission to discover to what extent these are well founded in economic analysis. Chapter 2 discusses vertical agreements (those between firms and their customers or suppliers), while Chapters 3 and 4 discuss horizontal agreements (those between firms producing substitute goods or services). Chapter 3 looks at cartels (explicit or implicit agreements to fix prices or divide markets), while Chapter 4 considers joint ventures, examining both the circumstances in which they may distort competition and the grounds for granting them exemption under the provisions of Article 85§3.

The distinction between vertical and horizontal agreements is not only conventional, but it is also very useful. For, as we explain in Chapter 2, whether the agreement is horizontal or vertical provides a powerful basis for determining the burden of proof in any argument about its likely effects on competition. Parties to horizontal agreements have much more reason to connive in each other's exercise of market power, while parties to vertical agreements will tend to have an interest in limiting the market power exercised by each other. Given the limitations on the capacities of competition authorities to pursue investigations, and the imperfect information available to them, quite different investigative strategies seem appropriate in the two types of case. Each chapter, therefore, compares the nature of the appropriate strategy suggested by economic analysis, with the strategy that appears actually to have been followed by the Commission (the European Union body charged with both investigation and decision).

In doing so we have faced a number of difficulties. First there is the fact that the confidentiality of the case material means that the strategy must be inferred from published decisions, which include less information than that available to the Commission itself (and which in any case cover only a small subset of the total cases investigated by the Commission, although probably including most of the interesting and challenging ones). Our assessment cannot, therefore, be interpreted as a judgement as to whether the Commission decided correctly in any particular case. What we are doing instead is to use the evidence of a number of cases to infer the character of the underlying rule the Commission is following in investigating cases and taking decisions about them. We then assess the consistency of this rule, both in the sense of its conformity to economic principles and in the sense of its consistency of application from one case to another (one might call these *external* and *internal* consistency respectively). Any inconsistencies we find cannot, by themselves, show that the Commission has been mistaken. It is desirable, however, that the implementation of competition policy be an accountable process, so inconsistencies are of concern both in themselves and because they call for some kind of explanation.

A second difficulty arises because the analysis of decisions over a period of time to support judgements about the implicit decision rule being followed by the Commission requires the assumption that the rule itself has not changed over this period. We have, therefore, faced a trade-off: analysing cases over a longer period of time gives more evidence on which to base our inferences, but it also runs the risk of attributing inconsistency to a policy which has evolved over the period in response to various pressures, quite possibly in a beneficial direction. We have chosen to focus primarily on cases since the beginning of 1989, though occasionally referring to earlier cases that illustrate aspects of the Commission's procedure that still appear to be relevant. Appendix 1 shows details of the cases covered in this way.

Chapter 5 examines the procedure of the Commission by means of a survey of firms subject to investigation. Once again and for similar reasons we have confined our attention to those firms that were subject to investigation after the beginning of 1989. Our purpose in this chapter is somewhat different from that in earlier chapters. Rather than examine the reasoning behind decisions, we investigate the procedure that determines how decisions are taken, in order to evaluate the efficiency of this procedure and to identify any biases to which it may be subject.

Chapter 6 of the book looks in more detail at the evidence from the survey about the ways in which firms seek to influence the procedure in order to ensure outcomes favourable to themselves. It includes an econometric analysis of the determinants of lobbying behaviour.

Chapter 7 briefly draws together the threads of the earlier chapters and concludes with implications for policy.

1.2   The Principles of European Competition Policy

When the founding members of the European Economic Community signed the Treaty of Rome in 1957, their wish to create a competitive economic environment was clearly stated in the third article of the Treaty. Indeed, Article 3§f stipulates that the action of the Community will aim at the 'institution of a system ensuring that competition in the Common Market is not distorted'. Much subsequent discussion has turned on what the distortion of competition might mean. To achieve the aim of the Treaty it was necessary to specify a competition policy more precisely. Articles 85 and 86 of the Treaty of Rome set out the basic principles. Each of these articles is concerned with one of the two types of behaviour monitored by competition policy, i.e. cooperative behaviour (formal or tacit agreements) and the abusive exercise of market power.

1.2.1   Article 85

In brief, Article 85§1[1] prohibits all agreements between firms that affect trade between Member States and whose object or effect is to prevent, restrict or distort competition. Some examples of prohibited agreements are also given, such as price-fixing agreements, market-sharing agreements and discrimination. In the formulation of Article 85, it is very clear that European competition policy is intended to promote and facilitate the integration of European markets. Due to this transnational aspect, the only agreements that are concerned by the provisions of the European competition policy are those that affect trade between Member States.

An agreement has to meet two conditions to be prohibited under Article 85§1. An agreement (or a concerted practice) is prohibited if:

1. it affects trade between Member States;
2. its object or its effect is to restrict competition inside the Common Market.

Some types of agreements are, however, exempted from the prohibition as long as they satisfy a number of conditions set out in Article 85§3. These conditions are supposed to have beneficial effects that outweigh the detrimental impact of the agreement on competition. In order to be exempted, an agreement must contribute to the improvement of production or distribution, or to the promotion of technological progress, while leaving a fair share of the resulting profit to consumers. However, while a transfer of benefits from producers to consumers is a necessary condition for an agreement to be exempted, it is not sufficient, for two further provisions were introduced in Article 85§3. Agreements satisfying the above criteria may not be exempted if they impose on the concerned firms restrictions that are not indispensable to the attainment of these goals, and if they allow the elimination of competition for a substantial part of the product market in question.

We can already see that the formulation of Article 85 leaves scope for a variety of interpretations. It requires considerable subjective judgement and it places wide discretion in the hands of the European Commission for the process of decision making. When do we consider that an agreement *affects* trade between Member States?[2] When does an agreement *restrict* competition? And what is a *fair* share for consumers?

1.2.3 Article 87 and Regulation No. 17/62

Article 87 of the Treaty of Rome stated that the Council of Ministers had to lay down, within a period of three years, all Regulations and directives necessary for the application of Article 85. Regulation No. 17/62[3] (hereafter Regulation 17) was the first regulation adopted under Article 87. Regulation 17 determines the administrative procedure for the application of Article 85. The procedure based on it will be described in Chapter 5. The European Commission (more precisely, the Competition Directorate-General, DG-IV) is in charge of the application of competition rules. The Commission has the power to investigate and to make decisions. As Van Bael (1986) points out, 'the Commission combines the functions of prosecutor, judge and jury'. Its decisions can, however, be reviewed by the Court of Justice, and now also by the Court of First Instance.

Competition rules do not apply in the same way to all economic sectors. For example, they do not apply to the defence industry (Article 223 of the Treaty of Rome). A series of regulations determine specific procedures for some economic sectors – agriculture (Regulation No. 26/62), coal, steel, transport[4] and nuclear energy. As far as agriculture is concerned, priority was given to the application of the Common Agricultural Policy. For transport, a series of regulations have been issued, setting particular competition rules and procedures. The steel and coal industries are subject to the rules set in Articles 65 and 66 of the ECSC Treaty, though this will merge into the EC Treaty in the year 2002.

Chapter 5 of this book describes in detail the procedure of application of competition rules in the European Union. This procedure relies mainly on the provisions of Regulation 17, but its implementation has also involved other communications with legal force. A series of Commission's and Council's Regulations and Directives completes the framework of competition rules. A number of communications have also been published by the Commission in order to clarify some stages of the procedure. Finally, the case-law established by the judgements of the Court of Justice and the Court of First Instance has clarified an important number of procedural issues. Table 1.1 presents all the legal provisions determining the application of European competition rules.

1.2.4   The Institutions

For European competition matters, the decision-making body is a ministerial type administrative body whose 20 Commissioners are appointed by common accord of the governments of Member States for a five-year term. One of these Commissioners is responsible for competition and is at the head of DG-IV. DG-IV has a Director General, two Deputy Director Generals[5] and a Hearing Officer, and is divided into five Directorates (Directorates A, C, D, E, F[6]). These Directorates are in turn divided into units. DG-IV concentrates all the powers for the application of competition rules: it is in charge of the initiating, investigating and deciding stages.

National courts and national competition authorities can also apply the provisions of Article 85. The granting of individual exemptions remains, however, an exclusive right of the Commission.

Until 1988, appeals against the Commission's decisions in competition cases were brought before the European Court of Justice. Due to the overwhelming number of appeals, a Court of First Instance came into being in 1989 with the main task of dealing with these private appeals. The possibility of further appeal to the European Court of Justice is nevertheless still granted. Yet the majority of competition cases fall outside this judicial review. In fact, most of the work of the Commission under Articles 85 and 86 is never made public and may not be challenged in Courts. The control exerted over the Commission's work by the Courts applies to only a small proportion of its decisions.

The possibility of judicial review does not, therefore, significantly alter the fact that the Commission enjoys substantial discretion in the implementation of competition policy. In addition to the statutory provisions of European competition policy, it is, therefore, important to examine the Commission's own policy statements to see what light they shed on the way the Commission has approached its task.

Table 1.1 Legal provisions for the application of European competition rules (by chronological order up to end 1997)

Council Regulations
(*) = rules for transports

Regulation	Provision	Reference
No.17/62	First Regulation implementing Articles 85 and 86 (amended and completed by No.59/62, No.118/63 and No.2822/71)	OJL 13/204 of 21 February 1962
No.26/62	Art.1: Non-applicability of 85 to agriculture	OJL 30/993 of 20 April 1962
No.27/62	Sets rules concerning the form, contents and other details of applications and notifications (modified by No.1133/68, No.1699/75, No.2526/85 and No.3666/93) REPLACED BY Commission Regulation No.3385/94	OJL 35/1118 of 10 May 1962
No.141/62	Exempting transport from the application of Council Regulation No.17 (amended by No.165/65 and No.1004/65)	OJL 124/2751 of 28 November 1962
No.99/63	On the hearings provided for in Article 19§1 and 19§2 of Council Regulation No.17	OJL 127/2268 of 20 August 1963
No.19/65	Enabling regulation for the application of Article 85§3 to categories of exclusivity agreements	OJL 36/533 of 6 March 1965
No.1017/68 (*)	Sets rules for the application of competition rules to the railway transport, inland transport and waterways	OJL 175/1 of 23 July 1968
No.2821/71	Enabling regulation for the application of Article 85§3 to categories of agreements concerning the setting of norms and types, R&D cooperation and specialization (amended by No.2743/72)	OJL 285/46 of 29 December 1971
No.2988/74	Concerning limitation periods in proceedings and the enforcement of sanctions under the rules of the European Economic Community relating to transport and competition	OJL 319/1 of 29 November 1974
No.4056/86 (*)	Sets rules for the application of competition rules to the maritime transport	OJL 378/4 of 31 December 1986
No.3975/87 (*)	Sets rules for the application of competition rules to the air transport (amended by No.1284/91)	OJL 374/1 of 31 December 1987
No.3976/87 (*)	Enabling regulation of the application of Article 85§3 to the air transport (amended by No.2344/90 and No.2411/92)	OJL 374/9 of 31 December 1987
No.1534/91	Enabling regulation for the application of Article 85§3 to the insurance sector	OJL 143/1 of 7 June 1991
No.479/92 (*)	Enabling regulation for the application of Article 85§3 to agreements between liner shipping companies	OJL 55/3 of 29 February 1992

Table 1.1 Continued

Commission Regulations

Regulation	Provision	Reference	Expiration date
No.67/67	Application of 85§3 to exclusivity agreements	OJL 57/849 of 25 March 1967	
No.1629/69	Sets rules concerning notifications and complaints made under Regulation No.1017/68	OJL 209/1 of 21 August 1969	
No.1630/69	Sets rules concerning hearings under Regulation No.1017/68	OJL 209/11 of 21 August 1969	
No.1983/83	Block exemption for exculsive distribution agreements	OJL 173/1 of 30 June 1983	31 December 1997
No.1984/83	Block exemption for exclusive purchasing agreements (rectified in JOL 79/38 of 23 March 1984)	OJL 173/5 of 30 June 1983	31 December 1997
No.123/85	Block exemption for the distribution and after-sale services of motor vehicles	OJL 15/16 of 18 January 1985	30 June 1995
No.2349/84	Block exemption for patent licensing agreements (rectified in OJL 280/32 of 22 October 1985)	OJL 219/15 of 16 August 1984	31 December 1994
No.417/85	Block exemption for specialization agreements	OJL 53/1 of 22 February 1985	31 December 1997
No.418/85	Block exemption for R&D cooperation agreements	OJL 53/5 of 22 February 1985	31 December 1997
No.2671/88 (*)	Block exemption in air transport	OJL 239/9 of 30 August 1988	
No.2672/88 (*)	Block exemption for computerized reservation systems in air transport	OJL 239/13 of 30 August 1988	
No.2673/88	Block exemption for assistance services during stops	OJL 239/17 of 30 August 1988	
No.4087/88	Block exemption for franchising agreements	OJL 359/46 of 28 December 1988	31 December 1999
No.4260/88	Sets rules concerning notifications, complaints and auditions made under Regulation No.4056/86	OJL 376/1 of 31 December 1988	
No.4261/88	Sets rules concerning notifications, complaints and auditions made under Regulation No.3975/87	OJL 376/10 of 31 December 1988	
No.556/89	Block exemption for know-how licensing agreements	OJL 61/1 of 4 March 1989	31 December 1999
No.84/91	Block exemption for agreements concerning joint planning and coordination of capacity, consultations on passenger and cargo tariffs rates on scheduled air services and slot allocation in airports	OJL 10/14 of 15 January 1991	31 December 1992

Table 1.1 Continued

Regulation	Provision	Reference	Expiration date
No.3932/92	Block exemption for agreements in the insurance sector	OJL 398/7 of 31 January 1992	31 March 2003
No.151/93	Regulation extending block exemptions No.417/85, No.418/85, No.2349/84 and No.556/89	OJL 21/8 of 29 January 1993	
No.1617/93	Block exemption for agreements concerning joint planning and coordination of schedules, joint operations, consultations on passenger and cargo tariffs on scheduled air services and slot allocation at airports	OJL 155 of 26 June 1993	
No.3652/93	Block exemption for agreements concerning computerized reservation systems for air transport services	OJL 333 of 31 December 1993	
No.3385/94	On the form, content and other details of applications and notifications provided for in Council Regulation No. 17	OJL 377/28 of 31 December 1994	
No.70/95	Amendment of regulation No.2349/84 (6 month extension of the block exemption)	OJL 12/13 of 18 January 1995	30 June 1995
No.870/95	Block exemption for agreements between liner shipping companies	OJL 89/7 of 21 April 1995	22 April 2000
No.1475/95	Block exemption for motor vehicles distribution and servicing agreements	OJL 145/25 of 29 June 1995	30 September 2002
No.2131/95	Amendment of regulation No.2349/84 (6 month extension of the block exemption)	OJL 214/6 of 8 September 1995	31 December 1995
No.240/96	Block exemption for technology transfer agreements (replacing No.2349/84 and No.556/89)	OJL 31/2 of 9 February 1996	31 March 2006
No.1523/96	Regulation amending Regulation No.1617/93 (air transport)	OJL 190/11 of 31 July 1996	
No.1582/97	Amendment of Regulations No.1983/83 and No.1984/83 (2-year extension of both block exemptions)	OJ L 214/2 of 6 August 1997	31 December 1999
No.2236/97	Amendment of Regulations No.417/85 and N°418/85 (3-year extension of both block exemptions)	OJ L 306/12 of 11 November 1997	31 December 2000

Commission Decision

Subject	Provision	Reference
Hearing Officer	On the terms of reference of hearing officers in competition procedures before the Commission	OJ L 330/67 of 21 December 1994

Table 1.1 Continued

Commission Communications

Reference	Subject
OJ C 139/2921 (1962)	Notice on exclusive dealing contracts with commercial agents
OJ C 75/3 (1968)	Notice concerning agreements, decisions and concerted practices in the field of cooperation between enterprises (corrected by OJ C 84 in 1968)
OJ C 111/13 (1972)	Notice concerning imports into the Community of Japanese goods falling within the scope of the Treaty of Rome
OJ C 1/2 (1979)	Communication concerning the appreciation of subcontracting agreements under 85§1
OJ C 251/2 (1982)	Notice on procedures for applying competition rules of the EEC and ECSC Treaties: Appointment of hearing officer
OJ C 295/6 (1983)	Notice concerning notifications pursuant to Article 4 of Regulation 17
OJ C 131/2 (1984)	Communication concerning regulations No.1983/83 and No.1984/84
OJ C 17/4 (1985)	Communication concerning regulation No.123/85
OJ C 231/2 (1986) replacing OJ C 313/2 (1977)	Notice on agreements of minor importance which do not fall under 85§1
OJ C 329 (1991)	Communication completing the 1985 communication concerning No.123/85
OJ C 121/2 (1992)	Notice modifying the 1984 communication concerning regulations No.1983/83 and No.1984/83
OJ C 39/6 (1993)	Notice on cooperation between national courts and the Commission in applying Articles 85 and 86
OJ C 43/2 (1993)	Commission notice on the assessment of cooperative joint ventures pursuant to Article 85
OJ C 177 (1993)	Notice concerning procedures for communications to the Commission pursuant to Articles 4 and 5 of Commission Regulation No.1617/93
OJ C 368/20 (1994)	Notice concerning the updating of the 1986 communication on agreements of minor importance
OJ C 207/4 (1996)	Notice on the non-imposition or reduction of fines in cartel cases
OJ C 23/3 (1997)	Notice on the internal rules of procedure for processing requests for access to the file in cases under Articles 85 and 86 of the EC Treaty, Articles 65 and 66 of the ECSC Treaty and Council Regulation No.4064/89
OJ C 372 (1997)	Notice on the definition of the relevant market for the purposes of Community competition law
OJ C 372 (1997)	Notice on agreements of minor importance which do not fall under Article 85§1 of the Treaty establishing the European Community (replacing the 1986 Notice)

When reading the Annual Reports on Competition Policy published by the European Commission, it is hard to avoid being struck by the multitude of objectives that are attributed to competition policy. They are very broad, and have involved substantial shifts of emphasis over time.

A final issue concerns the extent to which the principle of subsidiarity can be said to govern the application of Article 85. Unlike in the case of the Merger Regulation, where the allocation of jurisdiction between the Commission and Member States is determined by a careful and systematic consideration of the extent of policy externalities between Member States (see Neven *et al.*, 1993), powers in respect of Article 85 have been allocated on a fairly *ad hoc* basis. The involvement of national courts and national authorities in the application of Article 85 has been particularly encouraged by the Commission. There does not appear, however, to have been any systematic consideration of whether and in what circumstances these institutions will have incentives to take the Community interest into account in applying the law. This is a difficult question to which we do not pretend to offer an answer in this book, but which remains an important one for further consideration.

1.2.5   The Aims of the European Commission in Competition Policy

1.2.5.1 The Promotion of 'Effective Competition' and Consumer Protection

The primary goals of competition policy were affirmed in the Ist Annual Report on Competition Policy in 1972 and reasserted in 1980. The beneficial effects of competition are described in the 1st Report. Competition is said to be 'the best stimulant of economic activity since it guarantees the widest possible freedom of action to all'. Competition is also said to 'enable enterprises continuously to improve their efficiency, which is the *sine qua non* for a steady improvement in living standards'. Competition is described, in other words, not only as yielding beneficial results (efficiency) but also as being a beneficial process because it is the embodiment of liberty. The latter theme (the desirability of rivalry for its own sake) is taken up again in the XVth Report (Commission, 1985), where the Commission defines the concept of 'effective' competition. The definition puts the emphasis on the freedom of action. The definition is the following: 'effective' competition 'preserves the freedom and right of initiative of the individual economic operators and it fosters the spirit of enterprise. It creates an environment within which European industry can grow and develop in the most efficient manner and at the same time take account of social goals'. This emphasis is important because it both signals and provides an explanation for the significant attention given by the Commission to contracts which may limit (or appear to limit) the freedom of parties to take independent decisions.

The link between the desirability of competition as a process and the material benefits that result from it is given only sketchy argument in the Commission's reports. The Ist Report states that 'competition policy endeavours to maintain or to create effective conditions of competition . . . (and) encourages the best possible use of productive resources for the greatest possible benefit of the economy as a whole and for the benefit, in particular, of the consumer'. Competition policy is also seen as a means of fighting inflation and promoting employment.

In addition, the concepts of equity, loyalty and fairness in competitive behaviour constitute a prominent goal of European competition policy. Competition authorities should protect that freedom of action which characterises the situation of effective competition. The concept of economic equity is discussed further in the IXth Report (1980). It involves:

1. the preservation of 'equality of opportunity';
2. of a 'great variety of situations'; and
3. consideration of the 'legitimate interests of workers, users and consumers'.

The first argument does not rely on economic considerations. Equality of opportunity, whether it takes place in a social or in an economic environment, is a principle that finds its roots in philosophical thought and has a very indirect link with 'the greater profit of the whole economy'. The second argument has a quite obscure meaning and its justification is less than clear. The third point is very important in European competition policy. The protection of consumers and the achievement of the best conditions for them constitute fundamental purposes of European competition policy. In fact, it seems reasonable to say that the promotion of consumer welfare is one of the main goals of European competition policy. At least in its declared objectives, the choice has clearly been made to favour income redistribution from producers with market power to consumers.

One additional objective that has frequently been mentioned by the Commission is the promotion of small and medium enterprises. The XVth Report argues that 'such firms are an essential and major component of a healthy competitive environment, in view of their contribution to the competitive structure of the market, their flexibility and their role in technical evolution' (Commission, 1985, p. 29). Forrester (1998) argues that this goal has made an appreciable difference to Commission policy in a number of cases.

1.2.5.2 The Monitoring of the Restructuring Process

Over the years since the 1st Report, new objectives have gradually appeared. During the crisis period that followed the two oil shocks, competition policy had to 'support an industrial policy which promotes the necessary restructuring' (Xth Report, Commission, 1980). In fact, the Commission became involved in monitoring industrial rationalization programmes. The aim of this monitoring was to impede firms from using these restructuring programmes (which often took the form of joint ventures) as a means of making tacit pricing or market-sharing agreements. During that crisis period, competition policy was also seen as a means of favouring the adaptation of industrial structures to the new economic environment.

1.2.5.3 The Promotion of Innovation

At the beginning of the 1980s, the importance of innovation (to which reference is already made in Article 85§3) started to be given significant emphasis in the Annual Reports, and the promotion of innovation also became one of the main objectives of competition policy. Innovation was first seen as a way of overcoming the economic crisis. In the XIth Report (Commission, 1981), competition is described as a force pushing firms to innovate: 'competition is supposed . . . to encourage them (firms) to invent, develop and exploit efficiently new techniques and new products'. The importance given to innovation is even more emphasized in the XVth Report (Commission, 1985): 'Dynamic, innovative competition, led by enterpreneurs, is the life-blood of the economy'. In fact, such an argument is not a straightforward one in economics. The importance given to innovation has led the Commission to adopt a very lenient attitude towards cooperation between firms when an innovative activity is at stake. The XVIth Report (Commission, 1986) states that: 'subject to the maintenance of an adequate level of competition, it (competition policy) allows scope for cooperation between firms likely to further technological and economic progress, especially in research and development and the transfer of technology'.

1.2.5.4 Restoring the Competitiveness of European Industry

In the late 1980s, a new goal was attributed to competition policy, namely the promotion of the competitiveness[7] of European firms outside Europe. This goal was clearly stated in the XVIIth Report (Commission, 1987) where more competition is said to promote a 'greater competitiveness of EC firms both inside the EC, and in the third countries market'.

In the XVIIIth Report (Commission, 1988), it is again stated that: 'More competition will . . . strengthen the position of European industry in both world and domestic markets'. This idea is recurrent in the reports that followed. That period was characterized by the increasing internationalization (and globalization) of the world economy. This phenomenon can be defined as a geographical evolution of rivalry. Rivalry, which was previously mainly confined within national boundaries, was increasingly seen as becoming a world-wide struggle.

At the beginning of the 1990s, it appeared that European firms (particularly in high technology sectors) were facing a competitive disadvantage as compared to their American and Japanese competitors. The measurement of competitiveness is a complex task because many indicators have to be taken into account. Nevertheless the main indicators showed that European industry was losing ground in the world economy to the United States and Japan. Imports from outside the EU were growing much faster than Community exports to non-EU countries at the end of the 1980s. Labour cost differentials were in general cited as the major reason for the competitive disadvantage of European firms.

In this context, competition policy was supposed to help European firms improve their competitive advantage and acquire a strong position on the world markets. The adoption of this goal led to some contradictions in the implementation of competition rules. Indeed, this objective can be achieved by two different means. First, competition policy can be used to put pressure on production costs and product development strategy through a strengthened intensity of rivalrous behaviour between firms (see Porter, 1990). Alternatively, it can allow for more cooperation between firms in order to create large-scale ventures capable of competing on a world-wide basis. It has been this second perspective that has been the most influential in the Commission's thinking. In the XXIInd Report (Commission, 1992), the Commission clearly stated its intentions: 'The Commission is willing to facilitate . . . cooperation operations that allow firms to adapt and to improve their competitiveness in a global context'.

We can interpret this lenient attitude in another way. The external pressure exerted by competitors may be considered a 'substitute' to the intervention of competition authorities. In a global context of enhanced competition, the role of competition policy may become less justified since the pressure on costs and prices arise from the market itself. In any case, competition policy can be complementary to trade policy and they have the same objectives although their tools are completely different if not sometimes contradictory (for an evaluation of these arguments, see Neven and Seabright, 1997).

1.2.5.5 The Completion of the Internal Market

We will now end the description of the declared objectives of competition policy by presenting the most specific goal of European competition policy. This objective is the completion of the Internal Market. In the Ist Report on Competition Policy (Commission, 1972), the Commission stated that: '. . . the competition policy of the Community must be directed towards the creation and proper operation of the common market'. In the IXth Report (Commission, 1979), the completion of the Internal Market is presented as one of the major goals of competition policy.

In fact, European competition policy has been the first real experience of the application of a transnational competition policy. In this sense, European competition policy is closely related to transnational trade policies aiming at implementing free trade between nations. Whereas trade policies act on tariffs and on barriers that are institutionally set, competition authorities try to achieve similar goals by monitoring the behaviour of firms and by impeding the compartmentalization of markets due to private actions. One of the major tasks of European competition policy is, therefore, to remove all restrictions to free trade between Member States in order to achieve total integration of the European market. As mentioned earlier, this mission assigned to competition policy is unique to the European Union. In Chapter 2 we shall see how dominant this objective has become in the specific context of European Union policy towards vertical agreements.

As we have seen, the functions assigned to competition policy are numerous and not always consistent with economic theory. They may even sometimes be contradictory. For example, it is not clear how the promotion of the competitiveness of European firms through increased cooperation is compatible with the protection of the interest of consumers or with the protection of small competitors. In fact, as we have already pointed out, these objectives are so varied that competition authorities have very considerable discretion in the weight they give to each of the objectives in any particular case.

1.3 Concluding Remarks

Our overview of the declared objectives of European competition policy has demonstrated both their variety and their consequent potential for inconsistency. Our task in the next three chapters will, therefore, be to see to what extent modern economic analysis has been able to impose some coherence on the potential goals of government intervention in the process of competition between firms, and the various possible means of achieving these goals. Is it possible, for example, to analyse systematically the extent to which intervention involves trading off the different desiderata against each other? We begin with an analysis of vertical contractual relationships between firms.

2

Vertical Restraints

2.1 Introduction

Public policy towards vertical restraints has been subject to severe swings
in intellectual and political fashion in recent decades, and even now
remains one of the areas of competition policy where there is least clarity
in the public debate, and where it is hardest to see what are the issues
dividing those with different points of view. Vertical restraints are, loosely
speaking, contracts between firms at different stages in a production chain
that specify more detailed commitments on the parties than simply to
exchange a given quantity of goods or services at a given price per unit. In
the early days of competition policy in both the United States and Europe,
'free' market transactions were often seen as consisting intrinsically of no
more than an exchange of goods or services for money at a single unit
price. Therefore, any contracts specifying more than this were to be seen
certainly as restrictive, and presumably as anti-competitive (the very word
'restraints' captures the flavour of this approach directly).

Subsequently, however (and to a considerable extent prompted by the
writings of the Chicago school in economics and law), both research and
policy have accepted that beneficial economic transactions may take
many more varied forms that the two stark polar cases of administrative
command within a single enterprise and exchange between independent
economic agents for a common unit price on anonymous spot markets.
Vertical restraints are not a feature purely of twentieth-century business
practice or of the dealings of large firms with small suppliers and distributors: in the 1830s the novelist Honoré de Balzac used to stipulate in
contracts with journals publishing his stories that they should subsequently refuse to publish negative criticism of his work (Robb, 1994,

p. 203). There may, in short, be many good reasons why all kinds of economic agents should wish to enter into contractual relations that are more detailed than those embodied in spot contracts but fall short of full economic integration into a single firm. There has been an explosion of theoretical and empirical arguments demonstrating that such contractual relations may enhance the efficiency of the production process. The so-called Chicago approach (and its practical embodiment in US anti-trust policy under Presidents Reagan and Bush) has drawn from such arguments the conclusion that vertical restraints as such should not be proscribed, though the recent policy of the Clinton administration has modified the approach to some extent.[8] Competition policy elsewhere has typically been more cautious, but even the European Union has accepted that under a variety of circumstances vertical restraints may have significant beneficial economic consequences.

Most recent academic studies of vertical restraints have accepted that there are many circumstances under which they enhance productive efficiency, but most would also accept that there are significant circumstances in which they may indeed be anti-competitive.[9] Unfortunately the implications of such findings for practical policy are quite unclear. One conclusion that might be drawn is that public policy towards vertical restraints must be inherently highly discretionary and sensitive to the circumstances of particular cases. The following statements, each by an influential scholar in the field, are characteristic of such a point of view:

> Theoretically, the only defensible position on vertical restraints seems to be the rule of reason. Most vertical restraints can increase or decrease welfare, depending on the environment. Legality or illegality *per se* thus seems unwarranted (Tirole, 1988, p. 186).

> It should be apparent . . . that few general rules are appropriate in dealing with vertical restraints . . . since the same restraints may be, in different circumstances, beneficial or adverse in their impact, *ad hoc* assessment is inescapable . . . The best conclusion is that we should look principally at the consequences, rather than the form or first order effects of the restraints (Kay, 1990, pp. 560–1).

Tirole goes on to say that 'this conclusion puts far too heavy a burden on the anti-trust authorities', though he argues that before a different conclusion is warranted: 'it seems important for economic theorists to develop a careful classification and operative criteria to determine in which environments certain vertical restraints are likely to lower social welfare' (Tirole, 1988).

Given that assessment of the precise impact of a given vertical contract on competition will often be a delicate matter, the benefits of discretion in implementing competition policy in this field are important. Discretion, however, also has its costs. It makes decisions by the authorities hard for firms to predict, and increases the risk that firms may be breaking the law when they have been trying in good faith to abide by it. Discretion also increases the risk that decisions may be systematically tilted towards those parties with the resources to employ the cleverest lawyers and economists: in the field of vertical restraints good consultants can often devise economic models to support any desired conclusion about the impact of a given vertical restraint on economic welfare. More generally, discretion creates opportunities for regulatory capture and the distortion of policy towards those with the means to exert influence. The exercise of discretion also imposes administrative costs and costs of delay: a large number of agreements between firms with no adverse impact on competition have nevertheless to go through a lengthy vetting procedure, often lasting several years, before the firms concerned know whether the agreements are legally acceptable. Finally, the exercise of discretion increases the risk of inconsistency between decisions and between different branches of competition policy, with consequent distortionary incentives for the way in which firms plan their business strategies. For instance, as will be seen below, European Union policy towards vertical restraints is significantly more restrictive than its policy towards vertical mergers: if so, this may create artificial and inefficient incentives for full-scale merger purely in order to avoid the anti-trust risks posed by a vertical contract.

These considerations suggest that practical policy towards vertical restraints should seek to balance theoretical rigour with simplicity and predictability. It should attach significant weight to diminishing the extent of discretion exercised by the competition authorities. This chapter will, therefore, develop an approach to vertical restraints that consists of developing a sequence of rules of thumb that allocate a burden of proof, as well as determining the kinds of argument and evidence that might constitute such proof. It will outline reasons for thinking that vertical restraints should be presumed not to be anti-competitive unless certain conditions hold, and will then seek clear and relatively simple means of identifying in practice whether those conditions are fulfilled.

The structure of the chapter is as follows. Section 2.2 sets out a formal framework for analysis, describing what vertical restraints are and the issues they raise for public policy. It suggests that public policy should principally concern itself with external effects of vertical restraints. Section 2.3 then examines more systematically what those external effects might be, by looking at three types of third party that might be affected adversely by a vertical restraint. Section 2.4 outlines a procedure for competition authorities to use. Section 2.5 examines the decisions of the European Commission in cases involving vertical restraints since 1989, to see how far European Union policy differs from the procedure advocated in the chapter. Section 2.6 considers briefly to what extent the recent Commission Green Paper on vertical restraints recognizes and remedies the deficiencies we identify in the Commission's practice. Section 2.7 concludes.

The criteria by which vertical restraints are to be evaluated deserve explicit comment. Economic analysis tends to focus on considerations of efficiency, and US anti-trust law has also tended to give the main weight to efficiency over other considerations such as equity. In the European Union, as we discussed in Chapter 1 (Section 1.2.5), other considerations than efficiency play an important role. With respect to vertical restraints, we show in Section 2.5 that at least two other evaluation criteria can be discerned in both statute and case law. First there is an emphasis on protection of the interests of small and medium enterprises, and second (and particularly importantly for vertical restraints) an emphasis on the role of competition policy in promoting market integration. Of course market integration can be and often has been justified in terms of the promotion of long-run efficiency; nevertheless it is clear that it has come to assume a fairly autonomous status as a goal of competition policy in the European Union. It is not the purpose of this chapter to comment on the relative merits of these various criteria, but it is desirable to make explicit the terms of the trade-off between them. For instance, it is important to illuminate the circumstances under which the pursuit of market integration may involve a sacrifice of efficiency. The theoretical analysis will, therefore, evaluate vertical restraints from an efficiency point of view. Section 2.5 will seek to identify to what extent efficiency and other considerations have pulled in similar rather than different directions in the policy of the European Union.

Before turning to Section 2.2 let us summarize the argument to come. Although the pure Chicago view that vertical restraints virtually always enhance productive efficiency is not credible, the Chicago approach has yielded one particularly important insight that is sometimes overlooked by authors who call for context-sensitivity in public policy. This insight is that vertical restraints are agreements between producers of *complementary* goods or services (see Baxter, 1990). Agreements between producers of *substitute* goods or services are always and rightly suspect from the point of view of public policy, for the simple reason that the exercise of market power by one producer always benefits the producers of substitute products. If two of us produce goods that are substitutes we have an incentive to connive in each other's exercise of market power. However, the exercise of market power by a producer always harms the producers of complementary products, since (by definition of complementarity), anything that raises the price or reduces the output of a good will reduce demand for a complement. In particular, inefficiency in the production of a good will typically harm the producer of a complement.

To the extent that public policy is rightly concerned to prevent the abuse of market power, this simple insight makes it clear why, from an efficiency point of view, vertical contracts should indeed be presumed

innocent unless proven guilty: each party to such a contract has a fundamental interest in preventing rather than facilitating the exercise of
market power by the other. Each party to the contract is, therefore, in
some sense an ally rather than an enemy of the public interest, and can
shoulder some of the burden of policing the competitive process. From
time to time, of course, a firm may sign a contract that is harmful to its
own interests, but it is no part of the mandate of a competition policy to
tell firms how to manage their own business. It is precisely because firms
generally know better than the authorities how to do so, that in a modern
capitalist economy contracts freely entered into are generally presumed to
be acceptable unless they harm third parties. The most obvious mechanism for harming a third party available to producers of substitute
products, namely the exercise of market power, is one that producers of
complements ordinarily have no incentive to adopt.

This insight does not, however, imply the Chicago conclusion that vertical restraints can always be presumed innocent, period. There are three
reasons why not. First, and most fundamentally, a vertical contract may
indeed harm third parties. A variety of ways in which this may happen
will be described below, as well as some simple ways in which the danger
may be diagnosed in practice. Second, it is possible that, in the context of
long-term relationships between firms, one or other party may be coerced
into accepting contractual terms as a result of making relationship-specific investments that it would not have accepted had it known them in
advance. This is sometimes known as the 'hold-up problem'. More insidi-
ously, the fear of a weak *ex post* bargaining position, and the lack of
commitment mechanisms to prevent such a situation, may deter firms
from entering into long-term relationships in the first place. Such phenomena might well provide a rationale for ruling certain types of contract
illegal. However, it must be emphasized that there is nothing in this argument to imply that contracts embodying vertical restraints are any more
suspect than those merely embodying unfavourable prices (indeed, arguments of the kind just sketched have been used as a rationale for
minimum wage legislation). A theory of vertical restraints as such should
take as its benchmark case, contracts willingly entered into by both parties (this need not imply that they have equal bargaining power, merely
that each of them expects to be at least as well off in the presence of the
contract as in its absence). A diagnosis of the hold-up problem would
need to be based on the circumstances of the particular case.

The third reason why vertical contracts may be harmful in spite of their
being struck by producers of complementary products is that when one of
the parties to a vertical contract possesses market power in its own market, it
no longer always has an interest in ensuring efficiency in the provision of
complementary goods or services. Comanor (1985) demonstrates this
clearly. The reason is that its market power creates a division between the

interests of its marginal customers and the interests of its intra-marginal ones – that is, between the interests of those customers who are just on the point of indifference between the firm's products and those of a rival, and the interests of the remaining customers who have a clear preference for the firm's products. Both marginal and intra-marginal customers share an interest in the production of a given good or service at lowest cost, but they may have divergent preferences regarding the combination of characteristics embodied in that good or service (a matter of allocative rather than productive efficiency). There is no reason to expect a vertical contract between profit-maximizing firms with market power to reach an allocatively efficient trade-off between different aspects of a product's characteristics (price and quality of after-sales service, for example). One way to represent the intuition behind Comanor's argument is given in Figure 2.1, which uses an Edgeworth box to represent transaction possibilities between Firm 1 (a manufacturer) and Firm 2 (a distributor). The points in the box represent different combinations of retail price and after-sales service for a given wholesale price. In other words, we assume that, for a given price per unit at which the manufacturer sells to the distributor, the two parties are contemplating whether to have a high retail price and high service level or a low retail price and low service level. Different points on the contract curve represent combinations which, while all bilaterally efficient, divide in different proportions the surplus from the trade between the two parties.

Unbroken convex curves represent the preferences of marginal consumers as between price and after-sales service, and broken curves represent the preferences of intra-marginal consumers. Unbroken concave curves are the iso-profit curves of Firm 2 (which bears the costs of providing after-sales service and also receives the sales revenue). In this interpretation the indifference curves of marginal consumers are also iso-profit curves for Firm 1, since its profits depend solely on the numbers of consumers buying its product (given that the wholesale price does not vary). Point P, therefore, represents the profit-maximizing contract between Firms 1 and 2. This is clearly inefficient since a small movement in the direction of the arrow (drawn to be tangent to the unbroken indifference curves) yields a first-order utility gain to intra-marginal consumers while causing only a second-order loss to marginal consumers and to the profits of Firm 2. As drawn this shows the outcome where consumers who do not wish to pay for large amounts of after-sales service nevertheless have to do so. In sum, therefore, producers with market power have a group of consumers who are intra-marginal and are, therefore, disenfranchised (rather like minority shareholders) in matters affecting allocative efficiency. This differs from competitive markets where all consumers are marginal, and from considerations of productive efficiency where marginal and intra-marginal consumers have identical interests.

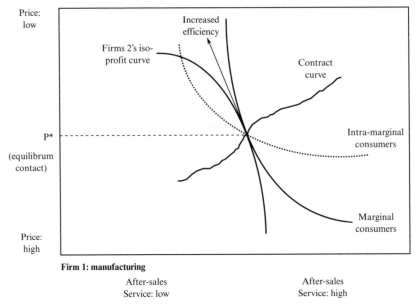

Figure 2.1 Intra-marginal combinations of retail price and service for a given wholesale price

Nevertheless, this potential conflict between the interests of marginal and intra-marginal customers affects all aspects of production where choices between combinations of product characteristics are concerned, and is as true of integrated firms as well as non-integrated ones linked by contracts. Integrated firms will choose combinations of product characteristics that do not reflect the preferences of intra-marginal consumers, and the fact that they implement these product choices by administrative command rather than by contract does not fundamentally change the character of the problem. Any potentially inefficient properties of the vertical contract are more properly thought of as a symptom than a cause of the market power concerned. Conversely, the imposition of restrictions on allowable contractual forms can be justified, if at all, only as an imperfect intervention made necessary by the inability of the authorities to alleviate the intrinsic problem which is the original market power. In addition, it will often be hard for the authorities to judge the nature of the distortion involved. Discussions of distribution contracts in the cosmetics industry, for example, are sometimes thought to be characterized by exactly this inefficiency: everyone has to pay for the glamorous sales ambience that benefits only the marginal customer. Other industries, however, have if anything the opposite tendency: in computer hardware, for example, after sales service is often lamentably poor because of the intensity of price competition for the marginal customer. This contrast illustrates just how difficult it is for competition authorities to use the argument just outlined as a guide to policy. There is no general presumption that the balance between price and non-price factors will be systematically distorted by market power in any particular direction.

Strictly speaking, the intra-marginal customers of the contracting parties can be thought of as among the possible third parties that may be harmed by a vertical contract. In the policy rule proposed here, therefore, vertical contracts are presumed acceptable unless there is a substantial adverse net external effect on a third party.[10] Third parties may be divided into:

1. customers;
2. competitors;
3. potential entrants to the industry.

Section 2.3 proposes ways of identifying circumstances in which such adverse external effects are likely.

In order to understand these circumstances, however, it is important to see first why vertical contracts are important to firms in the first place. This is the primary task of Section 2.2.

2.2   A Framework for Analysis

Consider a pair of (possibly multiproduct) Firms 1 and 2, each of which may be identified with a collection of human and non-human assets that are jointly controlled by each firm's owner(s). Firms 1 and 2 produce vectors of goods or services (hereafter 'goods') x and y. The two firms are said to be vertically related if one of them sells to the other a good which:

(a) is complementary to a good produced or owned by the other;
(b) is sold on to a third party together with the complementary good, or is transformed or used up with it in the process of producing a composite final good.

Note that it may sometimes be difficult to determine the direction of the vertical relation. Suppose, for example, that a manufacturer of beer distributes its product to a bar or other outlet on a sale-or-return basis. Is the outlet purchasing beer for resale or is the manufacturer purchasing distribution services? The answer would seem to depend on which party could claim ownership of the beer while it is in the custody of the outlet immediately prior to final sale. If, for example, the outlet goes bankrupt, does the stock of beer revert immediately to the manufacturer or does it count among the assets of the outlet to which the manufacturer may claim in order of precedence among other creditors? If the former, it is natural to say that the manufacturer has purchased services from the outlet; if the latter, the purchasing relationship is reversed. Either way, the basic economic characteristics of the relation between the two parties while they continue in business may be the same whichever of them is the 'upstream' firm, suggesting that it would be unwise to make prescriptions of importance turn on the direction of the vertical relation.[11]

Note also that two firms may be vertically related even if they are also horizontal competitors. Firm 1 may sell a good x in $\underline{x}$ to Firm 2; x may be complementary to a good y_1 in $\underline{y}$ even if it is also a close substitute of another good y_2 in $\underline{y}$. Thus, for example, Firm 2 may be a car manufacturer that produces its own spark plugs and also purchases spark plugs from Firm 1.

In the use of its assets to produce its vector of outputs, each firm has access to a set of strategies. These strategies may or may not be contractible (in the sense that the firm may credibly commit itself in an enforceable contract to choose among them in a certain way). Specifically, Firm 1 chooses a strategy which is a pair (s^C, s^N) from the set $\{S^C, S^N\}$, where S^C is the set of strategy components to which the firm can contractually commit itself, while S^N is the set of strategy components to which it cannot.[12] Likewise, Firm 2 chooses a pair (t^C, t^N) from the set $\{T^C, T^N\}$.

Contractible strategy components include the prices at which each firm sells its output, the total level of output transferred to, or from, the contracting partner, and (importantly) whether or not the contracting partner has other contracts, either with the same partner or with some third party. *Non-contractible* components may include the level of effort each firm puts in to producing or improving the quality of its goods, and the level of costs it incurs in doing so.[13]

A vertical restraint on Firm 1 by Firm 2 can then be defined as any contractual agreement such that:

1. Firm 1 and Firm 2 are vertically related.
2. Firm 1 undertakes to restrict its choice of strategy components to some strict subset $\{S'^C, S^N\}$ of its strategy set, this subset either fully specified in the agreement or left to the partial discretion of Firm 2.
3. The restriction of Firm 1's strategy affects the quantity or quality produced or sold of one or both of the complementary goods in virtue of which the firms are vertically related.

Condition three is intended to distinguish genuine vertical restraints from other agreements (e.g. horizontal cartel agreements) between firms that also happen to have a vertical relationship.

Different kinds of vertical restraint can then be characterized according to the subset of strategies to which they restrict Firm 1's choice (examples are given in the subsequent paragraphs).

1. *Price/quantity restrictions* In determining the price of the composite good (or the joint price for the two complementary goods), Firm 1 may choose only within the subset of strategies characterized by a given price p^* or set of prices P^* (e.g. those below some maximum or above some minimum). The choice of this price set is left to the discretion of Firm 2. Given demand conditions, price restrictions and quantity restrictions are two aspects of the same phenomenon. If there is uncertainty the two will differ in respect of the allocation of risk to which they give rise.

2. *Restrictions on dealing in substitutes* There are two main kinds of restriction:
   - The first consists of dealing restrictions: Firm 1 may not choose any strategy that involves purchasing from or selling to a competitor of Firm 2. When Firm 1 distributes the goods manufactured by Firm 2 this is usually known as exclusive dealing. When Firm 2 is the distributor it usually takes the form of territorial exclusivity, since the basis of Firm 2's market power is usually geographical. However, the exclusivity may sometimes refer to types of service or product (such as the mail order component of a certain retail business).
   - The second type of restriction on the purchase of substitutes is non-linear pricing: Firm 1 may pay a certain price in a transaction with Firm 2 only if it also purchases specified numbers of other units of the same or a substitute good at a different (actual or implied) price. At its simplest this may consist of a two-part tariff, in which the right to trade at all requires a franchise fee while subsequent units require only a fixed marginal cost.

3. *Restrictions on dealing in complements* Once again there are two main types:
   - First there are input restrictions: Firm 1 undertakes to use specified levels of inputs of certain types (e.g. advertising), or inputs purchased from certain sources (e.g. Firm 2). Such restrictions may take the indirect form of selective distribution, where Firm 2 supplies only through Firm 1 and a limited number of other outlets that it has selected as being likely to provide the appropriate inputs (usually complementary services).
   - The second type of restriction on dealing in complements consists of tying (this may also apply to goods that are neither substitutes nor complements). Here Firm 1 undertakes, as a condition of the contract, also to purchase or sell a certain number of units of a complementary good (other than an input into the composite good, which is already covered under input restrictions). Note that this

form of tying represents a restriction on one of the two firms; exclusive dealing can also be thought of as a form of tying, but a quite different kind, namely one that imposes tying on the final customer.

These three fundamental categories cover all the main kinds of vertical restraint that are practically relevant. For example, Dobson and Waterson (1996a) treat eight main kinds of restraint, which fall into the following categories under our classification.[14]

1. *Price/quantity*   Retail price maintenance, quantity forcing.
2. *Substitutes*   Non-linear pricing, exclusive distribution, exclusive dealing.
3. *Complements*   Service requirements, selective distribution, tie-in sales.

Having defined this terminology we can now go on to ask the two fundamental questions about vertical restraints. First, why should Firm 1 willingly submit to a contract restricting its freedom as an economic operator? To put it another way, how could the restriction of the strategy set of Firm 1 yield sufficient benefits to Firm 2 to enable Firm 2 to compensate it adequately for the losses that a restriction on economic freedom must entail? Second (and more centrally for competition policy) can we identify any general reasons why agreement on such a contract might be damaging to third parties?

To take the first question first, we can distinguish three types of reason why firms might wish to engage in vertical restraints:

1. there may be externalities between them in the exercise of their *contractible* strategy components s^C and t^C which they wish to internalize by agreeing to implement them according to a cooperative solution;
2. there may be externalities between them in the exercise of their *non-contractible* strategy components s^N and t^N which they are unable to internalize directly, but which they hope to offset by agreeing to choices of s^C and t^C that will give them private incentives to set (second-best) optimal levels of s^N and t^N;
3. the restriction on the strategy set of Firm 1 may enhance the credibility of certain threats or promises it may wish to make to some third party, and thereby benefit Firm 1 directly regardless of any additional beneficial impact on Firm 2.

These three motivations can be summarized as the direct externality motive, the indirect externality motive and the strategic credibility motive. The following include some common examples of vertical restraints designed with these motivations in mind.

1. *Direct externality*:
   • maximum retail price maintenance to avoid 'double marginalization', where an externality arising from pricing decisions (a contractible component of the strategy set) would lead to excessively high prices in the absence of the vertical restraint;

- agreements on the amount of advertising and promotion expenditure to be undertaken by either manufacturer or distributor.

2. *Indirect externality:*
   - two-part tariffs to avoid double marginalization (here the pricing decision for the final product is treated as non-contractible, either intrinsically or because it depends on information (e.g. about demand) that is itself non-contractible);
   - minimum retail price maintenance to provide incentives for investment by distributors in product quality, where such investments lead to a reputational benefit for both distributor and manufacturer.

One of the features of the indirect internalization of externalities is that there will often be several forms of vertical restraint that are capable of achieving the same goal. For example, the provision of incentives to a retailer to invest in pre-sale service and information may be possible through retail price maintenance or through the granting of exclusive territories in a way that guarantees a certain margin to the retailer. When there is no uncertainty in demand or in costs the two may have identical effects, though in conditions of uncertainty they will typically differ (Rey and Tirole, 1986). Nevertheless, the general similarity of their effects indicates that a policy which is based purely on the legal form of a restraint, and which rules illegal certain forms and not others, will be easily undermined by the substitution of one form for another with little if any amelioration of such anti-competitive effects as may exist.

3. *Strategic credibility:*
   - refusal to supply as a means of preventing arbitrage between distributor territories between which a manufacturer is practising price discrimination;
   - retail price maintenance as a way of making price collusion easier to observe and police by members of a cartel;
   - tying purchase of a monopolistically supplied good to the purchase of a more competitively supplied good to discourage entry by rival suppliers of the competitively supplied good (exclusive dealing is a special case of this).

If any of these three motives provides an explanation why a firm might submit itself voluntarily to a restriction on its future commercial freedom, what can be said about the welfare implications of such contracts, and the role of public policy? The fact that the two firms are producers of complements provides a strong *prima facie* reason to treat agreements between them as benign. The logic behind this is given a simple formal expression in Box 2.1.

The argument outlined in Box 2.1 can be seen as a generalization of the double marginalization argument for vertical restraints, one that may apply even if the firms concerned are not both pricing above marginal cost. What this indicates is that double marginalization is not just one among a range of phenomena with which vertical restraints can deal, but is in some sense typical of a very general problem that may arise between producers of complements. The exercise of market power by one will tend

---

Box 2.1 Complementarity and social welfare

Taking as a measure of social welfare the sum of profits and consumer surplus in the markets for two goods 1 and 2, the derivative of social welfare with respect to the prices of each of the two goods can be written, using obvious notation, as follows:

1. $\dfrac{\partial SW}{\partial p_1} = \dfrac{\partial \pi_1}{\partial p_1} + \dfrac{\partial \pi_2}{\partial p_1} + \dfrac{\partial CS_1}{\partial p_1} + \dfrac{\partial CS_2}{\partial p_1}$

and

2. $\dfrac{\partial SW}{\partial p_2} = \dfrac{\partial \pi_1}{\partial p_2} + \dfrac{\partial \pi_2}{\partial p_2} + \dfrac{\partial CS_1}{\partial p_2} + \dfrac{\partial CS_2}{\partial p_2}$

When the two firms are setting prices non-cooperatively it follows that:

3. $\dfrac{\partial \pi_1}{\partial p_1} = \dfrac{\partial \pi_2}{\partial p_2} = 0$

The terms $\partial CS_1 / \partial p_1$ and $\partial CS_2 / \partial p_2$ are always negative. The cross terms $\partial \pi_1 / \partial p_2$ and $\partial \pi_2 / \partial p_1$ are also negative if and only if the two goods are complements, and therefore the sign of the derivative of social welfare with respect to price is unambiguously negative. This means that, at the non-cooperative outcome, the derivative of Firm 1's profit with respect to the price set by Firm 2 has always the same sign as the derivative of social welfare with respect to that price (and analogously for Firm 2). In other words, at the non-cooperative outcome each firm always has an incentive to influence the price of the other in a direction that unambiguously improves social welfare.[15]

to harm the other, and therefore agreements between the firms are likely, in the absence of externalities, to rein in rather than exacerbate the market power which is at the root of the problem. For the authorities to treat vertical restraints as automatically suspect is to forgo the advantages of enlisting valuable allies in the task of policing market power.

Of course, as was discussed in Section 2.1, the conclusions of this simplified model will not necessarily carry over to a more sophisticated one. If non-cooperative price-setting is determined by some other mechanism than individual profit-maximizing by each firm (say because of collusion), or if consumer surplus depends upon more than one choice variable (say price and quality of after-sales service) between which marginal and intra-marginal consumers may have differing marginal rates of substitution, or if there is some competitor that suffers a negative externality, the unambiguous positive relation between the demands of social welfare and the incentives of each firm with respect to the other's choice will no longer hold. However, all of these cases involve some party other than the two firms who is adversely affected by the contract. It, therefore, seems appropriate to conclude that vertical restraints should be given the benefit of the doubt unless such adverse effects can reasonably be shown to exist.

To summarize, the important issue for competition policy is whether in engaging in such vertical restraints the parties impose additional negative externalities on any third party. When the motive is strategic this will often be the case (since by definition some third party must be affected, and the effect may be negative); when the motive is the internalization of externalities it need not be. We will treat third parties as falling into two main categories: competitors (actual or potential) in the market for the product of either firm, and customers in these markets. The negative externalities of greatest concern will, therefore, be those inflicted upon actual or potential competitors or upon customers. The former kind of externality will typically be of concern because it subsequently leads to costs imposed upon customers, but it is useful nevertheless to distinguish analytically between externalities inflicted directly upon consumers (e.g. via the facilitation of collusion), and those inflicted indirectly by damaging a competitor whose actions could have been beneficial to customers.

A different question about vertical restraints also suggests itself: why might firms wish to have a contractual relationship rather than full integration? Broadly speaking we can note that non-integration of the two parties may yield advantages due to greater credibility of their commitments. Duopolists may be able to maintain a more collusive outcome, via delegation of price-setting behaviour to distributors, than would otherwise be possible; an incumbent firm may be able to commit to a more aggressive response to entry if it is not vertically integrated; management may be able to set more credible incentives for distributors if those distributors are separately owned, and so on.

In implementing competition policy, the authorities would wish to ask whether vertical restraints impose significant negative externalities compared to a situation of non-integration without vertical restraints, and also compared to a situation of full vertical integration. Only if the answer to both questions is positive, or if the answer to the first is positive and the authorities would be justified in forbidding vertical integration, will there be a *prima facie* case for intervention. Section 2.3 now considers how the possible presence of negative externalities might be diagnosed.

2.3   Who Suffers from External Effects?

Under what circumstances are significant adverse net externalities are likely to occur? Let us classify such circumstances according to the identity of the affected party.

2.3.1   *Final customers*

Externalities may be inflicted on final customers in two distinct ways. The first, already discussed above, is when a distinct sub-set of customers (who are intra-marginal) is adversely affected by the terms of contracts designed to meet the preferences of marginal customers alone (for an example see Winter, 1997). For instance, customers who value pre-sales advice relatively little may be forced by retail price maintenance to consume more such service than they require.

The second way is when the terms of a vertical contract act to weaken competition between different types of final product (or inter-brand competition as it is usually known). This may occur for a variety of reasons, three of which can be distinguished in the literature. First, exclusive dealing may raise the costs to consumers of comparing products or obtaining relative price information: there is an established literature documenting the potential adverse consequences of 'switching costs' for social welfare (see Klemperer, 1987 and 1995). This is not the only way in which exclusive dealing can be damaging, since it may also harm competitors (see Comanor and Rey, 1997). Second, a vertical contract may allocate profits between manufacturer and dealer in such a way as to weaken the incentive of either link in the chain to steal business from rival brands by cutting prices. Rey and Stiglitz (1988) show that when there is competition between two pairs of manufacturers and distributors, a vertical restraint may lead to higher prices (because of lower marginal profits from price-cutting) than either full vertical integration or vertical disintegration with an ordinary linear contract. Third, measures such as retail price maintenance may make it easier for members of a cartel to police price-cutting behaviour by its members, and thus to enforce cartel discipline more effectively (see Jullien *et al.*, 1997 and Dobson and Waterson, 1996b for developments of this argument).

Specifying these possibilities theoretically does not imply that the relevant externalities are straightforward to diagnose in practice. In the example of the trade-off between price and service quality imposed by retail price maintenance, it would be necessary to establish that those consumers with relatively low willingness to pay for service quality were indeed intra-marginal (the opposite is equally plausible). Even if this were so, it would be necessary to establish further that, in consuming more service than they wished, they were significantly worse off than in the absence of retail price maintenance, when price competition could drive levels of service provision below what *all* consumers might wish.[16] Nobody with the experience of shopping around to have their car serviced cheaply can be wholly confident that price competition will lead to optimal outcomes.

The Rey-Stiglitz case is even harder to use to identify externalities in practice. Before the vertical restraint could be diagnosed as harming consumers, it would be necessary to establish either that full vertical integration between manufacturers and distributors would itself harm consumers, or that a vertically-integrated structure could not credibly duplicate (by means of an appropriately-structured commission payment system) the incentives to weaken price competition created by the vertical contract.

Like the Rey-Stiglitz case, the fear that retail price maintenance helps to enforce cartel discipline, if it is to inform practical policy, depends upon our having some confidence that we understand cartel behaviour and the circumstances that promote collusion. In practice we are a long way from being able to do so on a systematic basis. Nevertheless, the strength of inter-brand competition makes a difference: it is hard to see retail price maintenance in book-selling, for example, as having any potential for enforcing collusion.

The possibility that exclusive dealing weakens price competition by raising switching costs is probably the most straightforward of the three to identify in practice. It is most likely to lead to significant adverse net externalities when the costs in time and effort of comparing brands between different outlets is high relative to the value of the goods. This is more likely to be true for 'impulse' ice-cream than for cars (to take two examples relevant to European Union policy). It should also be noted that goods subject to significant repeat purchasing are less likely to be subject to switching costs merely because of exclusive dealing unless some important degree of territorial monopoly is involved: once a consumer has chosen which pub to visit there may be significant costs of switching to another pub, but relative prices may play a part in determining which pub to visit in the first place, provided there are enough pubs within con-

venient travelling distance (something that drink-drive laws may uninten-
tionally make less likely).

In all of these examples it is clear that the possession of significant
market power by each brand is a necessary condition for the vertical
restraint to damage consumers. So an important lesson for competition
policy is that only if inter-brand competition is weak will a negative
externality upon consumers is even worth investigating. A second lesson
is that weakening inter-brand competition by raising switching costs is
the most straightforward of these possibilities to diagnose empirically
with any confidence.

2.3.2 Existing competitors

The possibility that negative externalities may be inflicted on existing
competitors has been well explored in the literature under the label
'raising rivals' costs' (see Salop and Scheffman, 1983; and Krattenmaker
and Salop, 1986). The most common example is when access to a scarce
input is restricted by means of a vertical contract, so that rivals are
forced to use more expensive supplies. Their ability to compete is, therefore, weakened, and the market power of the parties to the vertical
contract is enhanced.

It is clear that, on its own, the fact that a contract prevents a supplier
from dealing with a rival does not inflict a significant externality. It is only
if the supplier enjoys market power such that the rival's costs are raised to
an appreciable extent that the fear may be justified. This is something that
may not always be easy to establish empirically,[17] but at least it is possible
to see what questions a competition authority needs to ask.

2.3.3 Potential entrants

When vertical restraints have the effect of raising rivals' costs to such an
extent that the rivals cannot operate profitably at all, some or all of them
may cease to be actual competitors and the result is known as 'market
foreclosure'.[18] This may happen because vertical contracts tie up scarce
distribution facilities, such as sole access to licences or the sole prime site
in a city. The result is damaging for exactly the same reason as raising the
costs of actual competitors is damaging.

A puzzle about such vertical contracts is why one party should willingly
submit to restraints that prevent it from seeking out more favourable terms
if such are available. Why should the owner of a prime retail site wish to
promise not to let it to a higher bidder than the present incumbent? Any
such promise will discourage entry by precisely the kind of bidders who

would drive up the value of the site. Why should a manufacturer write long-term contracts with suppliers or distributors that discourage the entry of other (presumably more efficient) suppliers or distributors? The literature on foreclosure provides two important answers. The first is due to Aghion and Bolton (1987). Long-term contracts, with liquidation damages, do indeed discourage some entry by more efficient suppliers (which disadvantages the purchasers of their goods). For those suppliers, however, who nevertheless enter, the damages represent a kind of entry fee that allows the combination of the manufacturer and the existing supplier to claim some of the rent that the entrant would otherwise obtain in virtue of its greater efficiency. The negative externality, in other words, takes the form of a tax on entry. Like all taxes its effects consist partly of a transfer and partly of a dead-weight loss (the latter being the entry foreclosed). The private benefits to the party imposing the tax consist purely of the transfer, but the social costs include the dead-weight loss.

The second reason why a manufacturer might wish to exclude the entry of other suppliers than those currently in the market has been discussed in detail by Rey and Tirole (1996), drawing on earlier arguments of Hart and Tirole (1990) and McAfee and Schwartz (1993). A manufacturer with market power (or, more generally, any owner of a bottleneck facility) faces in its dealings with distributors a commitment problem that tends to dilute the exercise of its market power. Having signed contracts with its distributor, it has an incentive to renegotiate these secretly so as to increase the amount of output sold, the benefits from this increase coming at the expense of a negative externality inflicted on the other distributors. Although the manufacturer is better off doing so, given the contracts it has signed with other distributors, the knowledge *ex ante* that it will be tempted to do so lowers its expected profits and increases the overall output in the market. This temptation is greater the more competitive is the distribution segment. Certain vertical restraints therefore act as a commitment device to prevent the manufacturer from conducting such secret agreements, by restricting the degree of competition in the distribution segment. The possibility of excluding a genuinely more efficient distributor is seen as a necessary price to pay for this commitment mechanism, but from the point of view of society as a whole, both the commitment mechanism and the exclusion of more efficient distributors have positive costs. The likelihood of vertical restraints playing this role is clearly increasing in the degree of market power enjoyed by the manufacturer, as well as in the ease with which such a manufacturer would be able, absent the restraints, to engage in secret renegotiation of contracts.[19]

It is often hard for the competition authorities to know whether the costs of potential foreclosure are significant when set against some of the benefits that vertical contracts may bring. Indeed, it is often hard for firms to know whether in writing vertical contracts they may risk damaging their own interests by discouraging entry by more efficient suppliers or discouraging experimentation in conditions of evolving demand. Martin (1993, p.350) argues that 'case study evidence supports the argument that vertical restraints are likely to outlast the period in which they are socially beneficial', and in fact some of the evidence he cites implies that they are no less likely to outlast the period in which they are privately beneficial. For instance, when a challenge by the Federal Trade Commission forced the Levi Strauss company to abandon its policy of retail price maintenance, 'stores specialising in jeans cut price, while Levi Strauss's sales and stock market value *increased* sharply' (*ibid.*, p.349, emphasis added). This poses a dilemma for competition authorities: they may believe that a given vertical restraint is not in the interests of the companies that have agreed to it; they may be right in their belief; but is it appropriate for competition authorities to be offering management consultancy advice to companies under the guise of enforcing the law?

Underlying the argument in this chapter is the view that competition authorities should avoid becoming management consultants in disguise. They should seek to identify significant externalities, and, where these can be shown with reasonable confidence to exist, they should be prepared to prohibit the contractual behaviour that threatens to inflict them. In principle, however, and in the absence of such externalities, the right to contract between parties that are not competitors (producers of substitute products) should be left to the wisdom (or the foolishness) of the parties themselves.

2.4   Policy Implications: a Practical Procedure

The arguments so far reviewed suggest that economic principles recommend a three-part rule:

1. Do the parties to the contract operate in the same product market or in markets for sufficiently close substitutes? If not, there is a *prima facie* presumption that their contract is legal. If they do, then their contract should be treated as a horizontal restraint with a (refutable) presumption of illegality.
2. When the answer to the first question is negative, is inter-brand competition sufficiently weak that, if the parties to the contract were vertically integrated, they would together possess substantial market power in the market for their combined final product? If not, then their contract is legal, unless it can be shown (à la Rey-Stiglitz) that the parties are seriously likely to exert more market power without vertical integration than in an integrated state.

3. When the answer to the second question is positive, is there any evidence of a substantial adverse net external effect exerted by this contract on any third party (compared with a situation in which the contracting parties simply traded goods or services at a given unit price)? Specifically, are consumers, existing competitors or potential entrants likely to be damaged by the contract in one of the ways outlined above? If not, the contract can be declared legal.

One final point of clarification should be made. It may be objected that, when the downstream party is a supermarket or department store, the question about vertical integration at step 2 makes little sense. In fact, the question makes perfect sense, but is merely a correspondingly stringent test for the contract to pass. If Coca-Cola owned all the stores in which it is sold, or Unilever all the outlets in which its impulse ice creams are sold, then market power might be substantial, even though this came from denying other brands access to distribution facilities rather than through the market power of the brands themselves (the case is probably stronger for Coca-Cola than for Unilever). Failing this test does not make the contract illegal, but merely passes it onto the third stage of the investigation, in which we enquire whether the contract poses similar risks to those posed by vertical integration itself.

The investigative work required of such a rule falls into clear categories. The first stage requires market definition similar to that undertaken in merger investigations. The second requires an assessment of dominance. The third requires an identification of actual parties and a quantification of likely harm. The third stage is more complex than is typically required in a merger enquiry, but one of the merits of the proposed rule is that the first two stages, which ought to suffice for clearing the great majority of vertical contracts from any competition concerns, can be carried out with a methodology that is entirely consistent, in speed as well as substance, with that employed in investigating mergers.

2.5   The Decisions of the European Commission

2.5.1   Introduction

The purpose of this section is to examine the principles implicit or explicit in the application of competition law by the European Commission in the field of vertical restraints, in order to determine how great a gap exists between the principles outlined earlier in this chapter and current law and practice. It is not intended to provide a systematic review of competition law in this field (a comprehensive treatment can be found in Whish (1993)). Nor is it intended to discuss, except incidentally, the extent to which the

Commission's practice is a necessary consequence of legal constraints or whether it represents merely a set of ingrained habits of analysis (this being a question more appropriately left to those with better legal qualifications than ours[20]). We shall concentrate on giving a general sense of the distance that would need to be travelled in order to implement principles such as those advocated earlier, rather than addressing the precise nature of the legal reforms that would be required to make the journey.

Before examining the decisions it is nevertheless worth outlining a few general features of the approach to vertical restraints in Community law. First of all, since the 1966 decision by the Court of Justice in the case of **Consten & Grundig**, it has been clearly established that Article 85§1 applies no less to vertical than to horizontal agreements, and that the criteria to be applied do not differ systematically according to whether the agreements are vertical or horizontal. This already means that economic reasoning on this distinction, according to which the effects of which horizontal and vertical agreements do differ systematically, has no ready purchase in Community law.

Secondly, the scope of Article 85§1 has been interpreted very broadly, in particular due to the **Technique Minière** decision of the Court in the same year. Article 85§1 prohibits agreements that have as their 'object or effect the prevention, restriction or distortion of competition within the common market'. In this decision the Court addressed the question how the words 'object or effect' were to be understood. It ruled that the phrase was to be read disjunctively: in other words, that provided it could be established that an agreement had an anti-competitive *object* (which might be determined solely by considering its legal form), there was no need for it also to be established that it had an anti-competitive *effect*. This interpretation was subsequently confirmed in **VdS vs. Commission** of 1987. The effect of this ruling (and possibly also its intention) has been to bring a very large number of entirely harmless agreements between firms under the scope of Article 85§1, and thereby to place a large burden on exemptions under Article 85§3 if European competition policy is not to be unreasonably restrictive. A large number of fish are caught entirely unnecessarily within the net of European competition policy, and have to be returned to the sea at the expense of considerable effort and uncertainty. There has been some mitigation of this tendency by the system of block exemptions, according to which agreements falling within the scope of Article 85§1 can be automatically exempted if they keep to a certain legal form. But it is a system that increases the emphasis in European competition law on form at the expense of effects, an emphasis that was entrenched in the original **Technique Minière** decision.

Third, market integration has long been an explicit and implicit principle of Community law. In other words, competition policy is intended to facilitate trade between Member States, even if trade between Member

States were in some circumstances to be antithetical to other goals such as efficiency of distribution or competition within Member States. What this has meant is that the prevention of parallel imports is virtually a *per se* violation of Article 85§1, even though the Article does not itself cite the prevention of parallel imports explicitly in its list of particular outlawed agreements. In theory there is no reason why the prevention of parallel imports should be antithetical to market integration (let alone efficiency), since it might be only under the guarantee of absolute territorial exclusivity that a distributor would be willing to take the risk of distributing. However, the form-based nature of the interpretation of Article 85§1 has in practice guaranteed that an agreement that prevents parallel imports can be construed as being anti-competitive in object even if not anti-competitive in effect. This interpretation has been carried over to the application of Article 85§3, in that exemptions cannot be granted for agreements that restrict parallel imports – an interpretation made explicit in Regulation 1983/83, which grants block exemption to exclusive distribution agreements that meet certain conditions.

These three broad features of European Community law with respect to vertical restraints may perhaps mean that it is unrealistic even to begin to assess the application of that law by economic criteria. For instance, the Commission's own recently published *Survey of the Member State National Laws Governing Vertical Distribution Agreements* reports in an admirably poker-faced way that 'certain major aspects in which [Member States'] systems are consistent in differing from the Community system can be identified. First, they hold that economic analysis should be employed in the first instance to determine whether an arrangement is prohibited' (Commission, 1996, p.1). However, if there is to be any realistic assessment of the scope for implementing economically consistent policies in this area, an assessment of the economic consequences of existing practices (even if these practices are not explicitly motivated with respect to their economic consequences) is undoubtedly of value.

2.5.2 The Decisions of the Commission since 1989

From 1989 to the end of 1995 the European Commission took a total of 27 decisions that concerned primarily the legality of particular vertical arrangements, most but not all of these being arrangements between a manufacturer and the distributors of its products.[21] These decisions are reported in Table 2.1. Although this is not a large number, both the character of the decisions taken and the written reasoning offered in defence of them provide an illuminating picture of the general principles behind the application by the Commission of Community law. In addition there

Table 2.1 Commission decisions concerning vertical agreements 1989–95

Case	Year	Features	Decision	Fine?
German TV film purchase	1989	Exclusive broadcast rights	Exemption with conditions	
Bayonox		Purchasing conditions	Infringement	Yes
Association Pharmaceutique Belge		Quality labels	Negative clearance	
Sugar beet		Exclusive purchasing	Infringement	No
Moosehead	1990	Exclusive licensing	Exemption	
Bayer Dental		Export ban	Infringement	No
D'Ieteren motor oils		Distribution agreement	Negative clearance	
Vichy	1991	Selective distribution	Applicability of Article 85§1 + withdrawal of immunity from fines	
Scottish Nuclear, Nuclear Energy		Supply agreement	Exemption	
Gosme/Martell-DMP		Export ban	Infringement	Yes
Viho/Toshiba		Export ban	Infringement	Yes
ECOSystem/Peugeot		Refusal to supply	Infringement	No
Yves Saint Laurent		Selective distribution	85§1 inapplicable with conditions	
Newitt/Dunlop Slazenger	1992	Exclusive distribution	Infringement	Yes
Viho/Parker pen		Export ban	Infringement	Yes
Givenchy		Selective distribution	Exemption	
World Cup 1990 package tours		Exclusive distribution	Infringement	No
Distribution of railway tickets		Distribution agreement	Infringement	Yes
Ford Agricultural		Export ban	Infringement	No
Jahrhundertvertrag		Supply agreement	Exemption	
Scholler Lebensmittel		Exclusive distribution	Infringement	No
Langnese-Iglo		Exclusive distribution	Infringement	No
Zera/Montedison & Hinkens/Stahler	1993	Exclusive distribution	Infringement	No
Grundig		Selective distribution	Exemption	
Pasteur Mérieux-Merck	1994	Exclusive distribution	Exemption	
Tretorn		Exclusive distribution	Infringement	Yes
BASF-Glasurit	1995	Exclusive distribution	Infringement	Yes

were a number of cases in which the Commission made public its reasoning behind settlements reached with companies (such as Microsoft, and the manufacturer of contraceptive pills Organon, which had imposed a pricing system discriminating against exports). The most striking features of the Commission's reasoning as revealed by these cases are as follows:

1. There is no consistent application of the distinction between inter-brand and intra-brand competition, in spite of the clear economic presumption that different analysis is appropriate to these two phenomena. This is apparent in three main ways:
   - In the interpretation of Article 85§1, the notion of a restriction of competition is applied indifferently to inter-brand and intra-brand competition.
   - The severity of the impact of a particular agreement on competition is sometimes discussed with no reference to whether inter-brand competition is affected (as in **Bayonox**, or the two ice-cream decisions, **Langnese-Iglo** and **Scholler**). Sometimes, however, the strength of inter-brand competition is cited as a mitigating factor (as in **Moosehead**, where the decision takes 'account of the existence of many similar competing beers', though curiously it does so in the context of an exemption under Article 85§3 rather than in determining the application of Article 85§1). The absence of inter-brand competition can be cited as an aggravating factor (as in **Railway ticket distribution**).
   - There is no attempt to identify particular circumstances where weakening of intra-brand competition might be a legitimate economic concern: for example, the fact that railways are state-owned and might, therefore, be insufficiently attentive to the benefits of intra-brand competition could have been cited as an argument in **Railway ticket distribution**.

2. Restrictions on parallel imports receive great emphasis in the decisions, both in the sense that they occupy a significant part of the written analysis, and in that they virtually guarantee an infringement decision with no exemption. Not only are there no examples of decisions citing agreements that restrict parallel imports, but which are nevertheless exempted. In some decisions (**Ford Agricultural**, for example) the discouragement of parallel imports is considered sufficient to justify an infringement decision without the need for further market analysis. In **Tretorn**, a tennis ball producer that prevented re-export by its exclusive distributors, was fined ECU 600,000 and its distributors were fined ECU 10,000 each. In the **Organon** case, the fact that a pricing schedule discriminated against exports was more important in determining the Commission's opposition than that it discriminated *per se*.

3. The imposition of fines is quite likely for infringement decisions in cases where the agreement was not notified prior to the opening of the case (after a complaint or on the Commission's own initiative).

4. The Commission does not consistently either define markets or assess dominance. Indeed, in cases where it seeks to consider the impact of a particular vertical agreement, it goes to some trouble to avoid using the

term 'dominance'. In the ice-cream decisions both the firms concerned are described as having 'prominent' and 'strong' positions on the German market for impulse ice-cream, but the word 'dominant' is not used. Legally there is some logic in this, in that an assessment of dominance is not required for an Article 85 decision, but the result is that the question whether and to what extent either firm can exercise market power is very confusingly treated. For example, the number of competing retail outlets in typical German towns, and the average distance between them, both of which would be important facts relevant to the assessment of market power, are not discussed.

5. The legality of certain types of agreement is determined by purely formal considerations without any reference *at all* to the market circumstances in which these operate. This is particularly apparent in the analysis of selective distribution agreements, such as those in a series of perfume cases (*Yves Saint Laurent, Givenchy* and *Vichy*). Here the Commission (with the support of the Court of First Instance in the *Vichy* case) has enforced rules on the allowable form of agreements even in markets where inter-brand competition is accepted to be strong: no firm has much more than 5% of the market in any Member State. (These rules refer in particular to the requirement that agreements may restrict dealing to approved dealers only if the criteria for approval are qualitative rather than quantitative.) The Commission's procedure is legally as well as economically strange, since in 1991 the Community Court ruled in **Stergio Delimitis vs. Henninger Brau** that a national court should make a realistic market assessment before holding that an agreement restricted competition in the sense of Article 85§1.

6. The Commission often finds itself in the position of deciding whether a restriction of intra-brand competition is justified in terms of overall benefits to the ultimate purchasers. That is, of assessing whether the commercial judgement of the upstream purchaser was sound rather than looking at market-wide implications for competition. Thus, in *Givenchy* the Commission gave a detailed opinion as to the benefits to Givenchy of a particular structure of selective distribution; in **World Cup Package Tours** it pronounced that the safety and other coordination benefits of using a single distributor were not worth the restriction of competitive pressure on that distributor.

7. In the instances where a particular vertical agreement has been exempted under Article 85§3, the reasoning is extremely superficial. In the **Jahrhundertvertrag** decision, for example, the purchasing agreement between the German electricity and coal sectors is justified in terms of contributing to Germany's 'security of supply'. Not only is no evidence given in support of this assertion, but there is no attempt to quantify

the cost of this method of assuring security of supply, or even to raise the question how much it is reasonable to expect German consumers to pay for this benefit.

What are the implications of these features of the decisions? Four conclusions in particular can be drawn:

1. There are significant risks of inconsistency between the Commission's policy on vertical restraints and its policy on vertical mergers, with the latter likely to be substantially more permissive. Vertical mergers are assessed (as they should be) by the dominance criterion (that is to say, by the likely impact on inter-brand competition). Any impact on intra-brand competition is ignored (by definition, since integration means that intra-brand competition is suppressed). Since parallel imports are also suppressed by vertical integration, this implies, of course, that the feature that is the single greatest driving force behind the Commission's reasoning on vertical agreements plays no part at all in its assessment of vertical mergers. This procedure is wholly indefensible in economic logic and is an invitation to firms to structure their deals purely to surmount competition law rather than in pursuit of intrinsic economic benefits.

2. The link between restrictions on parallel imports and distortions of competition is deeply confused: the Commission simply assumes that the one implies the other. This underlines the importance of making the right counterfactual analysis. It should not simply be assumed that in the absence of restrictions on parallel imports there would be the same distribution networks and greater trade between Member States (certain distribution networks might not exist at all). More generally, the emphasis on enabling parallel trade confuses symptoms with causes. The fact that price differentials may exist between national markets may well be a symptom of market power in those markets, but, conditional on the existence of that market power, it is by no means clear that parallel trade is welfare improving (a point that should be familiar from the literature on price discrimination). Exclusive distribution agreements may not be the cause of the market power in such markets as motor vehicles, which are after all easily transportable by the consumer to their final destination. At least in the European Union, the factor that prevents consumer arbitrage in the car market is the present system of national registration of ownership of vehicles. The system is an invitation to market segmentation that obliges consumers of one Member State to use intermediaries to purchase cars from another Member State; intermediaries whose position in the market requires the protection of competition policy.[22]

3. Far too many entirely harmless agreements are caught in the net of European competition policy. The resources of the authorities would be better targeted at policing genuinely damaging abuses of market power if they had to spend less time deciding whether limitations of intra-brand competition were on balance in the interests of the consumer or not. Upstream purchasers are far more suitable representatives of the consumer interest in respect of such questions, unless (by reason of state ownership or blatant monopoly position) it can be presumed that their interests in purchasing inputs diverge from those of consumers to an appreciable extent.

4. The Commission's existing procedures do not systematically identify the presence of market power, still less diagnose the extent to which vertical agreements contribute to strengthening or exploiting it.

2.6   The Commission's Green Paper on Vertical Restraints

In January 1997 the Commission published a *Green Paper on Vertical Restraints in EC Competition Policy* (Commission, 1997), which surveys (some of) the economic literature on the question and invites comments on a series of options for change. Three options are proposed along with retention of the current system. This is not the place to comment in detail on the Commission's Green Paper, but a few observations are worth making.

1. Under all the options for reform, both resale price maintenance and the prevention of parallel trade would continue to be treated as per se violations of Article 85§1 and would be unlikely to benefit from an exemption under Article 85§3. Enough has been said so far in this chapter to indicate how unsatisfactory this would be.

2. One option (Option II) proposes widening the system of block exemptions, via an increase in the range of clauses qualifying for exemption. This option essentially retains the emphasis of the present system on form rather than economic effects, with all the disadvantages we have described. In addition the option proposes setting up an arbitration procedure for distributors denied admission to a selective distribution network, a potentially nightmarish bureaucratic creation that involves the Commission seeking to intervene in private commercial arrangements without providing any rationale in terms of effects of these arrangements on competition in the market as a whole.

3. Option III proposes more focused block exemptions that would apply only where each party has less than a certain market share. This proposal completely misses the point of arguments about the importance

of inter-brand competition. The point is that in the absence of significant (inter-brand) market power there is no public interest in the detailed specification of which clauses are and which are not acceptable in a contract. Only the presence of significant inter-brand market power creates a defensible rationale for such intervention. So Option III uses the market share criterion in precisely the wrong way!

4. Option IV is the only one that makes any significant improvement on current arrangements, since it suggests that for parties with less than, for instance, 20% market share in the contract territory, there would be a refutable presumption of compatibility with Article 85§1. While clearly preferable to the existing situation, this falls a long way short of the reform implied by the kind of three-step procedure we have outlined.

2.7 Concluding Remarks

It is perhaps not very surprising that a system of competition policy which does not pretend to be implemented on the basis of economic analysis should reveal itself to have economically indefensible consequences. However, such a system is often defended on grounds of implementability: form-based reasoning is at least predictable, and avoids the dangers of handing competition policy over to unaccountable cliques of economists.

This chapter has argued that these dangers are real, but that the virtues claimed for the current European Union competition policy in avoiding the dangers are entirely imaginary. An economically defensible policy towards vertical restraints does not have to be highly discretionary; it can be based on simple rules of thumb that have a common-sense as well as a technical interpretation. The gap between such a policy and the present European Union system is wide, but that is an argument for taking reform more rather than less seriously.

3

Hard and Soft Cartels

3.1   Introduction

This chapter considers 'hard-core cartels'; explicit agreements to fix price or share markets between producers and sellers of substitute products. It is also concerned with what may be termed 'soft cartels', where the collusive agreement is merely implicit. Hard-core cartel agreements explicitly fall under the prohibition of Article 85§1. However, the range of soft cartels which may be covered by the prohibition is unclear. Much of the legal debate has, therefore, centred around evidence from which the existence of illegal agreements and concerted practices can be inferred. In the last ten years, important decisions by the Commission, the Court of Justice and the Court of First Instance have been taken which affect these legal concepts, and there has been much commentary about the direction of this evolution.[23] At the same time, the way in which economists think about informal understandings between firms has changed markedly over the last decade.

After reviewing the relevant economic literature concerning such agreements (Section 3.2), we outline in Section 3.3 a framework for the analysis of the case law towards these practices and discuss several policy issues. In particular, we emphasize the costs of implementing a legal standard that encompasses implicit understandings between firms. We argue that in principle a legal standard based on explicit coordination between firms may be preferable because the cost of type I errors associated with the implementation of this standard is likely to be relatively small. In Section 3.4, we characterize the current legal standards by reviewing important Court decisions while Section 3.5 analyses the recent case law. Section 3.6 concludes.

3.2   The Collective Exercise of Market Power

Firms' incentives to enter into an agreement or foster some informal understanding with competitors selling substitute products are clear enough: all firms benefit from an increase in price or a restriction in the output of their competitors and a collective exercise of market power such that all prices rise or aggregate output falls will raise individual rents. This will also give rise to some allocative as well as productive inefficiency (see Neven *et al.* (1993) for a summary of the arguments). In general, however, even if the exercise of market power will be in the collective interest of the firms, it will often be constrained by individual incentives.

For many constellations of prices or individual quantities involving a collective exercise of market power, individual firms have an incentive to take advantage of the output restrictions (or price increases) achieved by their competitors. Typically, individual firms will find it profitable to increase output or reduce price. Being inconsistent with private incentives, many outcomes involving a collective exercise of market power can thus be sustained only by some mechanism for coordination and enforcement of the collectively desirable behaviour.

The organization of an explicit mechanism, involving for instance a detailed agreement on output allocations and the imposition of penalties in case of deviations, presumably requires a fair amount of communication and negotiation between firms. Given that such explicit mechanisms have been illegal (at least in the United States), their organization has had to be concealed and they have not been enforceable by the courts. As a result, one would expect these mechanisms to be designed only with considerable difficulty and their implementation to be highly unstable. The view was commonly held in the 1960s and early 1970s that 'hard core' cartels did not raise important concerns for anti-trust policy (see for instance Stigler, 1965).

Box 3.1 Non-cooperative coordination in repeated games

Consider an oligopoly in which identical firms sell homogeneous commodities. Consider first a static game in which firms take each others' output as given. Denote q^C as the strategy used by each firm at the unique Cournot-Nash equilibrium of this game while π^C denotes the equilibrium payoff. Next, assume that the game is repeated for an infinite horizon. A strategy for this game is a complete plan of action; namely an action for the first period, a plan for the second period expressed as a function of what other firms have done in the first period, a plan for the third period as a function of what has happened in the first and second periods, and so forth. We look for a non-cooperative Nash equilibrium in this game, i.e. a set of strategies that are best replies to one another. A combination of strategies where all firms plan to play the Cournot output q^C for ever will be an equilibrium. If one firm plays Cournot at every period, the best reply of the others is to play Cournot and vice-versa. However, firms may do better than that.

Consider for instance the following strategy (Friedman, 1971): play a strategy of low output, say q^L in period 1; then carry on playing q^L in subsequent periods as long as the other firms also play q^L; however, if other firm(s) play a strategy other than q^L in a given period, play q^C, the Cournot output in the following period and for ever after. In order to check that this plan is a non-cooperative equilibrium if all firms play according to this rule, we have to show that if all but one firm play according to the rule, the best reply of the remaining firms will be to apply the rule. Let us define q^H as the best reply of a firm when all competitors play q^L when it considers only one period and π^H as the payoff associated with this strategy. π^L will denote the payoff which is earned by an individual firm if everybody plays q^L. In general, we expect that $\pi^H > \pi^L > \pi^C$.

Given that the other firms play the strategy described above, if the remaining firm adopts the same strategy it will obtain π^C for ever. In present value terms, this gives a payoff of

$$\Pi^L = \sum_{i=1}^{\infty} \alpha^i \pi^L = \frac{\alpha}{1-\alpha} \pi^L$$

where α is a discount factor. Let us now consider alternative strategies: if the firm plays anything different from q^L in a period, other firms will subsequently play q^C for ever. At that stage, the best that the firm may achieve is to play q^C itself. Accordingly, the best alternative candidate strategy is to play q^H for one period, thereby taking advantage of the other firms for one period (deviating) and q^C ever after. This strategy will yield a payoff:

$$\Pi^D = \alpha \pi^H + \sum_{i=2}^{\infty} \alpha^i \pi^C = \alpha \pi^H + \frac{\alpha^2}{1-\alpha} \pi^C$$

The strategy combination in which all firms play the strategy described above will thus be an equilibrium if $\Pi^D < \Pi^L$. This will hold if the discount term α is large enough, i.e. if

$$\alpha \geq \frac{\pi^H - \pi^L}{\pi^L - \pi^C}$$

In other words, if the interest rate is low enough, there will be an equilibrium in which firms apply a low output strategy for ever. This strategy has so far been left unspecified; a wide range of such strategies (and associated outcomes) will thus result in equilibrium. As indicated by the last inequality, strategies which involve large output restrictions (for instance close to the monopoly output, such that π^L is large) will only be used in equilibrium if the interest rate is relatively low. Strategies which involve less output restraints will be used in equilibrium for higher values of the interest rate.

Various types of threats can be considered besides reversion to the Cournot outcome. For instance, Abreu *et al.* (1986) suggests a more complicated punishment path which involves a phase of expanded outputs and a progressive reversion to the low output level. Some threats will, however, be unreasonable; consider for instance a threat to set output at a level which will minimize the profit of the firm that has deviated (given the anticipated best reply of this deviator to the strategy of the punishing firm). This threat, referred to as the minimax strategy, is not very plausible. Indeed, if the deviators expect the punishing firm to use a minimax strategy and set output accordingly, it will not be in the best interest of the punishing firm to use it. The threat lacks credibility and it seems reasonable to impose that the strategies used by deviators and punishing firms should in turn be mutual best replies, not only for the whole game but also in particular contingencies, which correspond to particular truncations of the game. The restriction that equilibrium strategies should be mutual replies in every truncation of the game, formally know as subgame-perfection, will indeed restrict the set of strategy combinations that result in equilibrium. Of course, the threat to use the equilibrium strategy of the Cournot game, will by construction be subgame perfect.

There are other possible restrictions on the credibility of punishment strategies. For example, those which would hurt the punishing as well as the punished firm might never be implemented since both parties would have an incentive to renegotiate (see Farrell and Maskin, 1989).

The collective exercise of market power may not always require elaborate explicit coordination. In particular, firms might resist taking advantage of competitors in the short term because by doing so they would risk jeopardizing a profitable arrangement in the long term. This idea, which had been discussed informally for some time both in the economics and in the management literature (see for instance, Scherer (1980) and Porter (1982) respectively), has been formalized by the theory of repeated games. The central result of this literature confirms that if firms interact with each other repeatedly, the pursuit of individual interests may be consistent with the exercise of substantial market power (see Box 3.1 for a simple formal account). Firms which contemplate deviating from some allocation involving collective market power will trade-off the resulting short-term gains against the long-term consequences of forgoing the rents associated with the initial allocation. The terms of this trade-off will also depend on various market circumstances as well as firms' discount rates (see Box 3.2 for a short summary of the circumstances that will make implicit coordination more likely). In particular, if competitors can credibly announce that a short-term deviation will be severely punished, for instance by sharply increasing competition for ever, the long-term cost may easily exceed short-term benefits. All firms will thus prefer, in their own best interest, not to deviate from outcomes which involve substantial market power.

If repeated interactions provide an adequate mechanism to enforce outcomes with substantial market power, 'soft cartels' may indeed become a significant concern for anti-trust policy, and possibly more so than 'hard-core cartels'. There are, however, at least two reasons why 'soft cartels' may not be such a concern. First, as in the case of an explicit enforcement mechanism, the operation of implicit mechanisms will require that firms be able to observe each other's behaviour. Indeed, the decision to trigger punishment relies on the observation that some firm has deviated from the equilibrium strategy. In practice, observing individual actions may be difficult and firms may have to rely on information regarding aggregate variables only. This is modelled by Green and Porter (1984).[24] They assume that firms can observe only the aggregate price level, where prices are subject to random shocks in demand. A drop in price can, therefore, be due either to a drop in demand or to a deviation by a competitor. In this context, outcomes with substantial market power can still be supported by individual strategies in which firms select a trigger price and engage in price wars (a period of low prices) if the observed price falls below that level. The range of outcomes that can be supported is, however, reduced and implicit coordination is less profitable as, in any period, there is a strictly positive probability that a price war will break out.

Box 3.2 The circumstances favourable to implicit coordination

The literature points to a number of circumstances which are favourable for the collective exercise of market power. First, information about the behaviour of competitors should facilitate the detection of deviation from the cartel outcome and hence improve the incentive properties of the equilibrium. Information on individual behaviour is in this respect much more useful than aggregate information.[25] Similarly, information on past behaviour may be more useful than price announcements, which carry no commitment (at least downwards), and increasing the frequency of information transmission will also help. As discussed below, 'meeting competition' clauses in contracts with customers will help in disseminating information. Trade associations may also play that role. Second, any circumstances which improve firms' inferences about the past behaviour of competitors will help:[26] for instance some symmetry across firms in terms of costs or product characteristics will be useful.[27] Third, competition in several markets at the same time will usually enlarge the range of outcomes that can be supported as an equilibrium, because it allows for stronger punishments.[28] Fourth, the presence of a competitive fringe will usually limit the scope for coordination.[29]

Second, implicit coordination through repeated interactions may, paradoxically, be ineffective because it is such a generic mechanism. As indicated above, many different outcomes involving market power can arise for a given punishment strategy. How will firms make sure that they focus on a particular outcome? This question has by and large not been treated formally so far[30] and it is not clear whether the selection of a particular outcome can be undertaken simply through market interactions. Schelling (1960) proposed a theory of focal points which does not require direct coordination between firms. According to this view, firms will select outcomes, or at least behavioural rules, which are self evident or 'salient', and firms may want to try and affect the perception of particular outcomes, or particular rules, as self evident. For instance, a prior announcement of a well-defined price increase (say, a given percentage) may be sufficient to establish a self-evident way to behave. Short of theoretical backing or empirical evidence, it is still difficult to assess how much weight should be given to these conjectures. At the very least, it seems that selecting a particular outcome through market interactions, if feasible, will be a highly imperfect process. Firms trying to improve on the selection of the outcome may have to resort to explicit coordination.

Overall, the prospect that firms may rely on implicit enforcement mechanisms (however imperfect) to exercise collective market power still raises a significant issue for anti-trust policy. Before considering the attitude of the European competition authorities towards such implicit mechanisms (Section 3.4), we first outline the cost and benefits of various policy options.

3.3   Alternative Standards of Prohibition

A number of issues arise with respect to the design of an anti-trust policy towards the collective exercise of market power. As emphasized above (and in Box 3.1), the collective exercise of market power can be supported either by an explicit mechanism or by implicit coordination. In contrast to explicit mechanisms, implicit coordination may be achieved simply through market interactions, without any communication or negotiation between firms. There will be no evidence of firms' having met or having discussed the coordination of market behaviour. The only evidence that will be available in this case relates to firms' market behaviour and the issue arises whether anti-trust policy should trying to make such implicit coordination unlawful.

Second, one can wonder whether establishing that some coordination between firms (whether explicit or implicit) has taken place should be sufficient for a violation to occur. Indeed, many forms of coordination could be ineffective in establishing market power. One might reasonably argue that a market power test should be added to evidence of coordination in order to establish a violation.

Third, consider the evidence that will required to establish that explicit coordination has taken place. In principle, two types of evidence can be used, namely evidence of firm behaviour and direct material evidence of coordination (for instance, evidence of firms having met or having debated the coordination of their behaviour).

3.3.1   Should Implicit Coordination be Unlawful?

If implicit coordination in the exercise of market power were prohibited, firms could be convicted merely for the pursuit of their own best commercial interest. This may not itself pose a significant problem, as it has long been accepted that some types of firm behaviour that maximize profit can be deemed illegal (fraudulent or predatory behaviour, for example). The main drawback of such a legal approach is associated with the cost of type I errors (those involving false conviction). It may be difficult to distinguish between firms consciously trying to support implicit coordination and those which interact in the market without such an intention, and the authorities are likely to make important errors. In particular, they may convict firms that have done no more than pursue profit-making opportunities without any attempt to support an implicit coordination agreement. Competition policy might thereby discourage that pursuit of profitable activity which is a central motive behind the operation of a market economy.

The evidence that can be brought forward to establish the existence of implicit coordination is also likely to involve large type I errors. As we have indicated above, firms involved in the such mechanisms will periodically engage in price wars (Green and Porter, 1984) and the question then arises whether the observation of price wars could be used as reliable evidence of implicit coordination between firms. As noted by Baker (1989), the main insight of the Green and Porter (1984) model, namely that firms will react to a negative demand shock by expanding output (engage in a price war), can be contrasted with that expected under 'competitive' conditions (for instance in perfect competition or in a static Nash equilibrium) where firms react by reducing output. This would suggest that a careful observation of circumstance surrounding price wars may be revealing. This methodology has been used by Porter (1985), as well as Baker (1989).[31]

Unfortunately, this method might involve important type I errors because price wars can be made consistent with environments where firms are not involved in implicit coordination. For instance, in the presence of search costs, it is easy to generate cycles in prices which look like price wars (see for instance Comanor, 1990).

Overall, it seems not only that the identification of implicit coordination between firms is subject to large type I errors, but also that such errors are potentially very costly. In addition, the costs of allowing implicit coordination in the collective exercise of market power may not be very large. As we have indicated above, instances where firms can successfully exercise market power solely through market interactions may not be very frequent. Much depends on whether firms will be able to focus on a particular outcome simply through market interaction. The theoretical literature has little to say on the matter. Nevertheless, it is likely that in the absence of explicit coordination any market power that firms are able to exercise collectively will be highly imperfect. Entry is also likely to make implicit coordination more difficult to achieve as it may take time before the entrants reach a common understanding with the incumbents. In the case of imports, the asymmetry between incumbents and importers might make this task particularly difficult.

3.3.2 Should a Market Power Test be Necessary?

Independently of the evidence that will be required for its implementation, a market power test would require the definition of a benchmark for what constitutes an acceptable degree of market power. The complete absence of market power is of course not a sensible benchmark, because in the presence of substantial fixed costs, a free entry equilibrium with zero profits may entail significant market power. The market power arising at the zero profit equilibrium is also an inadequate candidate for such a benchmark. In particular, (explicit or implicit) collusion between firms in the market may attract a new entry that unnecessarily duplicates fixed costs. Even though no profits result from this, it would have been desirable for there to have been no collusion in the first place.

In principle, all it takes to evaluate market power is a comparison between price and marginal cost. Profits can also be used as an indirect measure. Both approaches, however, suffer from the same shortcomings. They are subject to important measurement errors, and may systematically underestimate the extent of market power to the extent that firms may enjoy the fruits of market power in the form of high costs.

The dynamic behaviour of aggregate market variables may offer more scope for detection to the extent that the change in price (or other aggregate variable) which follows some change in demand or and cost will vary according to the degree of market power being exercised in the market. As explained in Bresnahan (1989), a rotation of the demand curve or a shift in marginal cost offers most scope for identifying market power. This method, which does not require data on costs, has been used in a large number of industry studies. Nevertheless it still suffers from the drawback that the level of marginal cost might also be a function of the degree of market power being exercised in the market. Even if it is possible to allow for the endogenous determination of marginal cost to some extent while preserving the identification of market power,[32] pure shifts in intercept of the marginal cost cannot be disentangled from the market power itself.[33]

Overall, it is likely that market power tests will involve large type II errors (in which the conclusion is mistakenly drawn that no market power exists). A prohibition involving such a test will thus give rise to a limited deterrence effect.

3.3.3 Explicit Coordination: What Evidence Should be Required?

Explicit coordination in the collective exercise of market power can in principle be established from evidence on firms' behaviour or from material evidence. The standards of proof that will be adequate will again depend on the cost of type I errors. The authorities may conclude that firms have undertaken some explicit coordination in the collective exercise of market power when they did not coordinate at all, or did explicitly coordinate some strategies but not for the sake of exercising market power. This will be costly when firms are thereby deterred from undertaking explicit coordination which brings strong efficiency benefits. It would seem, however, that there are few instances where explicit coordination between firms on prices and output brings such benefits (though we discuss this in more detail in Chapter 4). As a result, stringent requirements on the evidence necessary to establish explicit coordination may not be appropriate. Given the large type I errors associated with evidence on firm behaviour, the requirement for some material evidence of explicit coordination may still be warranted.

There is one instance where explicit price or output coordination between firms may bring significant efficiency benefits, namely when competition fails to bring about a stable market outcome (equilibrium); explicit coordination between firms may then be seen as an attempt to establish a stable outcome in an otherwise chaotic environment. A legal prohibition of coordination would prevent this reasonable attempt to maintain stability. As indicated in the simple example developed in Box 3.3, highly unstable outcomes can indeed arise when entry is costless and when firms operate with large capacities relative to demand, or in the presence of a large fall in demand.

Overall, it seems appropriate not to exaggerate requirements on the evidence of explicit coordination. Given that type II errors are in any event relatively large (because firms have ample opportunities to conceal their coordination) and relatively costly (because of reduced deterrence), and given that type I errors may not be very costly, reducing the latter at the cost of further increasing the former may not be desirable. A more cautious attitude may still be warranted in those industries where firms operate with large capacities relative to demand or in the presence of a large fall in demand.

Box 3.3 Is explicit coordination sometimes efficient?

Sjostrom (1989) provides a simple example where competition and free entry do not lead to an equilibrium. Assume that firms operate with a fixed cost (avoidable in the long run) and increasing marginal cost so that the average cost curve is U-shaped. Firms act independently and non-strategically so that the industry supply curve is the sum of individual supply curves. Consider a market outcome with two firms operating above the minimum efficient scale (with a market price above the minimum average cost). Such an outcome will attract entry because incumbents are making positive profits: entry by a couple of additional firms at a price equal to the minimum of the average cost might, however, trigger exit of the incumbent firms (their residual demand being insufficient). After exit of the incumbents, the new entrants will raise price to the level originally set by the incumbents. This in turn will attract new entry and the whole process starts all over again.

In this example (as in other cases of an 'empty core' – see Telser, 1985), the absence of an equilibrium is associated with an integer problem and with the absence of sunk cost (so that entry and exit are costless). If the capacity of the original incumbents at the minimum of the average cost were exactly equal to demand, no entry would ever take place. It is because demand is not a multiple of the capacity offered at the minimum efficient scale that entry and exit take place. If the fixed cost were sunk on entry, the equilibrium in this example could be restored: the prospective entrants would realize that entry would bring the price below the average total cost (including the sunk cost of entry) and would not enter. The long-run equilibrium would feature just two firms.

Allowing for sunk costs, however, a sharp fall in demand might very well precipitate a breakdown of equilibrium: consider for instance an initial configuration with n firms operating at minimum efficient scale. If demand falls, firms will keep on producing along their supply curve until the minimum of their avoidable average cost is reached. If demand falls further, however, there will be no equilibrium any more: some firms will become inactive, the price will increase, which will attract re-entry of some firms and so forth.

What should we learn from this simple example? First, even if it is undoubtedly feasible to restore equilibrium in these examples with appropriate assumptions about the strategy space of the firms, it serves as a useful reminder that competition may lead to highly unstable outcomes when entry is costless and when firms operate with large capacities relative to demand. Sjostrom (1989) indeed argues that the shipping industry is a case in point. Second, it underlines the effect of demand shifts on the competitive process: a large recession may indeed drive the industry into a situation where equilibrium no longer exists. This might serve as a justification for crisis cartels and in any event, sheds a particular light on coordination which, as revealed by the case law (see below) frequently takes place in certain industries. A further assessment is provided by Crampin (1997).

3.4 Agreement and Concerted Practices – the Legal Concepts

In this section, we turn to legal concepts and try to evaluate how the issues identified above have been handled in the case law. In particular, we try to evaluate whether unlawful agreements and concerted practices have been defined in such a way that implicit coordination in the exercise of market power is unlawful. We will review landmark decisions of the Commission, the Court of Justice and the Court of First Instance.

3.4.1 Contacts Between Firms

A couple of principles were firmly established in the early decision on *Zuiker Unie*.[34] According to the Court of Justice:

> The degree of 'coordination' and 'cooperation'. . . must be understood in the light of the concept inherent in the provision of the Treaty relating to competition that each economic operator must determine independently the policy which he intends to adopt on the common market . . . Although it is correct to say that this requirement of independence does not deprive economic operators of the right to adapt themselves intelligently to the existing and anticipated conduct of their competitor, it does however strictly preclude any direct or indirect contact between such operators, the object or effect whereof is either to influence the conduct on the market of an actual or potential competitor or to disclose to such a competitor the course of conduct which they themselves have decided to adopt or contemplate adopting in the market.

This statement established two important principles. First, it makes clear that interdependent decision-making by firms is in itself legitimate. From the economist's point of view, the recognition that strategic interdependence is not only a fact in most industries but is also an integral part of competition, is clearly welcome.[35]

The second principle established by the decision is one of prohibition: direct or indirect contact between firms to influence each other's behaviour (or that of a third party), is not legitimate. This decision thus provides a first definition of coordination, which can be seen as unlawful. It clearly covers the type of explicit coordination that was considered above (direct contacts). This definition, however, leaves an important ambiguity. It is not clear from this formulation whether some forms of market interaction between firms (which may be aimed at establishing a focal point for coordination or simply at the initiation of a punishment phase) can reasonably be seen as a form of indirect contact between firms. From this definition, one cannot exclude the possibility that implicit coordination could be seen as unlawful.

3.4.2   Agreements

Throughout the case law, the definition of an unlawful agreement has been relatively uncontroversial and has been clearly associated with a process of coordination between firms, for which there is material proof. The central element in an agreement seems to be an exchange of undertakings. For instance, the fact that firms may have expressed their joint intention to conduct themselves in the market in a specific way is sufficient to constitute an agreement.[36] It is also clear for the Court that the binding and rule-making character of an agreement is not due to legal factors[37] and that it does not have to be set down in writing.

3.4.3   Concerted Practices

The concept of concerted practices has evolved a great deal over time. Two important steps can be distinguished.

3.4.3.1 Concerted Practices and Individual Behaviour

In the early decisions, the concept of restrictive practices was meant to cover circumstances where there is no material evidence of coordination.[38] Concerted practices were associated with firms' behaviour indicative of a common policy being pursued.

This was expressed for instance by Advocate General Mayras in the *Dyestuff*[39] decision.

> It is my opinion that the authors of the Treaty intended to avoid the possibility of the prohibitions of article 85 concerning anti-competitive acts being evaded by undertakings which, while following a common policy, act in such a way as to leave no trace of any written document which could be described as an agreement

and

> such an interpretation . . . is of obvious interest as to the proof of the existence of a concerted practice which, even implying a certain manifestation of will of the participating undertakings, cannot be sought in the same circumstances as the proof of an express agreement.

> But there is need, first, for an objective element, essential to the concept of concerted practice: the *actual* common conduct of the participating undertakings . . . . However, the simple finding of a common conduct, parallel or concordant, of undertakings on the market clearly cannot suffice to establish a concerted practice within the meaning of Article 85§1. It is still necessary for that conduct not to be the consequence, or at least *the main consequence*, of the structure and the economic conditions of the market. There should be added a

certain will of the parties to act in common . . . but this common will may, according to circumstances, be deduced from all the informational data gathered on the conduct of the undertakings . . . .

This passage suggests that a concerted practice is indeed associated with evidence that firms follow a common policy that results from a hidden process of coordination. Rightly, the Advocate General also suggests that a solid analysis of counterfactuals should form part of the evidence on behaviour. However, the Advocate General also insists on evidence that parties have a certain will to act in common (and hence have coordinated their behaviour) while accepting fairly loose standards of proof (in particular that intention can be presumed from the outcomes).

In another important decision, *Zuiker Unie*,[40] the Court confirmed this approach but expressed the condition of a 'common will' differently by requiring that firms should be aware of the cooperative logic behind their behaviour. A concerted practice was defined as:

a form of coordination between undertakings which, without having been taken to the stage where an agreement properly so called has been concluded, *knowingly*, substitute for the risk of competition, practical cooperation between them which leads to conditions of competition which do no correspond to the normal conditions of competition of the market.

These quotations suggest that the Court came very close to prohibiting implicit coordination between firms; indeed, the requirements (beyond *ex post* behaviour indicative of coordination) that firms should be aware of the cooperative logic behind their behaviour is arguably fulfilled in the context of implicit coordination. Still, the insistence by the Court that the existence of intentions, or that of a common will, should be substantiated by material evidence has narrowly but effectively excluded implicit coordination from the scope of the prohibition.

The requirement that some evidence of intent (common will) is also needed for establishing the existence of a concerted practice is consistent with the perception (explicit in the passages above) that type I errors would be unacceptably frequent if concerted practices could be established solely on the basis of behaviour. It is indeed one of the fixed points in the case law since the *Dyestuff* decision that the Court has refused to consider evidence on outcomes and economic counterfactuals as sufficient.[41]

This approach is not altogether very different from that found in the US where additional factors are required in addition to parallel behaviour in order to find a conviction. Among those factors, evidence of anti-competitive intent behind the parallel conduct[42] and the absence of a credible explanation for the conduct in the absence of detailed communication or coordination are given heavy weight (see Baker, 1993).

The concept of concerted practice that emerges from these decisions would still be greatly clarified if it were stated explicitly how the economic counterfactual (the 'normal conditions of the market') should be treated. So far little has been said (except in *Polypropylène*,[43] where it was established that evidence on behaviour need not be limited to parallel behaviour but could include any conspicuous behaviour which could not be explained in terms of 'normal competitive conditions'). As a result, there has been some confusion in the case law (see below). Effectively, what the Commission has to do is to show that observed behaviour cannot reasonably be explained without some form of explicit coordination. This ought to be explicitly acknowledged. It should also be clarified, in particular, that behaviour which can be explained as the pursuit of a firm's own interest in the absence of explicit coordination will not be taken as evidence for the existence of a concerted practice.

3.4.3.2 Concerted Practices – Weak Direct Evidence of Coordination

Recent decisions by the Commission and subsequent reviews by the Court have extended the concept of concerted practices. In *Polypropylène*[44] as well as in later decisions like *Flat Glass*[45] or *LEDP*[46], the Commission argued that evidence on behaviour was not really necessary to establish the presence of a concerted practice. It sought to extend the concept to situations where the factual evidence on direct and explicit coordination between firms was insufficient to support the conclusion that there has been an agreement (for instance, no clear exchange of undertakings), but where there was still abundant evidence of communication between firms regarding anti-competitive actions. The Commission has thus perceived a gap in the coverage of the legal concepts, between situations that can qualify as concerted practices because of evidence on behaviour and situations that can qualify as agreements because of abundant factual evidence. It has tried to extend the concept of concerted practice in order to cover this gap. This reaction is presumably a consequence of the considerable frustration that the Commission must have felt in dealing with counterfactual behaviour in order to establish the existence of concerted practices (in its original definition).

For instance, in the *Polypropylène* decision, the Commission stated in Article 87 that:

> toute prise de contact direct ou indirecte entre elles ayant pour object ou pour effet, soit d'influencer le comportement sur le marché d'un concurrent actuel ou potentiel, soit de dévoiler à un tel concurrent le comportement que l'on est décidé, ou que l'on envisage soit même sur la marché . . . peut tomber sous le coup de l'article 85 paragraphe 1 en tant que pratique concertée.

The companies involved challenged the Commission's interpretation during the administrative procedure by stating that (Article 88 of the decision) 'la notion de pratique concertée suppose des actes manifestés sur le marché'. In their view, the Commission should have shown that companies had tried to put into effect what was allegedly concerted. The case was brought to Court essentially on these grounds (in addition to procedural issues).

The Court firmly rejected the argument of the Commission that concertation (i.e. exchange of information and opinions between firms which can be used as a vehicle to outline common views) could be taken as evidence of a concerted practice *per se*. It has suggested, however, that when there is evidence of concertation, the effects on the market could be presumed. As stated by Advocate General Versterdrof:

> It can therefore be maintained that in principle concertation will automatically trigger subsequent action on the market which will be determined by the concertation, whether the undertakings do one thing or another with regard to their market policy, that is to say regardless of whether they subsequently behave in a more or less uniform way in the market.

Effectively what this ruling has done is to declare that the Commission was wrong on principles but right in its practice. There is still a subtle difference between the Commission's argument that coordination is *per se* a concerted practice and the Court ruling that when there is evidence of concertation, behaviour can be presumed; in the latter case, it still possible for firm to overturn the presumption, namely to argue that the content of the concertation has not affected its behaviour, for instance because it has put in place commitment mechanisms to prevent the use of the knowledge gained in the concertation (like firing the executives concerned).

3.4.4   Agreements and Concerted Practices: Conclusion

The main conclusion which emerges from our review of these legal concepts is that implicit coordination in the exercise of market power cannot be seen as a concerted practice and hence is not unlawful. Such safe harbour is also probably desirable in light of the cost that type I errors would entail if it were prohibited. Admittedly, the early case law came close to such a prohibition but has evolved away from it.

Second, there is no evidence in the case law that a market power test is necessary when the existence of an agreement or a concerted practice has been established. As noted by Advocate General Mayras in **Zuiker Unie**,[47] to the extent that concerted practices will be established by outcomes, it is not necessary further to establish that a concerted practice has the effect of restricting competition. This is an integral part of the proof that there is a concerted practice in the first place. By contrast, where agreements are concerned, it is necessary to prove that they have the object or effect of restricting competition. This additional requirement has, however, not proved to be a major hurdle in the case law (see Guerrin and Kyriazis, 1992). Here again, it seems that the Community practice is sensible, in light of the large type II errors that a market power test would entail.

The concept of concerted practices has also evolved a great deal in recent years. A concerted practice can currently be found on two different grounds. First, by evidence on the conduct of firms (which includes parallel conduct but also any suspicious conduct which cannot be credibly explained in terms of 'normal' competitive behaviour) supplemented by evidence on intent. Second, by evidence on concertation (regarding practices which can have anti-competitive effects) from which conduct in the market can be presumed.

Because of this evolution, one can wonder whether the distinction between agreements and concerted practices is still very meaningful. Both can be established from direct evidence of coordination, and the only difference is that evidence may be weaker for concerted practices. Hence, it seems that any agreement is *a fortiori* a concerted practice. In this context, it would clarify matters a great deal if the Commission or the Court were to state explicitly that the legal standard is indeed one of explicit coordination, and furthermore that explicit coordination can be established either by direct evidence or by evidence on market behaviour for which coordination is the only reasonable explanation.

Overall, the preceding discussion also suggests a number of issues that should be kept in mind in analysing the case law.

1. If the legal rule which emerges seems relatively clear, the analysis of firms' behaviour and the standards that economic counterfactuals should meet have remained rather vague ('the normal conditions of competition'). It is, therefore, important to evaluate how this analysis has been undertaken in practice.

2. The case law reviewed so far has considered various types of contact between firms which can be seen as explicit coordination, but has not provided a clear distinction between lawful and illegal interactions. As discussed above, some types of explicit coordination may be efficient. It will be interesting to find out whether this is recognized in the case law.

3. As indicated above, stringent evidence requirements to establish the existence of explicit coordination may not be appropriate given that type I errors may not matter very much in this context. Such requirements might lead to large type II errors, which in turn reduce much of

the deterrence effect of the policy. It thus be important to evaluate these requirements.

4. As always in competition cases, the analysis of the market will matter a great deal. Issues like market definition and the factors affecting the plausibility of coordination will deserve attention.

3.5   The Recent Case Law

Many decisions by the Commission in the area of secret horizontal agreements and concerted practices are appealed in Court. In what follows, we review all decisions by the Commission in the period 1989–95 (whether or not they were appealed in Court) as well as all the important Court decisions in the same period, together with the original Commission decisions relating to those cases (which may accordingly have been taken prior to 1989). In what follows, we will comment on various aspects of these cases. In order to avoid repetition of the basic facts of each case, a summary of the important cases is presented in Box 3.4 (less important cases will be discussed in the text).

Box 3.4 Summary of recent cases

1. *Welded Steel* (OJL 260, 1989). Producers of welded steel throughout Europe coordinated sales in a number of national markets (Italy, Benelux, Germany, France) between 1980 and 1985. Part of the incentive to coordinate arose because a crisis cartel was established in Germany and allowed by the Bundeskriminalamt (BKA). In order to make it effective, imports had to be restricted. The Commission found ample factual evidence of coordination and 14 companies were fined, with fines ranging from 20,000 to 1,375,000 ECUs.

2. *Soda ash* (OJL 152/1, 1991). Whereas Solvay has concentrated its sales of soda ash on the continent, where it holds a large market share (>60%), ICI has a near monopoly in the United Kingdom and has never penetrated the continent. An agreement, known as 'page 1000', was struck between the companies in 1945 to maintain the actual market-sharing arrangements which prevailed at the time. The agreement was formally suspended by the time the United Kingdom joined the Community. The Commission held that the companies had continued to coordinate their behaviour to

---

maintain the market-sharing agreement thereafter. The Commission had evidence of sustained contacts between the companies but not factual evidence of coordination. The interpretation of parallel behaviour, namely whether market-sharing could arise in competitive conditions, was essential. Fines of 7 million ECUs were imposed on each company. They appealed and the decision was annulled by the Court of First Instance, on procedural grounds (OJC 341, 19 December 1995). This case is closely connected with an application for exemption under Article 85§3 by a US export cartel (under the Webb-Pomerene Act) and various anti-dumping decisions.

3. *Wood Pulp* (OJL 85/1, 1985). Producers of wood pulp from the United States (organized as an export association under the Webb-Pomerene Act), Canada, Scandinavian countries and several members states were found by the Commission to have coordinated prices, between 1975 and 1981. There was evidence of numerous contacts between firms but little factual evidence of explicit coordination: there was evidence of parallel quarterly announcements of prospective prise rises and in some cases of virtually simultaneous price rises. Much of the decision turned on the interpretation of parallel behaviour, in particular the pre-announcement of prices. As many as 36 companies were fined, with amounts ranging from 50,000 to 500,000 ECUs. The decision was appealed on several grounds. The question of Community jurisdiction over foreign firms was settled in the first Court decision (on 27 September 1988) in favour of the jurisdiction. The second Court ruling (31 March 1993) annulled most of the Commission decision, on the grounds that the behaviour was equally well explainable as individual rather than coordinated behaviour.

4. *Polypropylène* (OJL 230/1, 1986). Fifteen European producers of polypropylene were found by the Commission to have operated a market-sharing arrangement since 1977. The Commission found little evidence of parallel behaviour but ample evidence of contacts between firms, some of it relating explicitly to prices and output levels. Substantial fines were imposed (around 10 million ECUs for the main offenders). All companies but one appealed, partly on substantive grounds (regarding the interpretation of concerted practices). The Court of First Instance upheld most of the Commission's reasoning, confirmed the fines on eight companies and reduced them on another six because of insufficient standards of proof (CMLR 84, 1992).

5. *Flat Glass* (OJL 33/44, 1989). Three Italian producers of flat glass were found to have violated both Articles 85 and 86. Regarding Article 85, the Commission held that the three producers had coordinated prices and commercial policies both in the automotive and non-automotive markets. The Commission brought material evidence of coordination and of parallel behaviour. The companies were fined between 1.7 and 7 million ECUs. They appealed and the Court of First Instance annulled most of the decision (CMLR 302, 1992) because of insufficient proof. It also reduced the fines (cancelling the fine altogether for one firm and reducing them by as much as 6/7 for the other two).

6. *Cartonboard* (OJL 243/1, 1994). Nineteen producers of carton boards throughout the EC and EFTA were found to have violated Article 85. The Commission held that the producers had met at regular intervals to coordinate strategy, had agreed on price increases and had shared markets. The Commission had access to ample material evidence but did not bring evidence on market behaviour. Fines ranging from 1 to 22.75 million ECUs were imposed.

7. *Cement* (OJL 343/1,1995). As many as 42 cement producers throughout Europe were found to have prevented parallel imports, to have systematically exchanged detailed information and to have occasionally fixed prices. The Commission relied mostly on material evidence of coordination between firms. Fines ranged from 100,000 to 32 million ECUs.

3.5.1 The Analysis of Firm Behaviour

In cases where the Commission is trying to establish a concerted practice on the basis of behaviour, the analysis of the counterfactual will be essential. What the Commission has to show is that the behaviour of firms cannot be explained without resorting to some form of coordination. Importantly therefore, it is not enough for the Commission to establish that the behaviour of firms is consistent with some prior form of coordination; it has to show that the observed behaviour cannot be explained in terms of alternative competitive processes which do not involve coordination. This principle has been clearly stated by the Court in *Wood Pulp*.

The next sections consider some flaws in the Commission's reasoning that appear in a number of decisions.

3.5.1.1 Alternative Explanations not Involving Coordination

On a number of occasions the Commission has failed to consider whether the observed behaviour might be explained without appeal to explicit coordination. First, the evidence on behaviour brought forward by the Commission can sometimes be interpreted as the operation of implicit coordination, which arguably is not unlawful (as discussed above).

The *Welded Steel* case serves as an illustration of such an instance (admittedly, the factual evidence of concertation was so strong in this case that the Commission did not have to rely much on interpreting the behaviour). In particular, the case contains a detailed account of what economists would refer to as the trigger of a price war. For instance in paragraphs starting at 38, the Commission describes first an exchange of information between French and Italian producers. At some stage, official statistics are published with a significant discrepancy from the declaration of Italian producers. Suspicion then arises, which is confirmed when a Belgian producers warns its French competitors that is has found, by chance, evidence of substantial sales at low prices by an Italian producer through a small company in Briançon (France). This triggers a price war, in which French producers ('nous sommes en guerre') reduce price by 15%. After a few months, prices have returned to their original level[48] (as in the model of Green and Porter (1984)). Of course, all this evidence is consistent with the view that firms were acting in their own interest without explicit coordination. Reporting this evidence did not, in our view, strengthen the case.

In other cases, the Commission has indeed considered whether observed behaviour could not be explained without explicit coordination. The analysis is, however, sometimes unconvincing.

In *Wood Pulp*, the Commission also argued that the sequence of price announcements, as well as the level of prices, could not be explained in a framework without coordination. Regarding the sequence of price announcements, the Commission noted that the first price to be announced was almost always met by subsequent ones. The Commission claimed that such pattern could not arise in a competitive environment because firms would normally experiment with different prices before converging to some equilibrium level. The suggestion that independent firms would normally experiment with different prices seems intuitively appealing, at least for transaction prices; but as mentioned above, preannounced prices carry little commitment and serve mostly to establish a maximum price for consumers. In this context, after a first announcement has been made, the best strategy of an independent firm may be to quote the same price: it certainly has no incentive to quote a higher maximum price as customers would turn to the firm having made the first announcement. Quoting a lower price may also be unattractive as firms would foreclose the option of reaching agreement on an intermediate price (in between the original announcement and its lower reply). By meeting the first announcement, subsequent firms may not foreclose any option and thus keep open the freedom of providing rebates later. Altogether, it is far from clear that the sequence of prices could not be explained in terms of competitive interactions.

The Commission also considered evidence regarding price levels, arguing that uniform prices should not be expected in a competitive environment, given wide differences in the location of customers and the cost structure of firms, and large changes in exchange rates. According to the Commission, these factors should have led firms to quote different prices. The argument is, however, puzzling: first, it is clear that in a competitive environment, different suppliers will end up quoting the same price for a given delivery (say, for a given product, at a given place and time); low-cost suppliers will make some profit but will not charge lower prices. In this respect, the uniformity of prices, as quoted by suppliers, is thus perfectly consistent with a very competitive environment. Second, the Commission seems to argue that the variation of prices across different types of products and across space is low and that more variation would be observed if firms did effectively compete. Yet, some degree of discrimination across products and space is consistent with both competition and some form of prior coordination. It is unclear whether coordination will always lead to more discrimination. At the very least, the Commission should have considered the argument in more detail.

In *Flat Glass*, the Commission considered a somewhat unusual form of parallel behaviour which could prove useful in other cases. The Commission suggested that firms had classified their main customers in a number of different categories in order to define appropriate rebates. The Commission argued that such common classification was the result of an explicit coordination because they did not respect the specificity of the relationship between each firm and its main customers (for instance, customers were given rebates proportional to total purchases addressed to firms in the coordination agreement, rather then proportional to the purchases addressed to individual firms). In principle, the argument seems convincing. However, the Court rejected the evidence brought forward by the Commission as insufficient (and indeed, the factual claim by the Commission was weak).

3.5.1.2 The Distinction Between Coordination Itself and Resulting Behaviour

This distinction has sometimes been far from clear. For example, there is a puzzling analysis of coordination in *Wood Pulp*. First, the Commission considered the pre-announcement of prices that firms undertook before each quarter, emphasizing the simultaneity of the announcements (within a few days of each other), the similarity of price levels that were announced and the fact that the first price announcement was almost always met by subsequent ones. The Commission, however, adopted a very ambiguous interpretation of this evidence: effectively, it could not decide whether these announcements were the result of a previous process of coordination, and should be seen as an outcome, or whether these announcements should be seen as a process of coordination in itself. The ambivalence of the Commission is most apparent in the following excerpts from the decision (107–8):

> Les annonces de prix en succession rapide ou même simultanément auraient été impossibles sans un flux constant d'information entre les entreprises visées.

> Le système des annonces trimestrielles, que les entreprises ont choisi volontairement, constituait à tout le moins en soi un échange indirect d'information quant à leur comportement futur sur le marché.

Following the logic that price announcements were a process of coordination rather than the outcome of such a process, the Commission even went as far as to argue that 'prior information exchanges, should be seen as a separate infringement of Article 85(1)'. This confusion was not lost on the defendants and the Court of First Instance. For instance, the Advocate General Darmon states (paragraphs 242–3 of his opinion):

> Is the 'common price' the result of the concertation between the undertakings prior to the announcement themselves . . . ? Or does the system of price announcements constitute the machinery of concertation for fixing that common price? The lack of clarity in the Commission's position is unfortunate . . . The Commission's position in this case has the consistency of mercury. Just as one is about to grasp it, it eludes one, only to assume an unexpected shape.

In theory, the argument that the system of price announcements should be seen a process of coordination seems more appropriate. As emphasized by Kühn and Vives (1994), the prices that are announced by firms carry little commitment value. Indeed, the actual prices in *Wood Pulp* sometimes differed from the announced prices[49] (even though the Commission tried to argue that discrepancies were small). Accordingly, announced prices could hardly be seen as the decision resulting from a prior process of coordination. These prices should rather be seen as a form of what game theorists call 'cheap talk'. Accordingly, the firms' announcements can be interpreted as an attempt to establish some focal point (whether this should be seen a sufficient evidence of coordination will be discussed in the next section). This interpretation was considered by the Advocate General, in his opinion: he accepted the view that such indirect information exchanges could be seen as unlawful, but rejected the argument in the case at hand because of insufficient reasoning.

3.5.1.3 Acceptance of Weak Reasoning by the Defendants

In some cases the Commission could have dismissed more strongly arguments advanced by the defendants. An example is the argument by Solvay and ICI that market sharing could be explained as the equilibrium of a Cournot game. The firms argued that 'Cournot is characterized by the expectation of undertakings in an industry that other undertakings will maintain output whatever the individual does'. According to the expert witness, producers in the soda ash industry could thus be expected to concentrate on their home market and refrain from competition with one another. The Commission dismissed the expert witness because she proved (in the administrative hearings) to be unaware of the documentary evidence attached to the statement of objections. Being ill informed, the Commission argued, she could not reach a relevant conclusion.

Such a dismissal avoided confronting directly the arguments of the firm. These arguments could nevertheless have been seriously questioned by the Commission. For instance, the reference to Cournot in the firm's submission is clearly a misrepresentation. The firms seem to imply that because Cournot firms take rival output as given, any output configuration can be seen as the outcome of a Cournot game. This implication is clearly incorrect and misses the equilibrium condition, namely that firms' outputs have to be mutual best replies. The Commission could have argued further that most models of international trade which assume Cournot behaviour predict significant cross-hauling (bilateral exports). The absence of market sharing has actually been considered as a major attraction of the Cournot framework in international trade, such that it can account for (widely observed) intra-industry trade. It takes extremely large barriers to trade to obtain an outcome where firms stay in their home markets.[50]

3.5.1.4 Inconsistency with Burden of Proof

In some cases, the arguments of the Commission regarding firm behaviour do not seem to be consistent with the allocation of the burden of proof. *Soda Ash* is a case in point. The defendants argued that they did not penetrate each other's market (with ICI holding close to a monopoly in the UK and Solvay holding more the 60% of continental Europe), simply out of fear of retaliation. Indeed, the defendants could have argued that when firms potentially meet in several markets at the same time, successful non-cooperative exercise of market power will typically involve market sharing.[51] This is more likely to occur when domestic firms have a cost advantage at home, which certainly holds in the present case, given the evidence being provided on transport cost.

The Commission argued that this behaviour could also be seen as the outcome of explicit coordination:

> the possibility of retaliation which Solvay and ICI claim as the reason for their respective abstention from each other's home market in no way excludes the existence of an understanding. . . . retaliation was the normal sanction for any breach of the home market principles: the threat of retaliation thus served to encourage continued cooperation.

The point is well taken but it would help the prosecution only if it were for the firm to show that its behaviour could not be seen as the outcome of coordination.

3.5.2 Direct Evidence of Coordination

As discussed above, the type of explicit coordination between firms which is unlawful, and the evidence that is required to establish the existence of explicit coordination, both matter a great deal for the effectiveness of the policy.

3.5.2.1 The Legal Status of Communication Between Firms

The main issue at stake is whether, and in what circumstances, communication between firms can be seen as explicit coordination and hence will be deemed unlawful. As indicated above, there is a presumption against the frequent exchange of information about the past behaviour of individual firms (as opposed to aggregate market conditions).

In this respect, the analysis of coordination undertaken by the Commission in the *Soda Ash* case is remarkable. The Commission provides a detailed account of contacts between ICI and Solvay and interprets them, very convincingly, as a concertation through which firms attempted to remove uncertainty about each other's past behaviour and future intention. Such communication certainly contributed to improving the transparency on the supply side of the market and as such may have contributed to the stability of the coordination agreement.

In the *Wood Pulp* case, the Commission tried to support its interpretation that price announcements were a mechanism of coordination by arguing that the market was 'excessively' transparent. It is hard, however, to interpret price announcements in this fashion, as they relate to intentions for the future rather than records of the past. In addition, the Commission failed to consider that information is also good for consumers; indeed, it is a standard result in the economics of imperfect information that if consumers do not observe prices and have to search for the best deal, monopoly outcomes can be sustained without coordination (Diamond, 1971). As indicated by court hearings, it seems that informing consumers was a main function of price announcement in the case at hand. Overall, the concept of excessive transparency (which was not challenged by the Advocate General, who only disputed the degree of transparency) should have been considered more cautiously.

3.5.2.2 The Standard of Evidence Required

The effect of Court judgements has been to impose increasingly high standards of evidence on the Commission. In the ***Polypropylène***, ***Flat Glass*** and ***Cartonboard*** cases, the Commission had to rely on fragments of evidence rather than a systematic account of concertation between firms. Evidence was missing regarding some periods of time as well as regarding the identity of the firms involved in the concertation. In its decision, the Commission sought to 'interpolate' its evidence both over time and regarding participation of firms, arguing that the various bits it had gathered should be seen not in isolation but rather as a whole. For instance in ***Polypropylène***, the Commission stated (paragraph 81):

> La Commission estime que tout l'ensemble de plans et d'arrangements arrêtés dans le cadre d'un système de réunions périodiques et institutionnalisés a constitué un accord unique et continu au sens de l'article 85 paragraphe 1.

and in paragraph 83§2:

> L'essence même de la présente affaire réside dans une association de producteurs pendant un laps de temps considérable afin de réaliser un objectif commun et chaque participant doit assumer la responsabilité de l'accord dans son ensemble. Le degré de participation de chaque producteur ne sera donc pas déterminé en fonction de la période pour laquelle ses instructions de prix ont été retrouvées lors des vérifications, mais pour toute la période de son adhésion à l'initiative commune.

This question was debated by the Court of First Instance. The Court did not reject the idea of collective responsibility, emphasizing instead that legal systems should not require impossibly high standards of proof, particularly in situations where detailed evidence is difficult to gather. Nevertheless, the Court suggested that each gap in the evidence should be analysed individually (that is, for each period of time and for each firm) and that a presumption should at least be established for each case. By insisting on such standards of proofs, the Court effectively prevented the 'interpolation' of evidence that the Commission attempted. As a consequence, fines were reduced for a number of participating companies. Similar standards were imposed in the ***Flat Glass*** judgement by the Court of First Instance.

3.5.3   The Analysis of Markets

Both in the interpretation of firm behaviour and in the interpretation of direct evidence of coordination, a good understanding of the relevant market is essential. Two aspects are particularly important: market definition and an understanding of the factors affecting the plausibility of coordination.

3.5.3.1 Market Definition

The Commission has not adopted the discipline of defining the relevant market at the outset of its analysis. Such a practice would nevertheless be useful: it would help determine at the outset whether coordination between firms would be potentially damaging, and, therefore, help screen out the unimportant cases. Without such a discipline, the Commission might find itself concluding that firms had coordinated behaviour in a market where coordination was not profitable to start with.[52]

Various methods can used to define a relevant market but the general approach of the method used in US merger analysis, known as the 5% rule, is the most generally useful.[53] This would entail considering whether demand and supply substitution would prevent incriminated firms from profitably raising price, above some competitive level, starting from a narrow market definition and progressively enlarging the market until a configuration is found such that a price increase would indeed be profitable. Admittedly, the definition of a 'competitive price' is likely to be more problematic in the present circumstances than in merger analysis; one may have to rely on benchmark prices from countries which clearly fall outside the scope of the alleged coordination. Indeed, since merger analysis in the European Union is concerned only with the risk that a merger might 'create or strengthen a dominant position' it can afford to be relaxed about whether or not the existing market price is a reasonably competitive price; analysis of collusion cannot afford to be since that is precisely what is at issue.

There are three cases where market definition may have mattered. In *Soda Ash*, the Commission stated that imports from the United States (and from Eastern Europe) could be highly profitable:

> The United States producers of dense ash are viewed by European manufacturers as the major competitive threat in their home markets. At current exchange rates, it is possible for these producers to sell in Europe at prices substantially below the local market prices without dumping.

This would suggest that for the exchange rate prevailing at time of decision (about $1.25 per ECU in 1990[54]), the relevant anti-trust market should have included the United States.[55] Of course, it may be that in earlier periods, in particular in the mid-1980s when the dollar was considerably stronger (about $0.8 per ECU in 1985), imports from the United States would not have been profitable. In any event, the fact that such imports are profitable at some realistic exchange rates can be expected to affect domestic firms' ability to exercise market power – this issue should have been discussed.

The possibility that the relevant market could have included the United States or Eastern Europe seems particularly puzzling in light of the defendants' argument that the United Kingdom and continental Europe should be seen as separate markets because the lowest transport cost that can be achieved, namely between France and the United Kingdom, already amounted to 40% of the net selling price (at paragraph 42 of the Commission's decision).[56] Of course, it may be that the transport cost of dense soda (as typically produced in the United States) is much lower than transport cost of light soda (produced in Europe). Surely, however, this matter would have worth discussing; indeed, if it turned out that the United States should have been included in the relevant market, the Commission's claim that explicit coordination between ICI and Solvay had sustained a market-sharing arrangement would have lost some credibility.

Flat Glass is the second case in which market definition may have been important; admittedly, the Commission looked into the matter in the context of an infringement of Article 86 (which is part of the same decision as the infringement of Article 85). The Commission concluded that the relevant market for flat glass was Italy, despite evidence of substantial trade, at least for the non-automotive segment, where imports accounted for about a third of domestic consumption in 1986.[57] In the automotive segment, there is only one customer (Fiat), which is presumably well aware of prices outside Italy. It is hard to believe that it would have not have resorted to imports, or at least could not have threatened to do so, if domestic firms had exercised substantial market power. The Commission used the argument that because of the importance of just-in-time delivery, suppliers could not be far away from Fiat's main production site, and this would tend to exclude imports (except of course that Turin, Fiat's main production site is less than 100 km away from France). This argument was rejected by the defendants in Court. In fact the Commission's argument was rather weak: because of the production process itself, each variety of glass for a manufacturer has to be produced in large batches which substantially exceed the flow consumption of the car manufacturer over the time taken to produce the batch. Accordingly, glass manufacturers hold stocks of the varieties they produce and just-in-time delivery simply entails precise logistics for delivery. It does not require, as it often does in other industries, a deep integration of the production processes of input and output manufacturers. Precise logistics of delivery are something that importers should be able to handle. Overall, it is surprising that this matter was apparently never discussed with Fiat.[58]

Finally, in the *Cement* decision, the Commission decided that Europe was the relevant market even though transport costs account for a high fraction of total cost and it is usually unprofitable to ship cement (by road or rail) further than 2000 km. The Commission acknowledged that any given firm was likely to meet only a few neighbouring competitors but argued that competition would be transmitted across neighbours. The overall market could thus be seen as a chain of competitors. It argued that since any competitor was related to all others throughout the chain, the relevant market was Europe for all of them. This reasoning is somewhat puzzling and seems in contradiction with the method underlying the 5% rule. In any event, a more careful analysis would have been warranted.

3.5.3.2 The Plausibility of Coordination

In its decisions, the Commission has not tried to argue that circumstances were favourable to the development of coordination in the collective exercise of market power. Such arguments (known as economic plausibility factors) are, however, used routinely in US case law (see Ginsburg (1993) and references therein) and could serve at least to establish a shift the burden of proof.

In a number of recent cases there are reasons to think that industry characteristics made the collective exercise of market power particularly attractive and that explicit coordination was also likely to be necessary. Indeed, there are striking similarities between a number of the recent cases, in terms of industry characteristics. Cases like *Polypropylène*, *Flat Glass*, *PVC*, *LEDP*, *Wood Pulp*, *Welded Steel* and to a lesser extent *Soda Ash* are concerned with industries where there is excess capacity for a substantial period of time, where fixed costs are large and where marginal cost rises quickly as capacity utilization is reduced. In terms of demand, the aggregate demand elasticity is relatively low but the products are either homogeneous (like wood pulp, welded steel or soda ash) or differentiated but highly standardized and sold by several firms (flat glass), so that in all cases, the elasticity of demand at the firm level can be expected to be quite high. In some industries (like wood pulp or the automotive segment in flat glass), the concentration of buyers may also contribute to such high elasticities.

These characteristics will affect the prospects for the exercise of market power in the following respects: first, the high degree of market transparency, which follows from the standardization of products and the concentration of buyers and sellers, will improve the detection of potential deviations. The probability that some exercise of market power can be established is thus enhanced. Second, when there is excess capacity, there is little threat of entry. Third, the incentive to seek some market power is very high in those industries, in particular after a negative demand shock (which affects profits significantly given the rigidity of the production

structure – this is illustrated by prototype model of competition presented in Box 3.5). Given that aggregate demand is inelastic, relatively
large increases in prices can be achieved without much reduction in aggregate output. Note, however, that the incentive to cheat on the 'agreement'
will also be strong because of the shape of the cost function. In other
words, both the rewards from reducing output, and the incentive to deviate from the collusive outcome, will be exacerbated by the characteristics
of the industry. Circumstances are, therefore, such that one might expect
on theoretical grounds a large number of attempts to coordinate, and a
fair number of failures. These are typically the circumstances under
which firms resort to some form of explicit coordination.

Box 3.5 Incentives for the collective exercise of market power in
cyclical industries with rigid capacity

Consider a duopoly producing a homogeneous output. Aggregate
demand is linear and is written:

$$p = 1 - bQ$$

where $p(Q)$ is the aggregate price (output). Each firm is endowed
with a fixed capacity, denoted K_i and incurs a flow cost of capacity
of cK_i if it produces. In addition, there is fixed (sunk) cost denoted
F. This assumption about costs guarantees that a firm will always
produce, if at all, at full capacity, as long as marginal revenue is
positive. Note that as b falls, demand becomes more elastic (for any
given aggregate quantity). A fall in aggregate demand can also be
associated with an increase in b, such that the demand curve rotates
around the intercept on the vertical axis.

   For simplicity, assume that firms are endowed with the same
capacity and that the total capacity is K. We consider an initial situation of 'natural duopoly' where demand is such that firms produce
at full capacity and make zero profit and where they have no incentive to coordinate output. Denote b_0 as the value of the parameter b
such that the marginal revenue from the entire market is equal to
zero, when firms produce at full capacity. Namely:

$$1 - 2b_0K = 0$$

Where firms are endowed with capacity K and when demand has
a slope b_0, firms have no incentive to coordinate output because the
maximum revenue is extracted from the market (and because there
are no cost savings from merging capacity). This situation is perfectly consistent with zero profit (and hence no entry), as long as

fixed and capacity costs are large enough. Of course, the balance between fixed costs and capacity has to be such that $p(K) \geq c$.

Next, consider a downturn, such that b increases (demand becomes less elastic at any given quantity). Firms will keep on producing as long the parameter does not exceed the value, say b_1, for which the firm's marginal revenue turns negative. That is:

$$1 - \frac{3}{2} b_1 K = 0$$

For intermediate values of the parameter, and as long as $p(K,b) \geq c$, independent firms thus keep on producing but make losses. If firms coordinate their decisions, however, it may be preferable for them to produce some output for stocks or simply destroy some production (note that firms will not have the incentive to undertake this policy unilaterally until b has increased to the level b_1). If production can be destroyed costlessly, firms will have a collective incentive to keep sales at the level that maximizes market revenues, namely:

$$Q = \frac{1}{2b} < K \equiv \frac{1}{2b_0}$$

More generally, assume that there is a cost δ which is incurred for each unit of output which is produced but not sold. This additional cost can also be interpreted as the cost of operating below capacity. The level of sales which maximizes (joint) profits is then given by:

$$Q = \frac{1}{2b - \delta}$$

The incentive to coordinate can be measured by the extra profit per firm that can be earned from the collaboration. This can be easily computed as:

$$\pi = (1 + \delta) \left(\frac{1}{2b - \delta} - K \right) - b \left(\frac{1}{(2b - \delta)^2} - K^2 \right)$$

Differentiating this expression with respect to b, it is easy to check that:

$$\frac{\partial \pi}{\partial b} \geq 0 \text{ if } (2b - \delta) < 1$$

That is, as long as the cost of moving away from full capacity is not too large, firms have an increasing incentive to coordinate sales as demand in the industry shrinks.

In addition to industry characteristics, the Commission could have made better use of the history of coordination between firms as a significant factor in establishing a presumption. Of course, the Commission used this argument in the context of the *Soda Ash* case, regarding the famous 'Page 1000' memorandum, an explicit agreement which was enforced after the war and possibly up to the entry of the United Kingdom in the Community. The argument could have been used further by suggesting that evidence of explicit coordination was unlikely to be forthcoming in the industry precisely because of the presence of such an obvious focal point; the standard of proof required might reasonably be weaker in such circumstances. Nor did the Commission argue that if firms have undertaken some coordination in one market segment, there is a presumption that the coordination will have extended to other segments. This argument, which is also well accepted in US case law, can be easily justified. As discussed above, the collective exercise of market power requires the establishment of some understanding between firms, possibly regarding focal points, and it may be reasonable to assume that firms can carry over their experience across industries. In particular, the Commission could have used the significant overlap in the identity of firms involved in *Polypropylène*, *PVC* and *LEPD* and the similarities in the concertation found in these cases.

Finally, the Commission has rarely appealed to the existence of facilitating practices in order to shift the burden of proof, a practice which is also common in US case law, particularly when it can be shown that the facilitating practice has been established by the defendants. The most common facilitating practice that appears is recent cases is the establishment of a research and information centre on the industry (see *Wood Pulp*, *Polypropylène*, *LEPD*, *PVC*, *Welded Steel*). Invariably, these research and information centres have gathered information about firms' behaviour in addition to aggregate statistics and have organized or even hosted meetings between competitors. The Commission could have taken a stronger line against such institutions and made some inference of coordination from their mere existence.

3.6 Conclusion

The first conclusion to emerge from our analysis is that unlawful concerted practices do not encompass implicit coordination in the collective exercise of market-power. As argued above, such a presumption is probably desirable. The absence of a market power test in addition to establishing the existence of an explicit coordination is, in our view, also appropriate, given the high levels of error to which it is subject.

The recent case law has not considered so far that some form of coordination might be useful or necessary. One can seriously wonder whether a more refined rule would not be more appropriate; indeed, one cannot help noticing that a relatively large number of cases (***Polypropylène***, ***Flat Glass***, ***PVC***, ***LEDP***, ***Wood Pulp***, ***Welded Steel*** and to a lesser extent ***Soda Ash***) were concerned with situations of large excess capacity where coordination may have been necessary to avoid cycles of entry and exit. To the extent that such cycles are costly (for instance, in the presence of fixed sunk cost of re-entry and exit), some coordination may be efficient. There may thus be argument in favour of a special treatment towards industries in 'crisis'. Of course, 'crisis cartels' could be notified and benefit from an exemption (as in the artificial fibre industry or in the steel industry, which is, however, subject to different competition rules under the CECA treaty). The Commission, however, has been increasingly reluctant to consider such exemptions. It might be preferable to allow easier exemptions of notified crisis cartels, rather than waiting to grant special treatment towards whole industries in crisis in a context of *ex post* control.

Second, the concept of a concerted practice has evolved in such a way that the distinction between agreements and concerted practices may no longer have much point to it. In our view, it would clarify matters a great deal if the Court were to state explicitly that the concepts are equivalent (recent decisions in any case suggest the Commission no longer attaches any importance to the distinction).

Third, the analysis of the firms' behaviour which has been undertaken by the Commission in recent cases often appears unconvincing or even misguided. What the Commission has to show is that firms' behaviour cannot be explained without some underlying process of coordination. The Commission often overlooks alternative and plausible explanations behind firms' behaviour which do not involve a process of explicit coordination. In particular, the Commission sometimes overlooks implicit coordination (which is arguably not unlawful) as an alternative explanation behind firms' behaviour.

Fourth, the standards imposed by the Court regarding the direct material proof of coordination appear to be stringent, and increasingly so. As a result, type II errors in the implementation of the current policy are rather large. The observation that the frequency of agreements and concerted practices (see XXVth Report on Competition Policy) is still relatively high despite long lasting efforts on enforcement should be interpreted in this light. When type II errors are large, one would indeed expect that the deterrence effect of the policy is relatively small.

In our view, given that the cost of type I errors is relatively small in this context, less stringent standards could be applied. In particular, the

Commission and the Court could take a broader view of what constitutes an agreement, and the standards of proof imposed by the Court
could be relaxed.

Such a change of policy is all the more important because one can
expect that in the future coordination will need increasingly to be established by direct evidence, because evidence of firms' behaviour will be
increasingly difficult to interpret. Indeed, as the economic analysis of
repeated games further develops and is popularized in business and management education, one would also expect the task of the competition
authorities to become more difficult. Soon, as predicted by Baker (1993),
firms will argue that they would be irrational to leave any material traces
of concertation when it is known that market interactions suffice, and
accordingly might ask for ever stricter standards of proof. Given that
coordination solely though repeated market interactions is a legal safe
harbour, they incur little risk in putting forward such argument.

The scope of what constitutes coordination could, therefore, be
enlarged, particularly regarding facilitating practices. Some of these
could increasingly be considered as presumptively an infringement of
Article 85§1. For instance, exchanges of individual price and quantity
data between competitors could be considered a sufficient condition for
presuming the existence of explicit coordination.[59] Similarly, the creation
of trade associations which organize the exchange of individual data
could lead to a similar presumption. Other practices like most-favoured-
nation clauses, or meet-the-competition clauses, are more difficult to
handle. Although such practices may tend to reinforce coordination, they
can also be justified on efficiency grounds: as argued by Crocker and
Lyon (1994), such contracts will often reduce the scope for opportunistic
behaviour in incomplete contracts and allow for more efficient contracting outcomes. Yet the presence of such contracts, in particular if they are
combined with pre-announcement of prices, should be counted as an economic plausibility factor.

Finally, more emphasis could be placed on measures to make collusion
less likely in advance. Merger control may play an important role in this
respect, as it is by and large the only instrument that can be used to affect
industry structure directly. Particular attention could be given in merger
analysis to the risk of establishing industry environments conducive to
coordination. As Neven *et al.* (1993) show, such considerations were not
explicitly taken into account in the first years of enforcement of the
European Union Merger Regulation.

4

Article 85§3 and the Social Benefits of Coordination

4.1 Introduction

Chapters 2 and 3 have argued that there is an important reason why agreements between firms that produce substitute products should be treated with much more suspicion by the competition authorities than agreements between firms producing solely unrelated or complementary products. Nevertheless, agreements between firms producing substitute products yield benefits to the firms concerned, and these benefits do not always consist solely or even mainly in the exploitation of market power. Article 85§3 explicitly recognizes that cooperation between firms may yield productive benefits and be a reason for exemption of such agreements from the application of Articles 85§1 and 85§2. In this chapter we examine what kinds of productive benefit might be expected to result from agreements between competing firms.

It seems reasonable to begin with the benchmark case of a full merger between the firms concerned. Such a merger would normally involve some (possibly small) increase in the market power of the merged firms relative to that which they had previously exercised separately. It might also involve some gains in productive efficiency, through the exploitation of complementarities between their assets. The trade-off between these two factors in assessing the overall social desirability of a merger has been much discussed elsewhere (see, for example, Neven *et al.*, 1993, pp. 32–40) and we shall not devote further space to it here. Instead, we shall make the reasonable assumption that if the firms concerned are undertaking a cooperative agreement that falls short of a full merger, this is for one of two reasons. First, it may be that they fear the authorities would prohibit a full merger, on the grounds that the threat of increased market power would outweigh any productive benefits involved. In these circumstances, it makes sense to ask whether a cooperative agreement can be expected to yield a substantial proportion of the productive benefits of a merger without also granting the firms an equally substantial proportion of the market power the merger would create. Why might this be so? Unless a convincing argument can be made along these lines, the fact that a merger would be prohibited creates a strong *prima facie* argument for prohibiting a cooperative agreement between those same firms.

Second, it may be that a cooperative arrangement actually yields greater benefits to firms involved than a full merger would do. In such circumstances cooperation is the preferred choice of firms even when there is no obstacle to a merger on the part of the authorities. Why might this be, and is there any reason to think these benefits are more likely to involve the exercise of market power than of productive efficiency gains? Unless such an argument is made, the fact that a merger would be allowed suggests there is no case for prohibiting a cooperative agreement between the same firms.

It therefore makes sense to look more closely at these two sources of benefit to the firms concerned (namely market power and gains in productive efficiency) and to ask how the benefits expected from a joint venture compare with those that might accrue to the firms through a full merger. This will be the task of Sections 4.2 and 4.3. Before beginning this analysis, however, it is helpful to set out some of the various forms that cooperation between firms can take.

1. Price-fixing or market-sharing agreements. These have been discussed extensively in Chapter 3 and will not be considered further here, since properly speaking they do not create productive benefits as such (although the market power they create may enable other productive benefits to be realized indirectly, as in a crisis cartel).

2. Agreements to operate assets together, the assets remaining under the control of their original owners.

3. Agreements to operate assets together, with some transfer of ownership between the parties.

4. The creation of a new firm to operate the assets, with ownership of the assets being transferred to the new firm, and equity in the firm being owned jointly by the two parent firms.

5. A common agency agreement, in which assets owned by a third party are operated together with the assets of the two cooperating firms (as when they use a common distributor).

6. Some hybrid of points 2–5, such as joint operation of assets under continuing separate ownership, but together with some new assets jointly owned (which may take the form of goodwill).

In each case the term 'assets' is used broadly, and can refer to human as well as non-human assets, in which case ownership must also be interpreted broadly. For example, an agreement according to which employees of one firm are seconded to another firm to work on a specified project, while remaining contractually responsible to the first firm, would be an instance of point 2 above.

The purpose of setting out all these different agreements in this way is to emphasize that cooperation between firms can take very many forms, and consequently can have many possible consequences. For example, the term 'joint venture' has been used to refer to all of the agreements in points 2–6 above, though it should be clear that these involve a considerable difference in structures of ownership and control, and consequently in incentives. It is not possible, therefore, to make general claims about the effects of joint ventures as such. It requires an analysis based on the particular features of the individual case; the role of general principles is to clarify what such an analysis should look for.

In this chapter we shall follow this usage and use the term 'joint venture' to refer to any agreement between separately owned parent companies to operate jointly some subset of their assets. We can take for granted, at least for the time being, that a *necessary* condition for firms to wish to engage in a joint venture in this broad sense is that they own assets that will (at least potentially) yield higher returns when operated together than when operated separately.[60] Call them *complementary* assets. What is important is that these assets are jointly operated (under some combination of joint and separate ownership) while the remaining assets of the parent company are separately owned and operated. The separate ownership of these remaining assets may be a matter of regulatory constraint, or it may be the preferred choice of the parent firms.

4.2 The Impact of Joint Ventures on the Market Power of the Parent Firms

On the face of it, a joint venture appears to have much less potential for market power than does a merger. The parent firms continue to act non-cooperatively in determining their output prices, even though they act cooperatively with respect to the assets of the joint venture, which are the source of the potential gains in productive efficiency.

Appearances are, however, misleading. There are two reasons for this, one fairly obvious and one much less so. The obvious reason is that if firms have incentives for tacit collusion in output prices, the fact that they are allowed to behave cooperatively with respect to the joint venture may make it easier for them to conceal the evidence of this collusion. A joint venture may, therefore, make the phenomena discussed in Chapter 3 harder to detect (and may, therefore, increase the incentives to engage in such behaviour).

More significantly, though, the mere existence of a joint venture can in some circumstances change the incentives for the parent firms in determining their output prices, and specifically can create the incentive for the parent firms to set the fully collusive output price. Bernheim and Whinston (1985, 1986) have shown this in a model of common agency. A simplified version of their model is given in Box 4.1.

Box 4.1 Joint ventures and the coordination of parents' behaviour

Consider the following environment (adapted from Bernheim and Whinston, 1985). Two firms (i = 1, 2) sell differentiated products, incurring a marginal cost γ. In the original Bernheim-Whinston model there is uncertainty over demand, and firms (and the joint venture) are risk neutral, an assumption that is necessary for their result; here we derive the same result without uncertainty. The firms select an output price p_i (x_i denotes the output sold) facing a demand D_i (p_i, p_j, m_i, m_j); m denotes the output of some activity which shifts demands. It could be seen, for instance, as the output of marketing which enhances brands or the output of research which improves the quality of the product. The cost of producing m is denoted $c(m)$. The parents can delegate this activity to a joint venture. The incentive contract stipulated by each parent takes the form $I_i(x_i)$. Firms choose price and incentive contracts simultaneously. Formally, each firm will thus solve the following maximisation problem:

$$\max_{p_i, I_i, m_i, m_j} (p_i - \gamma_i) D_i(p_i, p_j, m_i, m_j) - I_i[D_i(p_i, p_j, m_i, m_j)]$$

subject to:

$$(m_1, m_2) \in \arg\max_{m_1', m_2'} I_1[D_1(p_1, p_2, m_1, m_2)] + I_2[D_2(p_1, p_2, m'_1, m'_2)] - c_1(m'_1) - c_2(m'_2)$$

$$I_1[D_1(p_1, p_2, m_1, m_2)] + I_2[D_2(p_1, p_2, m_1, m_2)] - c_1(m_1) - c_2(m_2) \geq 0$$

where the first constraint describes the behaviour of the joint venture with respect to m and the second constraint ensures that it earn non-negative profit. In this context, firms will manage to achieve a fully collusive outcome (with respect to p and m). The reasoning comes in two steps. First, consider the incentive scheme. For any price that it chooses (say p_i^*), each firm will always find it profitable to 'sell out', namely to give to joint venture the full marginal profit from sales and charge a franchise fee which extracts all profit from the joint venture. The optimal contract will thus take the form:

$$\tilde{I}_i(m_i, x_i) = (p_i^* - \gamma_i)x_i - K_i$$

and

$$K_i = \max_{m_i', m_j'} (p_i^* - \gamma_i)D_i(p_i^*, p_j, m_i', m_j') - c_i(m_i') + I_j[D_j(p_j, p_i^*, m_i', m_j')] - c_j(m_j')$$

Second, it is easy to see that whenever a firm chooses to set the collusive price and associated incentive scheme, the best reply of the other firms is to do the same. The intuition is straightforward: assume that firm one has set the cooperative price and is 'selling' out to the joint venture. As indicated above, the second firm will always want to sell out, for any price. This firm will thus pick a price which maximizes the amount that it can extract from the joint venture. This amount is equal to the total net variable profit of both firms minus the fee paid to Firm 1. Hence, Firm 2 will set its price at a level which maximizes the total net variable profit of both firms. If the first firm has chosen the collusive price, this entails choosing the collusive price for Firm 2 as well.

To understand why, it is helpful to begin with a specific example (which is Bernheim and Whinston's own). Two firms choose to delegate the marketing of their products to a risk-neutral common marketing agent. They offer contracts that specify both an output price and a remuneration scheme for the agent. Because the agent is risk-neutral, inducing an efficient level of effort requires the remuneration scheme to give the agent the full marginal return to effort; in effect each firm 'sells out' to the agent (as in a standard model of a single principal and risk-neutral agent).

This choice of remuneration scheme has an important effect on the incentives for setting output prices. In the absence of common agency each firm's pricing decision imposes an externality on the other firm, which is the reason why equilibrium in pricing decisions will typically not be jointly profit-maximizing. When the other firm has sold out at the margin to the agent, however, it is the *agent* that suffers the externality from the pricing decision.

Why does this make a difference? When setting its own incentive scheme for the agent the firm will recoup any externality, since it sets its offer in such a way as to force the agent down to its participation constraint. To put the matter another way, any change in the pricing strategy of the firm that changes the value of the agent's profits by some amount x, also changes by precisely x the amount the firm can demand for selling out to the agent. So the pricing externality is now internalized by the firm itself, which as a result will set the joint profit-maximizing price.

In the more general case, we can see that the existence of a joint venture will enable collusive pricing when two conditions hold:

1. The contracts between the parent companies and the joint venture transfer the full *marginal* profit from pricing decisions to the joint venture.
2. These contracts enable to the parent companies to capture all of the *average* profit above some threshold level.

It is important to note that condition 2 will hold when pricing and agency decisions are made simultaneously. It will not necessarily hold if agency decisions are made first, and pricing decisions after these agency decisions are known; unless the pricing decisions are foreseeable at the time the agency contracts are written in such a way that the contracts can be made dependent upon them. This is because, if the terms of the agency contract are already determined at the time that pricing decisions are taken, the amount received by each parent for selling out to the agent cannot be adjusted to internalize the pricing externality. This will turn out to be important in evaluating the application of the model to research and development joint ventures, a point we develop more fully below.

If the contracts described in these two conditions are indeed profit-maximizing contracts, then the conditions imply that common agency will be sufficient for collusion whenever collusion would enable the parents to write fully efficient agency contracts from which they extracted all the surplus. If there would be unavoidable inefficiency in the agency contracts, however, common agency will typically lead to less than fully collusive outcomes.

We can use these conditions as a test for the circumstances in which a joint venture is likely to pose collusive dangers. Marketing and distribution joint-ventures are particularly suspect because of two facts. First, the natural way of structuring incentives for such a joint venture will tend to leave a large share of the marginal profits from pricing decisions in the hands of the joint venture. This is particularly characteristic of joint ventures that involve the addition of value to the product in ways that cannot easily be verified independently of the impact on final consumer demand. It is *not* necessarily characteristic of those that produce components or other inputs whose addition of value to the product can be independently verified.

Second, marketing and distribution joint-ventures are typically ones in which the terms of the agency contract can be negotiated simultaneously with the terms on which the product itself is traded. This also tends to be true of production joint-ventures. They differ in this respect from such institutions as research joint-ventures, in which the agreement to undertake the joint venture is typically made before probable demand for the product, and even the characteristics of the product itself, are known to the parties.

This second consideration is important for the case of research joint-ventures, since these usually do retain a large proportion of the marginal profits from pricing decisions, and might, therefore, seem like natural candidates for collusion. For example, patents and licences resulting from the research typically belong to the joint venture rather than the parents; the value of these is directly related to the prices set by the parents for the output of the products concerned. However, since the parents' equity shares have normally been determined by the time pricing decisions are taken, each parent appropriates only the share of the marginal profit represented by its own equity share. There remains, therefore, an important pricing externality that tends to undermine collusion.

So, to summarize, marketing and distribution and research joint-ventures both tend to meet the first criterion for collusion-proneness, since both will typically accord a large share of marginal profits to the joint venture itself. Marketing and distribution joint-ventures and production joint-ventures will tend to meet the second criterion for collusion-proneness. However, neither research nor production joint-ventures will normally meet both criteria; only marketing and distribution joint-ventures will do so.

Finally, it should be pointed out that the arguments just outlined refer to the intrinsic incentives for collusion implicit in the mere existence of the joint venture. It is quite possible that even if these intrinsic incentives are weak, the parent companies may take other steps to incite collusion. For instance, there may be exchanges of ownership of various assets beyond those needed to set up the joint venture, the purpose of which may be to internalize pricing externalities. A possible example, according to Nye (1992), is the Renault-Volvo joint venture in which each parent took a substantial ownership stake in the other's truck manufacturing business. Nye even suggests, on the basis of a Cournot model of output determination, that such a joint venture could reduce output more than a merger, since the cross-ownership would ensure that each party internalized the pricing externality to a substantial degree, while receiving fewer of the private benefits of price reductions than would accrue to a normal Cournot competitor. This of course raises the question, which the article does not address, of why firms might wish to strike such a deal. Such a strategy might be privately rational if the short-run collusive price were below the dynamically profit-maximizing price. This might be because the good is durable and the monopolist is unable to commit to keeping its prices high once it has sold to those purchasers with the highest willingness to pay (as Coase, 1972 conjectured). The cross-ownership structure embodied in the joint venture would act as a kind of commitment device to the extraction of more market power than would be available to a monopolist on its own.

Analogous arguments suggest that, even if research joint-ventures do not satisfy both of the criteria for collusion-proneness (because equity shares are determined before pricing strategies), it might be possible for the firms concerned to write contingent contracts to internalize the pricing externality. For example, the revenues from the patents taken out by the joint venture might be allocated between the parents not according to the equity shares but according to the use made by the parents of the patented products or processes. In these circumstances, the joint venture would more completely internalize the pricing externality and be a more perfect vehicle for collusion between the parent firms.

Whether a joint venture allows for collusion between the parents will, therefore, depend in considerable detail on whether the terms of the contracts between the parents and the joint venture allow internalization of the pricing externality. Marketing and distribution joint-ventures and cross-ownership of subsidiaries are two significant ways of doing so.

4.3   The Impact of Joint Ventures on Productive Efficiency

Joint operation of complementary assets by two (or more) owners carries with it the significant risk of inefficiency, compared with their operation by a single owner, such as would occur with a merger between the parent companies. These inefficiencies typically arise because of non-contractible actions required from the owners. Most commonly these are thought of as investments that are privately costly but yield joint benefits that are relationship-specific. They can, however, also be interpreted as management decisions, the simultaneous choice of which by the two owners may lead to inefficiency.

For this reason it is tempting to conclude that even if joint ventures produce a lower risk of market power than does a full merger, they also yield definitely fewer of the benefits of asset complementarity. Such reasoning is belied, though, by the evidence that joint ventures may often be the preferred choice of the parent organizations even if there is no regulatory or other impediment to full integration.

To understand why parent firms may choose joint ventures as an organizational form, we need to appreciate the potential disadvantages of the alternatives. There are two alternatives to consider. One is the sole ownership of the complementary assets by one of the two parents. The other is the full merger of the two parent firms so that all of their assets are operated together.

4.3.1   The Disadvantages of Ownership by One Parent

The disadvantages of ownership by one firm alone can be grouped under the following headings. Both are instances of the phenomenon highlighted by Grossman and Hart (1986), namely that for one owner to buy out another will be costly if specific non-contractible investments are still required from the owner who has been bought out:

1. *Input-related disadvantages*   The assets transferred to the joint venture may continue to have complementarities with those of the parent firm. This is particularly important if there is an intertemporal aspect to the complementarities: for example, the asset may be skilled personnel whose future lies with the parent company after the work of the joint venture is complete. Joint ownership then functions as a commitment device enabling the re-integration of the relevant assets back into the parent firm (the assumption being that a complete contract could not be written determining the terms under which such re-integration would take place).

2. *Output-related disadvantages*   These occur when the terms of sale of the output of the joint venture cannot be contracted in advance. This will be a problem only if *both* parents may potentially be efficient users of the output, otherwise the output can simply be sold on the open market or used by the sole parent. Joint ownership, therefore, functions as a means of commitment to sharing the output. This is particularly important when use of the output requires complementary non-contractible inputs from both the parents (such as brand reputation or distribution facilities).

4.3.2   The Disadvantages of Full Merger Between the Parents

The disadvantages of full merger can be grouped under the following headings:

1. *The need for ring-fencing*   Joint ventures function as a commitment device to prevent either of the owners from being able to manage the joint assets in exactly the same way as its fully-owned assets. Why might they wish to do this? One advantage is reputational: if the venture fails the owners can credibly claim that the causes of failure do not taint the parent company as well.[61] Another advantage has to do with the inflexibility of corporate culture: setting up a joint venture may allow its assets to be managed by different rules from those that operate within the parent company. For example, two airlines may choose to set up a low-cost subsidiary that pays its employees less than has been negotiated with the employees of the parent companies. Or talented researchers might be paid more in a joint venture than would be possible without arousing resentment in the parent companies.

2. *The reduction of influence-seeking activities*   Joint ventures might also function as commitment devices that prevent the parent company from seeking to appropriate the benefits of the venture at an intermediate stage if these turn out to be higher than expected. This commitment matters if the ultimate success of the venture depends upon its being able to reinvest intermediate profits. Although related to the argument of Meyer, Milgrom and Roberts (1992) about demerger as a commitment device against influence-seeking, it is not quite the same. The latter argument predicts that firms will demerge subsidiaries when these are under-performing and, therefore, prone to devote resources to influence-seeking rather than production. These are not the circumstances in which they would typically wish to set up joint ventures. Instead, joint ventures may be appropriate instruments to use for highly risky projects that require a commitment to reinvestment. For further arguments along these lines, see Cassiman (1996).

4.3.3   Policy Implications

What are the policy implications of this reasoning? First, none of the arguments just outlined imply any new reasons (other than those already discussed in Section 4.2) to fear that joint ventures might increase market power. Second, the arguments suggest that the benefits of a joint venture in the presence of asset complementarity may be quite substantial. If one of these motives for undertaking the joint venture is indeed present, that might significantly increase the weight of argument in favour of exemption under Article 85§3 even in the presence of some slight increased risk of collusion.

Not everything, however, that looks like a real benefit to the firm turns out to be so upon closer investigation. Firms are coalitions of interest groups, and joint ventures may be mechanisms for benefiting some of these interest group at the expense of others, even at the expense of the value of the firm as a whole. Before apparent benefits from joint ventures are accepted at face value, therefore, it is important to determine their overall value to the firm.

This means we can no longer take for granted that complementarity of the assets is a necessary condition for firms to choose to launch a joint venture. If the assets are not complementary, however, why might a decisive group within the parent firm choose joint operation with another firm? Even though this might not lead to higher overall rents, it might lead to a different distribution of rents within the parent. For example, skilled scientists within the parent could choose to work on Problem A (which if successful would produce rents that accrue primarily to Group A) or on Problem B (which would produce larger rents but for Group B). If Group A is decisive in matters concerning outside projects but cannot readily redistribute rents *ex post* from Group B, it may choose a joint venture in order to steer the rents in its own direction.

Apparent enthusiasm for a joint venture on the part of certain fortunate interest groups within the firm should not, therefore, be taken automatically to imply that the joint venture is good for the firm as a whole. Unless, however, there is evidence of this kind of minority 'capture' of the firm, it does seem reasonable to conclude that the organizational benefits of joint ventures discussed in this section increase the weight of argument in favour of exempting them under Article 85§3.

How well does the application of European law to joint ventures (and more generally, to exemptions under Article 85§3) reflect the kinds of economic considerations we have outlined here? Section 4.4 will consider the legal framework, while Sections 4.5 and 4.6 will consider to what extent actual decisions of the Commission and the Court have applied a coherent approach to the risks of market power and the potential gains in productive efficiency to be expected from joint ventures.

4.4 The European Legal Framework for Cooperative Joint-Ventures

The Commission draws a distinction between *concentrative* and *cooperative* joint-ventures. So far, concentrative joint-ventures have been reviewed under the Merger Regulation, whereas cooperative joint-ventures have been reviewed under Article 85. The Commission has also issued a notice on the treatment of joint ventures as a block exemption for R&D projects. We take these topics in turn.

4.4.1 Concentrative and Cooperative Joint-Ventures and Market Power

The distinction between cooperative and concentrative joint-ventures has evolved a great deal over time. When the Merger Regulation came into force (see Article 3 of the Merger Regulation and the Commission 'Notice on the Distinction Between Cooperative and Concentrative Joint Ventures' of 25 July 1990), the distinction was defined as follows. A joint venture was considered concentrative if it performed on a lasting basis all the functions of an autonomous economic entity and did not lead to the coordination of competitive behaviour of the parties among themselves or with the joint venture. By contrast, a joint venture was considered cooperative if it led to the coordination of competitive behaviour of undertakings which remained independent. The Commission has experienced substantial difficulties in implementing this distinction, particularly in evaluating whether a full function joint venture would lead to the coordination of behaviour between the parents. This evaluation is important as it affects the scope of the regulation. As a result, the amendment to the Merger Regulation adopted in June 1997 stipulated that all full function joint ventures should be reviewed under the merger procedure. It added that full function joint ventures which lead to the coordination of behaviour between the parents should be assessed additionally under the criteria of Article 85 (both paragraph 1 and paragraph 3). Under this new regime, the scope of the regulation is thus easier to delineate, but the substantive criteria that will be applied to the evaluation of any particular full function joint venture have become uncertain. Indeed, what the amendment has achieved, in this respect, is to shift the uncertainty; rather than facing uncertainty about the application of particular laws, firms will now face uncertainty about substantive criteria.

The question of whether a joint venture involves the coordination of behaviour between the parents will, therefore, remain important. This question is intriguing. Indeed, it would seem that the very decision jointly to create a new common entity must involve a significant coordination of business strategies between the parent companies. Some insight into this matter is provided by the (1994) 'Notice on the Distinction Between Cooperative and Concentrative Joint Ventures' (which expresses the principles that have led to the amendment of the Merger Regulation). In this

Notice, the Commission specified further the types of circumstances where there would be a strong presumption that the parents are able to coordinate behaviour. In particular, the Commission acknowledges that coordination of behaviour will be a serious concern when the parents and the joint venture are in the same relevant (product or geographic) market.

If the concerns of Bernheim and Whinston are realistic, a reasonable evaluation of a joint venture might well require that analysis of its potential dominance should take into account the sum of the market shares of the parents and that of the joint venture. However, the Commission falls short of suggesting this. On the contrary, it suggests that when the activities of the parents (outside the joint venture) are of minor importance with respect to their main activities, coordination should be less of a concern. It is somewhat unclear what this means.

In cases where the parents are in the same relevant market and the joint venture in a different one, the Commission seems to be concerned only to the extent that the joint venture activities are important to the parents and when the market of the joint venture 'has an interaction' with that of the parent. Again, it is unclear what is meant by the importance of the joint venture and why this should matter. A joint venture may enable the parents to exercise market power even if the markets in which they do so form only a small part of their overall activities. In addition, not all forms of interaction between the markets give rise to reasonable grounds for concern: as we emphasized in Chapter 2, when the markets are related vertically there are far fewer reasons for concern than when they are related horizontally.

Finally, the Commission acknowledges that it is not concerned about situations where the joint venture and the parents all operate in different relevant markets. Such a positive attitude suggests that the Commission is not concerned about the coordination between parents on entry (but only on coordination after entry of the joint venture has taken place, or what one might call *ex post* coordination). Indeed, the creation of a joint venture in a market where parents are absent can be seen itself as a form of coordination (*ex ante*) on entry, namely an agreement that parents will stay in their own geographic markets and concentrate the sales of the joint venture in another. There are good reasons to fear coordination of this kind, particularly since the joint venture may simultaneously provide a mechanism for collusion *ex post*. It may well be that a market which is currently monopolistic, and which could have become competitive had there been entry by the parent firms, will be shielded from competition by an agreement on the part of those firms to launch a joint venture instead of entering in their own right.

Two conclusions thus emerge. First, given that joint ventures may in certain circumstances be effective vehicles for the coordination of parent companies' behaviour, the coordination criteria proposed by the Merger Regulation (to define its scope under the original regulation and to subject particular joint ventures to Article 85 in its amendment) do not appear to be very powerful. The possibility needs to be borne in mind that joint ventures may be able to exercise as much market power as a full merger between the parents; if in the particular circumstances under consideration this seems unlikely, there need to be explicit arguments to that effect. Second, coordination on entry should be explicitly treated as a form of coordination between the parents.

Two final remarks are in order. First, as we have indicated, the amendment to the Merger Regulation imposes on some joint ventures both the substantive criteria of the Regulation (namely that a concentration should not create or strengthen a dominant position) and the criteria of Article 85. It is not clear that these criteria are necessarily consistent. The analysis of the next section will indeed confirm that they may sit together quite uncomfortably. Second, whether or not a given joint venture is likely to lead to an increase in market power will depend on some quite detailed aspects of the incentives of the parent companies in setting their prices. It may not be useful to make very broad classifications of joint venture types (such as, for example, whether they are 'full function' joint ventures or whether they perform limited functions such as marketing or R&D). As the arguments of Bernheim and Whinston have emphasized, even joint ventures that are limited in scope may have substantial implications for market power.

4.4.2   Block Exemption for R&D Projects and the 'Notice on Joint Ventures'

The block exemption of R&D projects (initially adopted in 1985 and limited to cooperation on research, but extended in 1994 to include joint distribution) and the Commission 'Notice on Joint Ventures' provide some insights regarding the restrictions of competition that will be considered in the case of joint ventures, efficiency benefits the Commission will take into account and the appropriate balance between them.

Restrictions of competition

In terms of restrictions of competition, the 'Notice on Joint Ventures' defines a *necessary* condition (paragraph 18) for a restriction to occur, namely that the parents be either actual or potential competitors. In addition to this necessary condition, the Notice (paragraph 26) lists a number of factors that should be taken into account in assessing whether the restrictions of competition are significant. The market shares of the parent companies and that of the joint venture in the relevant market (which, according to paragraph 17, has to be properly defined at the outset) are included, together with barriers to entry and the level of concentration in the relevant market. These factors seem appropriate, though others like the scale and significance of the joint venture activities in relation to the parents, or the financial strengths of the parents, are harder to interpret. It will thus be important in reading the case law to assess how the significance of the restrictions has been evaluated, and in particular to evaluate the weight that has been given to each of these factors.

The Notice also offers some guidance about the evaluation of the necessary condition, namely that parents should be actual or potential competitors. For the latter case, it says that parents can be seen as potential competitors insofar as they could have undertaken the activities of the joint venture on their own. It further indicates that the complementarity of the assets owned by the parents is an important consideration in deciding whether they could have undertaken the activities of the joint venture on their own.

This approach (which is also advocated by Korah, 1990) is commendable to the extent that it focuses on a useful counterfactual: whether the joint venture introduces restrictions of competition must be assessed relative to what would have happened in the absence of the joint venture. What the parents could have done is an important element of that counterfactual. It is, however, not the only element that is potentially relevant. The actual and counterfactual behaviour of competitors also matters. It is also worth emphasizing that the interesting question with respect to the parents is not whether they could have undertaken the activities of the joint venture on their own, but rather whether they *would* have done so. The case law may, therefore, cast useful light on which of these two counterfactuals has been considered by the Commission.

The approach has two disturbing features, however. First, it is not clear that the existence of potential competition should be seen as a necessary condition for a joint venture to restrict competition. Indeed, this implies that if firms could not have undertaken the activities of the joint venture on their own, there is no restriction of competition. The justification for this view seems to be that a joint venture in those circumstances can only be pro-competitive because it somehow adds output relative to the counterfactual of no joint venture. Yet it is far from clear that all joint ventures will always do better than the status quo; instead, they may sometimes generate negative external effects in other markets (such as by allowing for closer coordination in the market of the parent companies).

Second, evaluating the counterfactual question of whether the parent firms would have entered the market in the absence of the joint venture involves the Commission in making conjectures about the profitability of alternative strategies. Inconsistencies can easily creep into such conjectures. For instance, the suggestion in the Notice that the existence of complementary assets implies the parents are not potential competitors (and hence that their joint venture cannot involve a restriction of competition) is unconvincing, because the complementarity of asset is a key dimension of the efficiency benefits associated with joint ventures (as we emphasized above). Hence, the approach seems to imply that if a joint venture brings efficiency benefits, it will not involve restrictions of competition. Conversely, it implies that if firms are potential competitors, and their joint venture is found to restrict competition, this joint venture does not generate one important type of efficiency benefit. In other words, the existence of a competition restraint seems to presume the *absence* of an important source of efficiency benefit associated with the joint venture. Such an approach is odd from a legal point of view.[62] It seems to suggest that if a joint venture falls within the scope of Article 85§1, it has little chance of benefiting from exemption under Article 85§3. It is equally odd from an economic perspective insofar as one would expect joint ventures that bring large efficiency benefits to involve large risks of market power, and not that these two are mutually exclusive.

How this apparent contradiction is dealt with in practice will be a topic for the analysis of individual cases.

Efficiency Benefits

The block exemption on R&D projects and the 'Notice on Joint Ventures' suggest that joint ventures may produce efficiency benefits through reduced duplication in fixed costs, the exploitation of scale economies and the exchange of complementary knowledge. Interestingly, these benefits are not specific to joint ventures. They could equally well arise in the context of a merger. None of the benefits specifically associated with joint venture discussed above are mentioned.

The Balance Between Market Power and Efficiency

The block exemption on research joint-ventures recognizes that efficiency benefits have to be traded off against the increased market power *ex post*, after the product has been developed and is marketed.

As a consequence, the block exemption imposes two constraints. First, there should be competition at the research stage (the Commission will not allow R&D cooperation if there is no rival project) and that there should be sufficient *ex post* competition. For the latter, the exemption imposes a 20% ceiling on the *ex ante* market shares of the parents in products related to those being researched, and the exemption is granted for five years. If after five years, the market share is still below 20%, the exemption is extended (apparently without limit). If firms undertake joint distribution, the market share limit is 10%.

Overall, the approach of the Commission can thus be cast in terms of the traditional approach towards research joint ventures pioneered by d'Aspremont and Jacquemin (1988). In this framework, the benefits of a joint venture are the same as those that would accrue from a merger in the research market. The justification for the view that such a 'merger' may be beneficial has to rely either on the identification of specific complementarities between the assets involved, or on the presumption that there is excess entry in the research market and consequently too many firms currently involved. It is well known that in the presence of strong scale economies in the production of a commodity, free entry will often lead to excessive entry (see Von Weizsäcker, 1980); this applies with particular force in the context of research output, which is subject to ever declining average cost. There are too many firms in equilibrium, all producing at some inefficient scale. In this context, a reduction in the number of firms, admittedly giving rise to the exercise of some market power, would still be beneficial because of the lower cost level enjoyed by all firms. A 'merger' between two research units will achieve exactly this.

In the market for research, however, other forces are simultaneously at work. Most significantly, the tendency towards excess entry will be somewhat offset by difficulties in appropriating returns, i.e. in selling the output. To the extent that the output spills over to users, including competitors, for free, marginal incentives to undertake research will be reduced. It is unclear whether, on balance, entry into the research market will be excessive or insufficient, and the development of the literature since d'Aspremont and Jacquemin has abundantly illustrated this (see for instance, Suzumura, 1992; De Bondt, 1997 and others). As a consequence, this approach does not offer clear policy conclusions; the desirability of research joint-ventures will very much depend on the appropriability of the results and on the type of interactions between the parents (and between the parents and other firms) in the output market. In this respect, as pointed out by Ordover and Willig (1985), much will hinge on whether the parents have more to lose each other's advance or from falling behind other competitors (see also Grossman and Shapiro, 1986). The assessment of this contingency may be particularly difficult.

Overall, one may conclude that the desirability of research joint-ventures for the sake of reducing duplication is from generally clear, and the identification of those joint ventures that are beneficial is likely to be difficult. How the Commission has handled this matter is again an issue to consider in the analysis of the case law.

A couple of final remarks are in order. First, it may be important in evaluating the desirability of a research joint-venture to consider whether the output from the research is patentable and whether the parents can anticipate the use that they will make from the results. In this context, as we argued in Section 4.2 above, the scope for exercising market power may be much greater. Secondly, the counterfactual against which a joint venture is assessed has to be carefully specified. In general, it is not sufficient to simply look at the market share of the joint venture *ex post* and compare it with the situation prevailing *ex ante*. What is necessary is to make a comparison with the situation that would prevail in the future if the joint venture does not form. This requires an assessment of the developments in other competing firms.

4.5 The Case Law: Restrictions of Competition

4.5.1 *Potential Competition as a Necessary and Sufficient Condition*

As was discussed above, the Notice on joint ventures and the block exemption on R&D have suggested that, for the Commission to deem that a restriction of competition has occurred, the parent firms should be actual or potential competitors. This is a necessary condition, but in a number of cases it appears to have been considered also a sufficient condition. That is, the decisions do not attempt to evaluate with any depth whether the restrictions of competition are significant. The finding that firms are potential competitors appears to be sufficient to bring the joint venture within the scope of the prohibition of Article 85§1. *Eirpage*, a joint venture between Motorola and Telecom (the former monopoly operator of telecoms in Ireland) to provide paging services is a case in point. The Commission found that because Motorola had experience in the provision of paging services in other countries, it could have provided the service on its own. Similarly, because Telecom had been able to provide other types of valued-added services, like cellular communications, on its own, it could be presumed to be able do so for paging. As a consequence, 'au lieu d'avoir deux sociétés communes qui offrent le service en question, il n'y en a qu'une, ce qui doit être considéré comme une restriction de la concurrence'. Without any further consideration, the Commission decided that the joint venture by itself was a restriction of competition falling within the scope of Article 85§1.

In *Pasteur-Mérieux/Merck*, a joint venture effectively merging the vaccine operations of the parents in the EU, the Commission considered various products including polyvalent vaccines, like the ROR for which Merck has an effective monopoly world-wide (because competing vaccines generate serious side-effects). The Commission considered that

Pasteur-Mérieux was a potential competitor because it could have decided to develop an ROR vaccine on its own. As a consequence of the joint venture, no competing development would take place and this by itself was deemed to be a serious restriction of competition (paragraph 60), hence falling within the scope of the prohibition of Article 85§1.

In other cases, the Commission did consider whether the restriction of competition associated with the joint venture was significant, but the analysis remains very general. For instance, in *Ford/VW*, a joint venture created for the development and production of a multi-purpose vehicle (MPV, currently marketed as the Galaxy by Ford and the Sharan by VW), the Commission considered that both Ford and VW had the 'financial, technical and research capacities' (paragraph 19) to produce an MPV on their own. Since product development is, according to the Commission (paragraph 20) a key element of competition in the industry, this agreement was considered to be a serious restriction of competition without any further evaluation.

In *BT/MCI*, a joint venture to provide value-added telecommunications services to large companies, the Commission concluded that the parent companies were potential competitors. In this context, it was 'necessary to assess whether the creation of Newco (the joint venture) falls under Article 85(1)' (paragraph 43). The Commission then argues that because 'it has not been demonstrated that the creation of Newco is the only objective means for the parents' to enter, and because (given the existence of the joint venture) each parent company is unlikely to enter by itself, the joint venture falls within the scope of Article 85§1. The first of these arguments seems simply to repeat the fact that the parents are potential competitors but further suggests, surprisingly, that it is for the parties to show that they are not. The fact that the parents would not enter by themselves in the event of the joint venture, appealed to in the second argument, does not seem particularly relevant to evaluate the market power that could potentially be exercised. Indeed, if the parents did enter, one would expect them to coordinate their own behaviour with that of the joint venture.

It seems highly inappropriate to allow the application of Article 85§1 to hinge solely on whether firms could have undertaken the activity of the joint venture on their own. If that standard were applied to mergers, almost all of them by definition would be seen as unduly restricting competition. In following this approach, the Commission seems to lose sight of the fact that restrictions of competition only matter to the extent they allow for the exercise of market power. There are indeed many instances where the coordination of behaviour between firms (or even a full merger between them) simply does not matter because it does not affect any third party.

4.5.2 The Counterfactual for Potential Competition

In most instances, the Commission has failed to consider in its evaluation of potential competition between the parents whether they *would* have entered on their own. Rather, the Commission has simply considered whether firms had the *capability* to enter on their own. In other cases, like ***Eirpage***, the Commission explicitly presumed without justification that both parents would have entered in absence of the joint venture (see quote above). Similarly, in ***Asahi/Saint Gobain*** (a joint venture created for the development of new glass for motor cars), the Commission suggested that without the joint venture the parties would carry out parallel and differentiated developments on their own.

There are a number of cases where one can seriously doubt whether firms would have entered on their own. For instance, in ***Ford/VW***, the size of the market (about 350,000 units in Europe in 1995) together with the degree of scale economies (a minimum efficient scale of about 150,000 to 200,000 units a year) suggest that a substantial market share would be necessary to make the project viable. Given the very high degree of customer brand loyalty in the automobile market, it is unlikely that one manufacturer on its own would have achieved such market share. Arguably, it is only by pooling the brand loyalty of two manufacturers (which account for about 25% of the European car market) that the project became viable.

4.5.3 Potential Competition and Spillovers in Other Markets

As suggested above, it may be inappropriate to conclude that a joint venture does not restrict competition when the parents are not potential competitors, because the joint venture may have external effects outside the market of the joint venture. Of course, there are few published cases where the Commission has considered that firms were not potential competitors, so that instances of important external effects that may have been overlooked are relatively difficult to find in the case law. ***Elopak/Metal box-Odin*** may be such a case. It involves the creation of a joint venture to develop a new packaging technology between two companies that are both active in the packaging markets. The Commission has not considered the possibility that the joint venture may help the parents to coordinate their behaviour in the packaging market.

4.5.4 Complementary Assets and Potential Competition

As indicated above, the presumption that parents are not potential competitors when they bring complementary (non-tradable) assets to the joint venture is intriguing and illustrates the drawbacks of trying to second guess the relative profitability of alternative business strategies. A finding that parents are potential competitors (and hence that their joint venture involves a restriction of competition) may thus prejudge the existence of efficiency benefits (under Article 85§3) or risk introducing some internal inconsistency in the decisions. Such inconsistency is apparent for instance in *BT/MCI*, where the Commission first suggested in the analysis of competition that BT and MCI had similar competences and were involved in similar activities, but later argued that it was necessary to form a joint venture to enter the value added market successfully (see paragraph 58). This success presumably originates from the joint operation of complementary assets. Similarly, the Commission found in *Fujitsu/AMD* that the parents had substitute assets for the development and production of electronically programmable, read only memories (EPROMs). Later on, however, the Commission argued that AMD was rather better at the development of the new memories and Fujitsu was rather better at their production. In *Fiat/Hitachi*, a joint venture for the development, production and sales of hydraulic excavators, the Commission found that the parents had similar capabilities but admitted later that 'the joint venture would develop better excavators as each party will incorporate technically better components at its disposal'.

4.5.5   Evaluation of Specific Restrictions

The Commission not only evaluates whether the formation of the joint venture is of itself a restriction of competition, but in many cases it also considers particular contractual provisions of the joint venture agreements. In what follows, we cannot review all the types of provisions that have been considered but rather focus on the most prevalent ones.

4.5.5.1 Freedom to Choose

There are a number of cases where the Commission considers that restrictions in the freedom of parties to choose should be seen as *ipso facto* restrictions of competition. This approach, which is also found in the analysis of vertical agreements and horizontal agreements outside joint ventures (see Chapters 2 and 3), is misleading because many restrictions in the contractual freedom of the parents simply do not affect third parties. For instance, in *Olivetti/Digital* (see also *Auditel* for an alternative illustration), Olivetti committed to use the Alpha AXP technology developed by Digital for all its RISC-based applications (where RISC stands for reduced instruction set computing). This was not considered to be a restriction of competition because it was in the interest of Olivetti to commit to a single technology for these applications. Olivetti, however, also committed to purchase a certain proportion of its non Intel-based platforms (a component entering in the production of computers) from Digital. The Commission considered this to be a restriction of competition because, in part, it restricted Olivetti in its freedom to choose a particular supplier (paragraph 21). This vertical restraint does not, however, seem to affect any third party and in particular does not affect consumers because of intense inter-brand competition in the market for non-Intel-based hardware.

4.5.5.2 Essential Facilities

The Commission has also reviewed a number of cases involving access to an essential facility, and in particular three cases associated with the operation of the Channel Tunnel. The first case (*Eurotunnel*) involved the commitment by the tunnel operators to grant all traffic rights within the tunnel (outside those necessary for the operation of the shuttle) jointly to British Rail and the SNCF. In return, the SNCF and British Rail would invest in port facilities and the necessary rail stocks. The consequence of this contract is a complete foreclosure of the market for the operation of through trains in the tunnel. It also stands in contradiction to the directive on the liberalization of services on European rail networks (at least for freight). By selling traffic rights to a single operator, Eurotunnel has also presumably been able to extract the rent associated with monopoly operations of through trains in the tunnel. The importance of this rent admittedly depends on competition with alternative modes of transport such as ferries and aeroplanes, but it could still be substantial (see Kay *et al.*, 1989).

In addition to this agreement, BR and the SNCF have formed one joint venture (ACI) with IC (a company specialized in the operation of combined rail/road transport) to provide integrated freight services through the channel and one joint venture (Night Services) with a number of rail operators in the Community to provide sleeper trains through the tunnel. The Commission found in both cases that there were restrictions of competition because other service providers (in freight or sleeper trains) were put at a disadvantage. It is hard to see how the additional joint ventures can make matters any worse; the market for through trains (whatever their load) is completely foreclosed by the original award of monopoly rights jointly to BR and the SNCF. Given the (disputable) original decision, the additional joint ventures should have been waved through.

4.5.5.3 Intellectual Property Rights

In joint ventures involving new research or the production of items requiring the use of proprietary knowledge, many contractual provisions relate to the allocation and the use of intellectual property rights. In those cases, the Commission is often very concerned about the number of licences the holder of a property right will award. A commitment to an exclusive licence is often seen as a serious restriction of competition, and at times the Commission has required that the number of licences should be increased. In taking this view, the Commission apparently fails to accept that a patent is a monopoly right that in normal circumstances entitles a holder to realize its full value for a given period of time, in the expectation of which a firm will undertake its research and development in the first place. The willingness to pay of licensees of course depends on the number of licences that are awarded over the same product and geographic market. By insisting that the holder of a patent should provide several licences to competing firms, the Commission thus prevents the patent holder from realising its full value. This will of course discourage investment in research and the development of proprietary knowledge, which is itself recognized as a key objective of Article 85§3 (see also the block exemption on research and development).

The Commission has been particularly reluctant to accept exclusive licences when they have a geographical dimension. Patent holders are thus prevented from selling their monopoly rights by country because this has the apparent effect of preventing trade between the Member States (an absolute anathema for the Commission). This gives patent holders an incentive to award rights for the Community as a whole, which may not be efficient (for instance because there is no single licensee with adequate facilities across the Community), and in any event will not foster integration of EU markets any further. As a compromise, the Commission has also accepted exclusive geographical licenses as long as passive sales (by firms holding rights in other territories) are accepted. This regime adds to uncertainty for the licensers and licensees about the real value of the patent, does little to enhance efficient contracting between them and presumably still undermines the incentives to generate proprietary knowledge.

For instance, ***Mitchell/Sofiltra*** (admittedly a case dating back to the mid-1980s) involved the creation of a joint venture producing filters for the UK market. Sofiltra was the holder of a patent covering a technology that is essential for the production of these filters. It had committed, as part of the joint-venture agreement, not to grant any further license on the use of its technology in for the UK market. The Commission disputed this. It is, however, clear that this provision was essential to protect

Mitchell from opportunistic behaviour by Sofiltra, preventing it from trying to sell monopoly rights associated with its innovation several times round; in the absence of this provision, Mitchell could thus not determine the value of its licence. The prospect of passive sales which the Commission insisted upon still introduces uncertainty about this value.

A similar issue has arisen in the context of *Pasteur-Mérieux/Merck* where the joint venture obtained all property rights over existing vaccines. In some product and geographic markets (France and Germany), the pooling of patent rights in the joint venture led to substantial market shares. In one case, where Merck and Pasteur-Mérieux held the only competing vaccines, a duopoly was replaced by a monopoly. Presumably in anticipation of the problems that such pooling would entail, the joint venture granted exclusive licenses in France and Germany to manufacture and sell one of the vaccines. The value of this licence in each market thus presumably reflected duopoly rents and arguably the situation has not changed in terms of competition relative to what prevailed before the joint venture. Surprisingly, the exclusive licences granted by the joint venture, which seem to improve rather than aggravate the outcome in terms of competition, were considered by the Commission to restrict competition.

4.5.6   Conclusion

Overall, one cannot help concluding that in many instances the Commission follows a very rigid approach: the finding that a joint venture falls under the prohibition of Article 85 is very much a matter of abstract principles and not the outcome of a structured evaluation of the significance of the restrictions involved. Whether parents could have undertaken the activities of the joint venture on their own is often the sole focus of this enquiry. This approach neglects the question whether the joint venture would have any market power. It also involves frequently arbitrary judgements of the relative profitability of alternative business strategies. The approach also tends to cultivate a confusion between efficiency and market power issues. As a result, there have been a number of decisions where joint ventures were deemed to fall under the prohibition of Article 85 where there is little doubt that the alliance would have been allowed under the Merger Regulation (see for instance, *Fiat/Hitachi*, *Fujitsu/AMD* or *Exxon/Shell*).

An alternative to this approach would be to adopt the approach followed for the evaluation of mergers. This would entail adopting the presumption that if firms that are choosing to form a joint venture, this must be privately profitable. The analysis then focuses on whether the joint venture can lead to the exercise of market power. The presumption here would be that if the parents were present in the market of the joint venture, they would do their best to coordinate their behaviour with that of the joint venture. Therefore, in the absence of arguments to show that it would be difficult for them to do so, the combined market share of the parents and the joint venture should be considered in the analysis of dominance.

A number of recent decisions confirm that such an approach would be effective and feasible in the context of the current legal framework. For instance, the approach followed by the Commission in *Exxon/Shell* parallels in many ways the typical treatment of a merger. In that decision, the Commission defined the relevant market, considered rightly that the parents would coordinate their behaviour in the market of the joint venture and wondered whether the market share of the joint venture would be unduly large. In the event, one could regret that the Commission did not consider the sum of the market share of the parents and the joint venture in its analysis, but the overall approach seems reasonable. Interestingly, the question of whether the parents could have undertaken the activities of the joint venture is considered but does not play a central role.

The joint venture between Lufthansa and SAS is also a case in point. There again, the Commission started with a careful analysis of the relevant market, presumed that the airlines would coordinate behaviour, analysed their combined market shares and considered potential entry barriers. The analysis of the restrictions of competition in this case in effect closely parallels the analysis that the Merger Task Force has undertaken in cases like *Sabena/Air France* or *Sabena/Swissair*.

4.6   Efficiency Benefits

A number of formal conditions are listed in the Treaty for efficiency benefits to entitle an agreement to exemption under Article 85§3, namely that the production and distribution of goods should be improved, that the benefits could not accrue without the agreement, that consumers should obtain a fair share of the benefits and that competition should not be suppressed.

All exemption decisions under Article 85 inevitably follow this list of conditions. Their evaluation is, however, rather formal and it is only the first conditions relating to the existence of efficiency benefits which are considered in some depth. As indicated above, scale economies, a reduction in the duplication of fixed costs and the association of complementary assets are considered by the block exemption on R&D agreements as important efficiency benefits. These considerations also play an important role in individual exemptions.

4.6.1 Complementary Assets

The argument that complementary assets enable joint ventures to achieve better results than the parents could achieve on their own appears in a number of cases. However, the Commission sometimes loses sight of the fact that a joint venture is necessary for bringing complementary assets together only when these assets cannot be traded. When assets can be bought freely in the market, the joint venture does not necessarily bring additional benefits.

For instance, in *Pasteur-Mérieux/Merck*, the fact that the parents produce complementary antigen agents is listed as a source of efficiency in the development of new vaccines combining these antigens. Yet, at the same time, the Commission acknowledges that there is an active open market for these antigens. Similarly, in *Fiat/Hitachi*, the Commission refers to the availability of different components for the production of hydraulic excavators, but it is far from clear that these components cannot be traded. In *Lufthansa/SAS*, the Commission argued that the two companies' fleets would complement each other, and in particular that SAS had many of the small planes that were necessary to serve low density intra-Scandinavian routes. It ignored the fact that aircraft can hardly be seen as specific assets that cannot be traded: there is an market for the leasing of aircraft of all sizes.

In *Ford/VW*, the Commission considered that the partners brought complementary assets to the joint venture, but failed to argue that consumer loyalty was the main element of complementarity (see above). Rather, the Commission focused on technical aspects, even though the joint venture envisages a complete separation between the development of the MPV (undertaken by VW) and its production (undertaken by Ford).

4.6.2 Scale Economies

The argument that a joint venture will benefit from scale economies and a reduction in fixed costs is often quoted but rarely quantified. *Philips/Osram* is an exception. A joint venture was formed to produce leaded glass for lamp bulbs, after one of the parents (Osram) decided to close down its European factory. Before the joint venture, the parents had similar capacities, each accounting for about one third of European production. The remaining third of the output was produced by a relatively large number of small firms. The Commission endorsed the view, put forward by the parties, that the joint venture, which would produce about 70% of European sales, would achieve scale economies such that average cost would fall by at least 10%. It seems to us that the Commission could have taken a more critical look at this claim. Indeed, it is hard to square the observation that many small firms can profitably produce a third of market output with the view that the minimum efficient scale may be as high as 70% of the European market. The amount of excess entry that this scenario would imply seems quite unreasonable.

4.6.3 Competition as a Benefit

In the same way that efficiency arguments creep up in the evaluation of competition, increased competition is at times used in as an efficiency consideration. For instance, in *Fiat/Hitachi*, the Commission argues that the joint venture will prove to be a more effective competitor than the parents would be on their own and will 'bring about a more balanced market structure'. The fact that the joint venture will have a market share of 16% is seen as a benefit. In *BT/MCI*, after concluding that the joint venture would involve a restriction of competition, the Commission argued that competition in the market would be enhanced (paragraph 55) and that 'consumers would benefit from lower pricing'.

In *UIP*, the Commission concluded that the cooperation between Paramount, MCA and MGM in the distribution of films restricted competition, but argued at length that an exemption should be granted because the restriction was not very serious. For instance, it argued that the market share of the joint venture would not be excessively large, and the vital element of competition in the film sector would be preserved (paragraph 54).

4.6.4 Other Benefits

A number of other benefits are recurrently cited. In particular, the fact that the joint venture allows for a transfer of technology from third countries (especially Japan) is quite popular (see for instance *Olivetti/Canon*, *BT/MCI*, *Asahi/St Gobain*, *Olivetti/Digital*).

Somewhat more exotic arguments are sometimes put forward: for instance, in *Ford/VW*, not only employment but also the installation of robots in Portugal are seen as significant efficiency benefits. The contribution to the success of the Channel Tunnel is also raised in *Eurotunnel*, *ACI* and *Night Services*. An increased demand for telecommunications services as well as the development of small and medium size enterprises in rural areas are cited in *Eirpage*. The stimulation of the production of non-English movies is recognized in UIP.

Interestingly, there are also some cases where potentially important efficiency benefits have not been spelled out by the Commission. For instance, *Auditel* is a joint venture for the collection of data relating to television audiences in Italy. These audience measures are used in order to set advertising rates *ex post*. The joint-venture agreement includes a commitment by the main television stations and the advertisers not to dispute the measures put forward by Auditel. It is effectively a standardization agreement which arguably reduces transaction costs between television stations and advertising agencies. This benefit was not recognized by the Commission which refused an exemption.

4.6.5   Conclusions: The Treatment of Efficiency Benefits

Overall, it is striking that the range of efficiency benefits referred to in Commission decisions is large, but that hardly any of them is given a serious hearing. Some of the arguments refer to genuine externalities which might enhance efficiency. Others refer in vague terms to general objectives having a remote and unspecified link with economic efficiency. In all cases, the arguments are simply stated and there is no attempt to evaluate their significance, let alone to quantify their importance. Interestingly, the benefits that are commonly appealed to do not appear to be specific to joint ventures. They could equally well apply to mergers.

4.7   Concluding Comment

Overall, it is hard to avoid the conclusion that there is little systematic reasoning behind the Commission's approach to the exemption of joint-venture agreements under Article 85§3. To some extent this is unsurprising, because theoretical and empirical work on joint ventures has itself been rather scattered and unsystematic. We have, however, suggested that certain clear themes have now emerged from this literature, making a more systematic approach possible.

5

The Procedures of the European Commission

5.1 Introduction

Chapters 2, 3 and 4 have examined the principles according to which vertical and horizontal agreements are scrutinized by the European Commission, from the perspectives of both economic theory and the law. They have compared the Commission's actual decisions with those that an economic and legal analysis would recommend. The purpose of this chapter is to examine the Commission's procedures directly, and to ask two questions about them. First, are these procedures likely to lead, on balance, to good decisions? Second, do they operate efficiently, in the sense of minimizing the time and other resource costs (both to the authorities and to the firms they investigate) of reaching decisions?

Our main source of evidence about these procedures consists of a survey of firms involved in competition cases since 1989. As we shall see, the procedures of the Commission are complex, and it is important to discover the factors that influence them at each stage. It is by now a commonplace that the outcome of regulation in practice will be influenced not merely by the formal requirements of statutory rules, but also by a whole range of more or less informal pressures on the individuals and institutions responsible for the implementation of these rules (see Neven *et al.*, 1993, Chapter 5). There is nothing in itself reprehensible about this, but it does imply that investigation of these informal pressures is as important a task as consideration of the rules themselves.

This chapter is organized as follows. Section 5.2 describes the survey. Sections 5.3 and 5.4 describe and analyse the procedure on the basis of the information gathered with the survey, using also information published by the Commission. Section 5.5 considers the incentives that firms have to notify agreements and to bring complaints, and what this implies for the kinds of case opened by the Commission on its own initiative. Section 5.6 considers evidence about contacts between firms and Commission officials. Section 5.7 reports firms' opinions about the procedure. Section 5.8 reports the extent to which firms' behaviour is likely to be changed by the experience of a competition case. Section 5.9 concludes.

5.2   The Survey

As part of this research we carried out a survey of firms involved in completed competition cases since the beginning of 1989. The aim was to obtain further information from firms about the actual operation of the Commission's procedure, both about its formal aspects (such as published decisions) and its more informal aspects.

The number of firms engaged in a competition procedure that was closed between 1989 and 1994 is very large: 4720 cases were terminated within that period (most of them concerning more than one firm). The identity of the firms involved in these cases is, however, usually confidential to the Commission (that is, except where the Commission makes their identity public as part of the procedure, for example by publishing a decision). For us to have relied entirely on the published information would, however, have biased the coverage of our survey against the informal parts of the procedure. Consequently we directed our survey to firms from two sources. First, those whose names appeared in the published material of the Commission about Article 85 cases (the 'published list'); and second, the largest European Union firms not in the publication list but included in the European Top 5000 classification of Dun & Bradstreet (the 'unpublished list').

The initial sample constructed with these two lists consisted of 874 firms. Of these, 50 firms replied that they had been involved in no competition cases with the Commission (and were, therefore, not concerned by our survey). A further 24 firms replied that they had had no direct involvement in the case concerned. Of the remaining 800 firms, the response rate to our questionnaire was quite low: 11%.[63] Most of the other firms did not reply at all, and those who replied but declined to fill in the questionnaire (12%) cited the costs in time and effort of responding to such a survey. In their survey on the merger procedure, Neven *et al.* (1993) obtained a response rate of 29.8%, so this lower response rate was a considerable disappointment. The reasons for it are probably threefold. First, at the time of *Neven et al.*'s merger survey, the European merger control procedure had recently been implemented; firms were fairly willing to give their point of view about these new rules. By contrast, the application of Article 85 is an old procedure that firms are used to having to go through, despite the frequent criticisms they express. Second, most Article 85 cases concern small agreements that are closed by an informal decision. We suppose that many firms were, therefore, unwilling to spend time answering a questionnaire concerning an agreement with a minor impact on their business. In contrast, under the merger procedure all cases had a significant impact on the firms concerned. Third, there is evidence from other sources that firms in Europe have begun to experience 'survey fatigue', especially in connection with Single Market issues.[64]

The sample used for the analysis consists of 88 firms and covers 74 different agreements. The number of files opened by the Commission for these agreements is 78. The number of files is higher than the number of cases because some agreements may involve both a complaint and a notification.

Some comments should be made about the representativeness of the sample, given the low response rate. Table 5.1 shows that in terms of formal decisions, the sample has captured a reasonable proportion of the cases (26%). By contrast, the sample captures only 1% of the cases settled informally. Nevertheless, this is less disappointing than it might appear, since the cases settled informally undoubtedly include a great number of unimportant cases. In particular, during the period covered by our survey a large number of cases were terminated following the issue of a new block exemption in the insurance sector (in 1992) and thanks to a backlog-clearing effort by the Commission.[65]

In Table 5.2, the structure of the Commission's workload and the structure of the sample are compared. As far as new files are concerned, our sample reflects reasonably faithfully the proportions of the Commission's workload. As far as terminated cases are concerned, formal decisions have a very important share in the sample whereas they are marginal in the Commission's workload. These figures imply that it should be kept in mind that the survey findings are likely to be a more accurate reflection of the character of formal than of informal procedures. Nevertheless, cases settled informally represent 57.2% of the sample.

Table 5.1 Representativeness of the sample

	Commission (1989–94)	Survey %
Total number of terminated cases	4720	1.6
Cases terminated by a formal decision under Article 85	126	26.0
Cases terminated by an informal decision	4594	1.0

Source: XXIVth Report on Competition Policy (Commission, 1994) and *Survey*

Table 5.2 Origin and destination of cases: Commission workload vs. Survey

	Commission (%)	Survey (%)
Cases opened following notification	61.5	66.2
Cases opened following complaint	27.1	20.8
Cases opened following own procedure	11.1	14.3
Cases terminated by settlement	76.2	26.0
Cases terminated by comfort letter	2.1	31.2
Cases terminated by formal decision	2.5	42.9

Source: XXIVth Report on Competition Policy (Commission, 1994) and *Survey*

The classification of responses by nationality is reasonably representative (although non-European Union firms – mainly American and
Japanese – have a somewhat greater share in our sample). Table 5.3.
compares the structure of nationalities in our sample and in the total
number of cases closed between 1989 and 1994 for which there has been
some publication.

Table 5.4 breaks down responses by economic sector. In the survey
most agreements were concluded in the chemical sector (17.6%), transport services (14.5%) and electrical machinery (12.2%). In terms of

Table 5.3 Nationalities

	Commission (%)	Survey (%)
British	28.9	23.9
French	13.6	17.0
German	10.7	14.8
Other European Union	36.2	26.1
Outside European Union of which	10.5	18.2
American	5.6	10.2
Japanese	1.5	5.7

Source: List of cases having led to some publication (available from the Commision) and *Survey*

Table 5.4 Economic sectors

	Commission (%)	Survey (%)
Chemical products	14.8	17.6
Transport	14.8	14.5
Electrical machines	11.1	12.2
Food, drink and tobacco	8.6	5.4
Other	50.7	50.3

Source: Article 85 Decisions published in the *Official Journal* (1989–94) and *Survey*

Article 85 formal decisions, these sectors also have the most important shares: chemical sector (14.8%), transport services (14.8%) and electrical machinery (11.1%).

To summarize, in spite of the low response rate, and the over-representation of cases that were settled by formal decision, the sample appears to be fairly representative in terms of the means by which the procedures were opened, firms' countries of origin and the economic sectors in which they operate.

Finally, Table 5.5 shows the relationship between the way in which cases in our survey were opened and they way in which they were concluded. No comparison with the overall Commission caseload is possible, though comments can be made: for example, the majority of notified cases are cleared (98%) and this seems consistent with the Commission's activity although formal clearance decisions are still over-represented. In the survey, a quarter of cases opened by complaint led to a prohibition decision (higher than the proportion of total cases). Prohibition decisions are similarly over-represented among the cases initiated by the Commission itself, though once again this probably suggests that our sample has captured a particularly high proportion of the difficult or important cases.

Table 5.5 Conclusion of cases according to means of opening

	Settlement (%)	Comfort letter (%)	Formal clearance (%)	Formal prohibition (%)
Notification	16.0	45.0	37.0	2.0
Complaint	66.7	6.7	6.7	20.0
Own procedure	25.0	0.0	12.5	62.5

Source: Survey

5.3 The Opening of a Case

5.3.1 Notification

Figure 5.1 describes the European Union procedure for firms that choose to notify their agreements to the Commission.

Pre-notification Stage

Firms choose to notify their agreements to the Commission in one of two circumstances. Most often, they do so after signing an agreement (and presumably on the advice of their lawyers). In the survey, these notifying

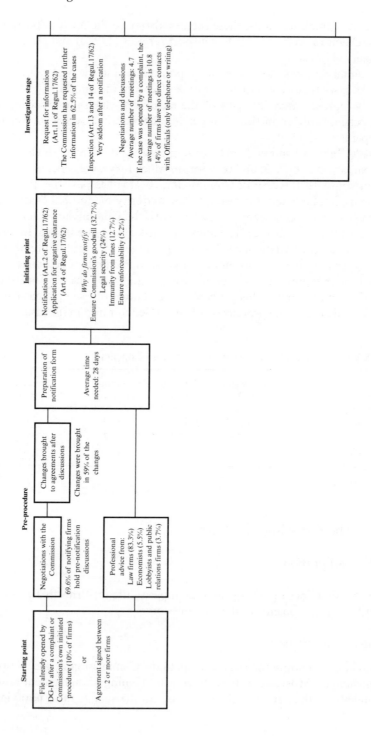

Figure 5.1a Early stages of the procedure when the case involves notification

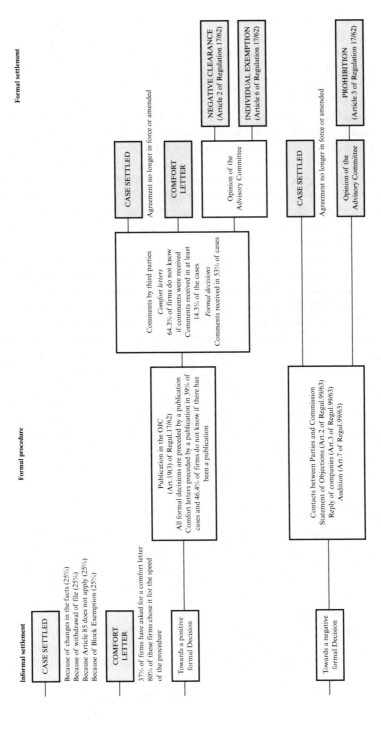

Figure 5.1 b Final stages of the procedure when the case involves notification

firms were asked what advantages they thought notification would bring to them. The willingness to obtain the Commission's 'goodwill' (32.7%) and legal security (24%) were the main advantages put forward by firms. Immunity from fines does not appear to be an important incentive to notify (only cited by 12.7% of firms). Finally, 5.2% of notifying firms answered that they wished to ensure the enforceability of their agreement.

Alternatively, firms may decide to notify an agreement because they are already suspected of infringing competition rules. In such cases, the immunity from fines can be an important incentive to notify. In our sample, 10% of all notifying firms adopted this strategy. They decided to notify their agreement *after* the Commission had already opened a file on its own initiative or subsequent to a complaint. This strategy also appears in the published decisions. In ten of the cases leading to formal decisions since 1989, agreements were notified *after* a file had already been opened by the Commission.

The survey reveals that there is an important 'pre-notification' stage: that is, most firms (69.6%) have contacts with the Commission before they submit their notification form. One firm claimed that seeing the Commission before the notification was 'invaluable', but gave no explanation. What is the purpose of such discussions? First, firms may hope to obtain hints about the position the officials from DG-IV are likely to adopt. Second, such contacts may also save time by allowing agreements to be modified in order to speed their clearance. In the survey most of these pre-notification discussions (59%) led to modifications of the agreement, though the modifications were described as 'major' in only 7.7% of cases. Nevertheless, pre-notification discussions certainly do not guarantee clearance: three of the firms in the sample faced infringement decisions in spite of such discussions. Two of them notified an agreement that was already under examination by the Commission. Their agreement was prohibited despite the changes they brought.

The Notification and the Investigation Stages

After these informal contacts, firms need to fill in the notification Form A/B, a task that may require significant management resources. We asked firms how many people were involved in this task and the total number of person-days required. The range of answers was from 1 to 25 people (with an average of 5 people), and from 1 to 180 person-days, with an average of 26 person-days.

The A/B Form requires firm to disclose commercial information to the Commission, including not only the detailed provisions of the notified agreement, but also information about the market, about prices and sales, etc. The Commission often requests further information (62.5% of our survey were asked to supply this), and this request was principally for market information. Most of these (74.3%) considered the Commission's request was reasonable. In fact such supplementary requests are likely to become less frequent now that there is a new A/B Form. It has been inspired by the CO Form (the notification form for merger operations) and is, therefore, substantially longer. Firms are requested to give information with a high degree of detail. In fact, one part of the analysis has been transferred to them. More precisely, they are now asked to give their definition of the relevant product market, of the relevant geographic market and they have to evaluate their position on that market (with market shares) as well as the position of competitors. If market shares on the relevant market exceeds 15%, they are also asked to evaluate barriers to entry and potential competition. This new A/B Form allows the Commission to obtain most of the relevant information in the earliest stage of the procedure and it also standardises the type of information received for all notifications.

An average of 258 notifications are introduced each year and on average, there is only one formal infringement decision per year prohibiting a notified agreement. This suggests that firms naturally tend to notify agreements that are likely to be fairly 'safe'. This selection process will be analysed later in this chapter.

5.3.2 The Complaint Procedure

There is only one complainant in our sample, so our account of the complaint procedure is heavily based on the information supplied by firms against whom complaints were filed.

Figure 5.2 presents the procedure according to the information given by firms. It appears that most complaints are lodged by customers (42.1%) and competitors (31.6%). As pointed out previously, some firms notify their agreement once it has been detected by a third party. However, in the majority of cases (76.5%), suspected firms do not bother to start a notification procedure.

Most suspected firms have contacts with officials from DG-IV (88% of them) during a complaint procedure. The average number of meetings in the sample was just under six per firm. However, they do not systematically have discussions with the complainant (only 41.2%). No rules define the contacts between the plaintiff and the defendant. The right to anonymity obviously makes such discussions less likely, and when they take place they are effectively negotiations. Overall, firms involved in complaints considered that the Commission had given a fair hearing to both parties, though this may have reflected the fact that only 20% of complaints resulted in prohibition and the fact that our sample contained hardly any complainants.

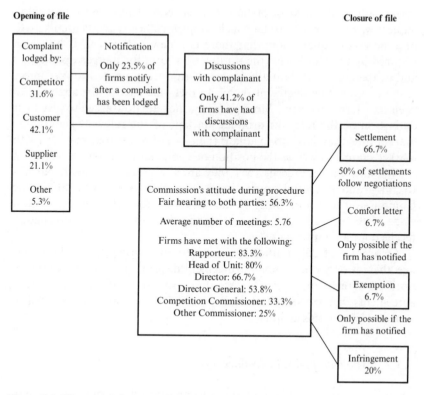

Figure 5.2 The complaint procedure

5.3.3   Proceedings Initiated by the Commission

In the sample, there are only eight cases that were opened on the initiative of the Commission. The majority of these cases led to infringement decisions. Due to this small number of cases, and the strong bias towards formal procedures, we report no chart for such proceedings. This procedure will be analysed later in the light of the published information.

5.4   The Decision-Making Process

5.4.1   Investigation and Analysis

Investigation

The task of the Commission in an investigation varies according to the way a case was opened. For notifications, all the information is provided by the notifying firms. The right to request information (under Article 11 of Regulation 17) is used for all types of case. The right to make inspections of company premises (Article 14 of Regulation 17) is used only the case has been opened by a third party. More specifically, most inspections occur when the Commission investigates on its own initiative.[66] For notified agreements, the Commission only has to assess the *effect* of an agreement on competition. When an infringement is suspected concerning an un-notified agreement, the type of evidence sought by the Commission is different and more difficult to gather: the *existence* of infringing provisions has to be proved, before their impact on competition can be evaluated. Since firms are unlikely to provide the evidence of their infringement (if committed), the Commission has to use its inspection powers. Most inspections are carried out when price-fixing and/or market-sharing agreements are suspected or when export bans are informally imposed by a manufacturer to its distributors.

Analysis

Once the information has been gathered, the analysis begins. The Commission's economic analysis has been assessed in detail in the chapters on vertical restraints and collusion, so we make only a few general procedural comments here. The only source of information that is available about the economic analysis performed by the Commission lies in the published decisions and notices (and very broadly in annual reports). Since published decisions concern only the few agreements[67] that are prohibited or formally exempted every year, the most important part of the Commission's analysis remains secret.

The analysis of Article 85 cases appears also to be much less systematic than is the case for merger decision. There are no clear rules concerning economic features that the Commission may consider.

After the first stage of analysis, most cases will be settled informally. In a small proportion of cases, the procedure will continue.

5.4.2 *The Settlement Stage*

5.4.2.1 *The Comfort Letter*

The comfort letter is an administrative informal letter signed by an official of DG-IV which informs the notifying firms that, according to the elements in the possession of the Commission, there is no need to engage in any formal procedure.

The advantages of the comfort letter A comfort letter allows firms to be granted a rapid clearance of their agreement. In the A/B Form, firms are asked if they would be satisfied with a comfort letter. Surprisingly, in our survey 56.5% of firms who had received a comfort letter said they were not given the choice between a comfort letter and a formal decision. The majority of firms having chosen a comfort letter claimed that their choice was mainly guided by the willingness to see their case settled rapidly. Figure 5.3 shows that the average length of the procedure leading to the issue of a comfort letter is of 20 months (58% of them were issued less than one year after notification).

The second advantage of comfort letters is to allow firms to avoid publicity about their case (15.4% of firms also gave this justification for their choice).

Finally, a comfort letter perpetuates the immunity from fines granted by the notification,[68] but this aspect was not cited by any firm in our sample.

To summarize, comfort letters offer two main advantages:

- The procedure is significantly faster.
- No information (or only little) is disclosed about the case.

Even if the issue of a comfort letter appears to satisfy most firms, there are still some problems associated with the procedure.

The costs of the comfort letter First, the adoption of this informal procedure by the Commission has no formal legal basis. Consequently, the protection offered by comfort letters is far from perfect. A comfort letter is not binding for national courts, national antitrust authorities and third parties. Nor is it binding for the Commission, which has the right to reopen the file if, for example, new information comes into its possession or after a request by a third party[69] (which could even be a party to the agreement). The Commission has expressed the view[70] that national courts 'may take into account' the issue of a comfort letter when assessing a case under European competition law, but this is far from constituting legal protection.

Second, comfort letters cannot be appealed to the Court of Justice under Article 173 of the EC Treaty, unlike letters sent by the Commission definitively rejecting a complaint. This asymmetry has led Stevens (1994, p. 85) to the conclusion that 'Complainants, it would appear, receive rather more protection than parties to an agreement'.

Following repeated criticisms on the weak protection offered by comfort letters, the Commission decided to publish the essential content of agreements that would be granted a comfort letter. This publication was aimed at increasing the protection offered by comfort letters since third parties could give their comments and the possibility of subsequent challenges was therefore reduced. Whish (1993), however, pointed out that only a marginal share of comfort letters have been preceded by a publication despite their growing number (3.4% of comfort letters issued in 1992; the percentage was still only 9.3% in 1995). In our survey, 37.5% of the comfort letters were preceded by a publication. The choice of published cases is made by the Commission, except if firms clearly wish to avoid publicity.

Our survey shows that firms are not properly informed about the participation of third parties during the informal procedure. First, an important proportion of them (45.8%) do not know if third parties have been invited to make comments. Second, an even larger proportion (66.7%) are not informed about the comments that may have been received. One firm in the sample answered that the Commission did ask for comments and received some, but did not officially inform the notifying parties.

When deciding whether or not to be satisfied with a comfort letter, firms face a trade-off between legal certainty and the speed of the procedure. The high number of comfort letters suggests that most of them favour the rapid settlement of their case. Moreover, firms appear to be satisfied with the protection conferred by a comfort letter. In the survey, 74% of them answered they felt assurance about the legality of their position with the comfort letter. However, one of them added that this assurance is temporary while another considered the comfort letter offers legal protection only in certain (unspecified) circumstances.

5.4.2.2 The Informal Settlement

The main factor underlying the decision to settle a file is a judgement that the competition rules do not apply to the case in question. This may be for one of two reasons:

1. The agreement obviously conforms to competition rules (it may be of minor importance or covered by a block exemption, or an investigation reveals clearly that there is no restriction of competition).
2. The original agreement as notified did indeed infringe competition rules, but the necessary changes have been brought in order to make it conform. Walbroeck (1986) calls these 'negotiated settlements'.

Of the cases in our survey that were settled informally, most had been opened by complaints: 55% were settled on the grounds that Article 85 was judged not to apply, while 45% were settled because of some change in the facts of the case. These figures suggest that negotiated settlements are frequent, but they should be taken cautiously because of the relatively small number of settled cases in our survey.

The costs of a settlement Bringing the necessary changes may allow a settlement to be reached, but it is not a sufficient condition. Terminating an infringement is not systematically a safeguard against prosecution. The Commission has complete discretion about the choice of the cases it will settle by an informal decision rather than a formal one. Its choice is ruled, *inter alia*, by the willingness to set legal principles by case law and to clarify particular points of law. In fact, the decision to bring a case is not necessarily directed by economic reasoning, or the wish to achieve particular economic outcomes. This may owe something to the fact that 'there are more lawyers than economists in DG-IV', as Temple Lang (1981, p. 353) points out. This point is developed in the paragraph on formal decisions. Nevertheless, despite the uncertainty due to the Commission's discretion, there is still a high probability of settlement if the infringing provisions of an agreement are removed.

The mean length of settlement procedure for firms in our survey was quite short (see Figure 5.3). The variance is, however, enormous (the minimum is of 10 weeks and the maximum is of 15 years) and such an average should be taken cautiously. The only conclusion is probably that great uncertainty characterizes the time needed to reach a settlement.

Finally, the legal value of settlements presents the same problems as the legal protection of comfort letters. Settlements are often decided by officials from DG-IV and are, therefore, capable of review at any time if new elements come to the knowledge of the Commission or if there is a complaint by third parties.

The advantages of a settlement For notified agreements, the settlement has the same characteristics as a comfort letter with the only difference that notification was in fact not necessary.

For infringing agreements that have not been notified, the settlement is the most favourable outcome. When the infringing firm is informed about the Commission's doubts concerning the compliance of the agreement with competition rules, its best strategy is to negotiate the necessary changes in order to obtain a settlement of the file. Such a settlement offers the following advantages:

- There is no minimal disclosure of information about the case.
- The procedure is (usually) faster and no fines are imposed. The termination of the infringement is negotiated with the Commission (and sometimes with the complainant).

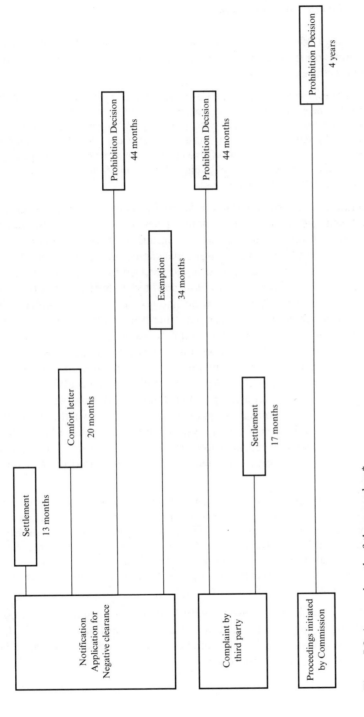

Figure 5.3 Average length of the procedure*

* The average was computed according to the information available in published formal decisions between 1989 and 1995. For settlements and comfort letters, the means were computed according to the answers to the survey.

4.4.3 The Formal Decision Stage

Temple Lang (1981, p. 352) has classified some of the factors influencing the Commission in its choice of which cases should be treated under the formal procedure:

> the aim of establishing legal principles by case law of the Commission and the Court, if appropriate by test cases; the need to deal with complaints; the need to deal with notifications which were important or urgently required by the parties or by national court; the need to prevent division of the Common Market, and to end clearly unjustifiable infringements; the need to adopt a certain minimum number of formal published decisions each year, to show how the law is applied in particular cases.

The Commission clearly stated in the **Scottish Salmon** case[71] that a decision may be taken in order to clarify a point of law. For example, in the **Bayer Dental** case,[72] Bayer Dental imposed conditions on its buyers that did not allow them to resell the product after repackaging, nor to export it. These clauses were removed by Bayer after it had received the statement of objections, but the Commission nevertheless adopted a short formal decision. The prohibitions of resale and of export had not been clearly formulated in the original agreement and Bayer had, therefore, claimed there was no infringement of Article 85§1. The Commission's decision sought to establish that even an unclear formulation could constitute an infringement.

In brief, clear and important infringements (terminated or not) as well as cases which may clarify the rules are most likely to be dealt with under the formal procedure. According to Van Bael (1986), however, even the type of offence under consideration does not determine whether a formal decision will be adopted. Over the years, similar cases have been dealt with differently, some by formal decisions, some by informal settlements. The most obvious example of unequal treatment is cited by Van Bael (*ibid*, p. 66):

> Likewise, in the recent John Deere case, the American manufacturer and its EEC dealers had taken steps to remove export bans from their contracts and Deere begun to instruct its European employees how to comply with EEC competition rules . . .. Nevertheless, the Commission not only issued a decision, but it also imposed the unusually heavy fine of 2 million ECU . . . . However, at least fifteen cases involving export bans/restrictions, have been settled in the past.[73]

In addition, complainants have no right to request a formal decision, nor do notifying firms (except in some cases of exemption). Overall, the Commission enjoys virtually unfettered discretion in deciding which cases to treat under the formal procedure.

5.4.3.1 Clearance Decisions

Once an agreement has been judged to conform to competition rules, two main reasons may lead the Commission to follow a formal clearance procedure: the willingness to create case law and the need to clear a restrictive agreement satisfying the conditions of Article 85§3.

Once the choice to move towards a formal decision has been made, the Commission must publish a notice in order to invite third parties to give their comments. This request for comments constitutes a further fact-finding stage. The Commission does not systematically receive comments (and did so in only 43% of the cases in our survey). The additional information brought by third parties may modify the Commission's attitude. Modifications of the agreement can sometimes be requested by the Commission on the basis of the comments it received. In the **Givenchy** case,[74] some distributors expressed reservations about a number of clauses. These clauses were modified or even revoked. Such changes, however, are not frequent. In our survey only 11.4% of exemptions were granted after firms had brought the modifications suggested by third parties' comments. This may show that third parties rarely bring new relevant evidence about the case or that the Commission rarely takes into account comments if it has decided to grant an exemption. Comments mainly come from competitors (42% of the comments received) or customers (26.3%).

The average length of the procedure for a clearance decision in our survey was 34 months (see Figure 5.3).

Negative clearance Negative clearances are the best example of formal decisions whose aim is mainly to create case law and to clarify specific issues. The agreements concerned could have been settled informally since the meaning of a negative clearance is that competition rules are not infringed. The small number of negative clearances decisions is therefore not surprising. Since 1989, three out of seven negative clearances concerned creations of joint ventures implying technological cooperation[75] (two of them in the telecommunications sector), one concerned agreements in the insurance sector, one in the betting market and the remaining two were small vertical agreements in very specialized areas: distribution of motor oil and distribution of parapharmaceutical products in pharmacies (both in Belgium).

From the firms' point of view, a negative clearance is similar to a comfort letter and offers little more legal protection. National authorities are free to apply their competition rules (and prohibit the agreement, for example) despite the issue of a negative clearance by the Commission. There are, however, some differences from the comfort letter procedure.

First, a negative clearance is always preceded by a publication whereas this is rarely true for a comfort letter. Although this disclosure may be unsatisfactory for the concerned parties, it still may reduce the risk of subsequent challenges. Under the informal procedure, firms may ask the Commission not to publish a notice.

Second, the negative clearance can be reviewed under Article 173 of the Treaty of Rome whereas the comfort letter cannot. The advantage conferred by this right to appeal the Commission's decision is less clear for the notifying firms than for the complainant. A rejection of a complaint is a decision contrary to the complainant's interests and, therefore, it is important for plaintiffs to be allowed to contest it. As far as negative clearances are concerned, the decision satisfies the interests of the firms that requested it. A challenge to the legality of the agreement might, however, subsequently come either from one of the parties or from a third party. The publication preceding the granting of a negative clearance normally reduces the probability of a subsequent challenge, but a change of circumstances might nevertheless provoke one.

Third, since it is a formal procedure, the granting of a negative clearance takes more time than the issue of a comfort letter (twice as long: an average of 38 months for the seven negative clearances granted since 1989).

Finally, the decision to grant a negative clearance requires consultation with the Advisory Committee on Restrictive Practices and Dominant Positions, and the agreement of all Commissioners, whereas the decision to issue a comfort letter does not.

The individual exemption Like the negative clearance, an individual exemption has the effect of formally clearing an agreement under competition rules. The procedure for the adoption of these clearance decisions is the same, but there are important differences in their substance.

First, whereas firms have a limited interest in gaining a negative clearance (as opposed to a comfort letter), they benefit from an exemption if their agreement falls within the scope of Article 85§1. This is because, when an agreement infringes Article 85§1, it can only be enforced if exempted.

Second, exemption decisions confer strong legal protection. They are binding for national competition authorities and courts. They constitute a 'positive measure' and should, therefore, be respected by national competition authorities and courts. This asymmetry of legal protection between negative clearances and exemptions has been described as 'paradoxical' by Van Bael (1986, p. 69) who writes: 'It is anomalous, indeed, that the less restrictive agreements or practice enjoys less legal certainty, compared with a more restrictive agreement that has received the benefit of an exemption'. The reason for this difference seems clear: the strong protection offered to exempted agreements is intended to increase the incentives to notify agreements that infringe competition rules. The legal certainty obtained with the exemption is of great value for the implementation of an agreement containing infringing provisions. In some cases, the willingness to acquire this legal security outweighs the costs of the notification. While the provision of strong protection to exempted agreements is coherent with the objectives of competition policy, the asymmetry of protection between exempted infringing agreements and non-infringing agreements has no justification.

Third, an individual exemption is limited in time and this may constitute a problem for firms entering into long-term agreements. However, since requests for renewal of exemptions are very rare, it may be assumed that firms are usually satisfied with the duration of individual exemptions. (It might be, though, that if the agreement has been exempted once, firms do not bother to start a second notification procedure in order to obtain a renewal.)

Finally, exemptions may be subject to conditions. These have two main objectives: first, monitoring firms during the exemption period (firms can be requested to send reports about their activities and/or to inform the Commission if some modifications are brought to the agreement); second, limiting the threat to competition posed by the exempted agreement. For example, in 1994,[76] British Railways, SNCF and Intercontainer created a joint subsidiary (ACI) which would offer combined transport via the Channel Tunnel. The exemption was granted on condition that the railway companies should offer on a non-discriminatory basis the possibility for other operators to offer the same service. Firms may ask for the amendments to the conditions. In the ***Bayer/BP Chemical*** case,[77] the Commission decided to change a condition imposed in an earlier exemption decision. Bayer, BP Chemical and Erdölchemie had signed a technical cooperation agreement in the polyethylene sector which was exempted in 1988. One condition was the closure of a particular plant at the end of 1991. The Commission accepted postponement of closure until the end of 1994.

5.4.3.2 Prohibition Decisions

When investigations reveal that an agreement infringes competition rules, the Commission can move towards a prohibition decision. At various stages of the procedure, the Commission may still settle the case informally if the firm puts an end to the infringement after the reception of a statement of objections.

Prohibition decisions result either from the failure of the firm to terminate the infringement or from the wish of the Commission to take a formal decision on other grounds (which as we argued above are not always clear).

Infringement decision without fines   Under Article 85, the Commission
can declare that the infringing agreement is void and require firms to terminate it (if this has not already been done). There is a significant
difference here between infringement decisions taken under Article 85
and those taken under Article 86 for the abuse of a dominant position.
Under Article 86, the Commission condemns behaviour that is abusive
and requests the firm concerned to modify its behaviour. Whish (1993, p.
307) gives the example of a refusal to supply. If a prohibited agreement
includes a refusal to supply (an exclusive vertical contract), the
Commission can only request the termination of the agreement and has
no power to order to supply. If the refusal to supply is condemned as an
abuse of dominant position, the condemned undertaking can be ordered
to supply. However, in the *Wilkinson Sword* case,[78] in order to terminate
an Article 85 infringement, Gillette and Eemland were requested to re-
assign Wilkinson Sword businesses to Eemland in some countries.

Infringement decision with fines   In addition to the termination of the
agreements, firms can be fined. Once again, the Commission has complete
discretion in the imposition of fines. Article 15§2 gives no clear indication
as to the factors to be taken into account. The only criteria mentioned are
the duration and the gravity of the infringement. In fact, termination of
the agreement is no safeguard against fines. The Commission may still
impose fines if it considers that the infringement was serious and perpetrated for a long period of time. For example, in the *Eurocheque* case,[79]
important fines were imposed in 1992 on the Groupement des cartes ban-
caires and Eurocheque International (5 million and 1 million ECU
respectively), although the agreement had been abandoned a year earlier.
The infringement had lasted for more than six years.

The 1996 *Notice* on fines[80] has set some guidelines concerning the
imposition of fines in cartel cases. Until 1996, previously published decisions were the only source of guidance as to the Commission's likely
practice. Van Bael (1995, pp. 239–41) lists the aggravating and mitigating
circumstances leading at the imposition of higher or lower fines. The
intentional aspect of the infringement, its nature and the profits generated
by it are some of the aggravating circumstances. Early termination of the
infringement, a cooperative attitude during investigation and the introduc-
tion of a compliance programme within the firm are some examples of
mitigating circumstances. Before 1996, the Commission was sometimes
'rewarding' cooperative attitudes (the acknowledgment of the infringement and the provision of evidence) with a reduction of fines.[81] Such a
practice is called plea bargaining. Plea bargaining has sometimes been
criticized for its lack of clear legal basis and consequently the scope it
allows for unequal treatment of different firms. The 1996 Notice has

clarified this practice. It sets a guideline for the reduction of fines. These reductions range from 10% to total exemption from fines according to the behaviour of the firm. This practice is supposed to save time and resources. It is a clear incentive to provide evidence and, therefore, it could be interpreted as a delegation of the fact-finding powers of DG-IV to the incriminated parties.[82]

Almost half of the infringement decisions since 1989 involved the imposition of fines. The probability of being fined depends on the way the case was opened, with the risk highest under proceedings initiated by the Commission (75%), compared to 39% for an infringement initiated by a complaint, and a low risk for an infringement following a voluntary notification.

Is the Commission's practice in accordance with the optimal public enforcement theory of Becker (1968)? According to this theory; the probability of detection can be lowered without sacrificing deterrence if higher fines are imposed. In other words, imposing important fines in cases that are not easily detectable achieves 'optimal' deterrence. Two major practices are condemned by the Commission: cartels (price-fixing and market sharing) and export bans. Cartels are not easily detected. Since 1989, 44% of cartel cases were opened by the Commission itself, and the great majority of them led to the imposition of fines. Export bans are much easier to detect since most of them (70%) were detected by complaints. The probability of a fine for an export ban is not significantly lower than for a cartel cases despite the fact that the probability of detection is higher. The absolute level of fines is, however, higher in cartel cases. Since 1989, the highest fine imposed for an export ban has been of 5 million ECU[83] whereas the highest fine imposed in a cartel case has been of 32 million ECU.[84]

5.4.3.3 Comparison of the Procedure for Clearance and Prohibition Decisions

There are some differences between the procedure leading to a formal clearance decision and the procedure leading to a prohibition decision.

First, during a procedure leading to a formal clearance decision, more information will be disclosed: a notice has to be published before the adoption of a formal exemption decision. No such provision exists for prohibition decisions. The Commission may publish the statement of objections (Article 2§2 of Regulation 99) but this is extremely rare. Third parties have the right to take part in the procedure provided they they prove their legitimate interest in the case, but they will not necessarily receive information about the case to allow them to do so.

Second, infringements are mainly detected by third parties. Since 1989, there have been only six cases of prohibition following notification (out of 42 infringement decisions under Article 85§1). The reasons are twofold: first, infringing agreements are rarely notified; second, notifying firms are usually willing to modify their agreements to receive clearance.

Since 1989, the mean length of procedure for an infringement decision was of 45 months. This greater length is easily explained by the fact that most cases are opened by a third party, meaning that the fact-finding stage (request for information and investigations) is much longer. Preparing a statement of objections is also a time-consuming exercise. Moreover, oral hearings may be organized with the incriminated parties as well as with third parties. Provisional measures are supposed to compensate for long duration of the procedure when a third party is seriously harmed.

5.5 The Incentives to Start a Competition Procedure

Sections 5.3 and 5.4 presented a detailed picture of the successive stages of a competition procedure under Article 85. One important question to be asked of such a procedure is this: what are the incentives to start such a competition procedure? Why exactly would a firm notify an agreement? What are the incentives to lodge a complaint? And why does the Commission itself choose to open a case?

5.5.1 The Decision to Notify

This is the most straightforward part of the question since the answer is already implicit in the description of the procedure. Table 5.6 summarizes the benefits and costs to a firm contemplating notification.

The various costs of notification are self-explanatory, but the benefits require some further comment. The statistics of the Commission's activity clearly show that almost every notified agreement is cleared. This

Table 5.6 Benefits and costs of the notification procedures

Benefits	Costs
1. Immunity from fines	1. Uncertainty
2. Limit subsequent challenges	• Outcome
• by participating firm(s)	• Type of decision
• by third parties	2. Absence of deadlines: length of procedure
• by national competition authorities	3. Changes to the agreement/renegotiations
• by the Commission	4. Disclosure of information
	5. A/B Form

observation suggests that firms only notify when they think that their agreement is very likely to be cleared. An obvious question then arises: given the costs of the procedure, why would firms bother to notify an agreement that is highly likely to be cleared? What do they expect from the procedure?

The most direct consequence of the notification is immunity from fines: even if the notified agreement infringes Article 85§1, no fine should be imposed for the infringement for the period starting from the notification. The survey has shown that immunity from fines is not an important influence on firms' decision to notify. There seem to be two main reasons for this. First, immunity from fines is not complete since the Commission may decide to revoke it.[85] Second, as pointed out by Brown (1993), decisions imposing fines are extremely rare and they represent a negligible part of the terminated cases. Between 1989 and 1995, fines were imposed in only 20 decisions taken under Article 85 (0.4% of all the terminated cases over that period).

There is one case where the immunity from fines can be an incentive to notify. When the Commission has started a procedure on its own initiative or if a complaint has been lodged, the suspected firms may then notify their agreement in order to reduce the possible fine. The notification does not protect them from an infringement decision, but it may lower the probability of being fined or reduce the amount of the fine. There are three cases in which firms notified an agreement already suspected and were finally granted a formal clearance after the necessary changes were brought.[86] It follows that immunity from fines is an incentive to notify in cases where the agreement is likely to infringe Article 85§1, and the Commission has already opened a case.

In the survey, firms stated that they had notified their agreement for two main reasons: ensuring the Commission's goodwill and obtaining legal security. Once the Commission has declared that the agreement conforms to competition rules, firms feel protected from subsequent challenges. Firms may want to rule out the possibility of a complaint lodged against them; they may fear prosecution by the Commission or by national competition authorities. Alternatively, since unlawful agreements are void, the parties to an agreement containing restrictive clauses are not bound to respect them if they have not been cleared under competition rules. As Brown (1993, p. 334) points out: 'Should the parties subsequently fall out, there is the risk that neither of them would be able to enforce rights and obligations against the other due to the agreement being void'. Temple Lang (1981, p. 337) lists some examples of possible situations: 'a partner in a joint venture may wish to avoid being bound by a clause prohibiting competition; a technology licensee may wish to disclose the technology licenced to him to a third party, contrary to his non-disclosure obligation'. It should be added that one firm in the sample answered that the clearance helped it in obtaining financial guarantees.

The individual exemption is the only decision that satisfies a need for legal certainty. A comfort letter only allows an assurance of the Commission's goodwill.

5.5.2 The Incentive to Lodge a Complaint

The complaint procedure is an important part of the application of competition rules. It represents a delegation of part of the task of detecting prohibited behaviour to the potential victims of such behaviour. The Commission does not have the information or the resources to monitor behaviour completely. On any specific market, however, firms and especially harmed firms (or individuals) do have information about situations that infringe competition rules. Therefore, the complaint procedure is a way of transferring the information to the Commission, and a very useful one at that, since complaints constitute the most important source of information about subsequent infringments. Since 1989, 55% of the infringement decisions under Article 85 concerned cases opened following a complaint.[87]

Competition rules should bring the correct incentives to lodge complaints, encouraging the reporting of real infringments and discouraging frivolous or malicious complaints.

The main benefit a third party may expect from a complaint to the Commission is the termination of the behaviour against which it complains. The Commission possesses important powers of investigation and intervention and can, therefore, bring the infringement to an end if it so chooses. This can be achieved through negotiations with the parties or by the imposition of interim measures[88] if the complainant incurs important damages. The procedure is administrative, so plaintiffs receive no compensation for the damages they have incured before the termination of the infringement. In the United States, private anti-trust suits are handled by courts and victorious plaintiffs receive treble damages if they manage to prove they have suffered from the effects of the agreement. In comparison with the US system, European rules offer a very limited benefit to a successful complainant.

The reason it is important to protect against frivolous complaints is not just that these waste the time and resources of the Commission. More seriously, the complaint procedure may constitute a strategic tool against competitors or partners in an agreement. Third parties can complain about a situation that does not directly damage them, or they can use the complaint procedure as a means to increase their bargaining power (for example, they may wish to obtain more favourable clauses in an unnotified contract that is being renegotiated).[89] As Baumol and Ordover (1985) suggest, anti-trust rules can in fact be used by firms to protect themselves against competition. They cite the example of Chrysler pressing a private anti-trust action against a GM-Toyota joint venture approved by the Federal Trade Commission. A similar example has occurred in the European Union. In 1992, Matra lodged a complaint against an exempted joint venture set up by Ford and Volkswagen for the development and the production of a multi-purpose vehicle (MPV).[90] In fact, Matra had developed the 'Renault Espace' (the MPV leader with a market share of 55% in 1990) and is the assembler and distributor of the vehicle. Leaving aside the possible risk of facilitated collusion between Ford and Volkswagen, this complaint clearly indicated the threat of increased competition for the leader on the market. The complaint was rejected. Such complaints constitute an attempt to be protected from new competitors and if successful (as they may be given the risk of type I errors) they can bring important benefits to the plaintiff. Baumol and Ordover suggest that the likelihood of competitors being favourable to an agreement normally increases with the monopoly power induced by the agreement since it will enable them to benefit from higher prices in the market.

Complainants have to fill in an application (the Form C) in which they describe the behaviour that infringes Article 85 and/or 86 and the legitimate interest they have in the case. They also have to provide evidence. The condition that the complainant should be harmed by the behaviour concerned or likely to incur damages is one safeguard against frivolous complaints. The cost of the filling in the Form C can be considered as low. In the United States, private anti-trust suits are handled by courts, and therefore, parties have to bear legal costs. If the plaintiff wins, however, its legal costs are paid by the defendant.

As in the case of notification procedures, the absence of deadlines is a major cost for the plaintiff. When infringements are indeed perpetrated, the procedure often lasts more than three years before the publication of the formal decision. Between 1989 and 1995, the average length of a procedure following a complaint and leading to an infringement decision has been of 44 months (see Figure 5.3). If important damages are incured by the plaintiff, interim measures provide for a rapid termination of the infringement but the conditions associated with the imposition of such measures are rarely satisfied. Consequently, the length of the procedure is a greater disincentive to genuine than to frivolous or strategic complaints, especially since the lodging of a complaint may worsen relations between the parties and make informal negotiation more difficult.

Does the European Union system create excessive incentives to lodge complaints? Estimating the number of frivolous (or strategic) complaints is extremely difficult. What do the statistics on the Commission's activity suggest? First, the number of complaints leading to infringement decisions is very small. The Commission receives an average of 111 complaints per year and on average, three infringement decisions following complaints are taken every year. Second, more than half (57.4%) of the formal decisions taken following a complaint are rejections of complaints. These figures may suggest that frivolous complaints are frequent but such a statement is not straightforward.

In fact, the majority of complaints lead to informal settlements. Such settlements are reached for one of two reasons:

- The parties reach an agreement: that is, an infringement was committed but the infringing party prefers to modify its behaviour in order to avoid prosecution. For example in the *CICRA/Fiat* case,[91] CICRA (an Italian association of spare parts manufacturers) lodged a complaint against Fiat because of the conditions attached to the granting of discounts to its distributors. Fiat was offering discounts on its spare parts if no competing spare parts were sold by the distributors. Moreover, the discounts were contingent on a minimum level of purchase. The Commission informed Fiat of its intention to start a procedure against these practices and Fiat finally abandoned the restrictive conditions. The case was settled.
- The Commission finds no infringement after a brief investigation,[92] so the complaint is informally rejected (and the case settled). For example, in 1990,[93] the Commission found no evidence of an export ban imposed by Kuhn SA on its dealers. One of its dealers had lodged a complaint alleging it was prevented from selling products from the Netherlands into the United Kingdom

It is impossible to tell from publicly available information to what extent complaints consist of the former rather than the latter type. It is clear, however, that the Commission wishes to see the number of complaints decrease. The 'Notice on Cooperation between National Courts and the Commission'[94] states a willingness to see more cases handled by national courts. The Notice presents all the advantages offered to the plaintiff by the application of European competition rules by national courts: availability of compensation for damages, quicker settlements, the ability to combine a claim under Community law with a claim under national law and the possibility that legal costs may be awarded to successful applicants (in some countries). In brief, national courts may offer a higher benefit to a *successful* complainant. Despite the publication of this notice, no decline has been observed in the number of complaints. Not only is the cost of the European Union procedure lower, but according to Riley (1993), national courts impose an additional uncertainty for the plaintiff because of the lack of competence of national judges in competition matters.

Who lodges complaints? It is interesting to see if successful complaints (those leading to infringment decisions) are lodged by the potential victims identified by economic theory. For horizontal agreements, customers constitute an important source of complaints, though not the major one. One explanation for this lack of complaints from customers may be that they have no information about the real costs. Not surprisingly, a closer look at the decisions shows that customers are attacking such agreements on the grounds of discriminatory pricing or excessive pricing. In fact competitors are the main source of complaints against horizontal agreement. These agreements are attacked on the grounds that they are aimed at preventing entry or inducing exit. For example, in 1992, the shipping companies members of the French-West African shipowners' committees[95] had cartelized the transport of general cargo between French ports and some African ports. They managed to exclude independent shipowners from the routes they were sharing. In 1991, Screensport[96] lodged a complaint against some members of the European Broadcasting Union and News International Plc for the agreements related to the setting up of the Eurosport joint venture. It should be noted that this horizontal agreement presents the characteristics of vertical foreclosure. According to these agreements, Eurosport was granted a privileged access for the broadcasting of sport events from which Screensport was foreclosed (or its access was restricted). In other words, Screensport was excluded from a major source of input.

For vertical agreements, the great majority of complainants are existing competitors too. More precisely, the most frequent successful complaints concerned export ban provisions in vertical agreements. The detection of such provisions arises from competing distributors that are the victims of these bans.

5.5.3 Cases Inititiated by the Commission

The discussion of the incentives to notify and to lodge a complaint suggests that the cases least likely to be brought to the Commission are anti-competitive agreements with a low probability of detection. For such cases, the Commission has to act on its own. So how does the Commission become aware of 'suspect' situations?

The sources of information are various. According to officials from DG-IV, the business press is an important source of information. DG-IV also has contacts with consumers associations that scrutinize prices in order to detect distortions or imperfections on specific markets. Trade statistics (intra-community and extra-community exchanges) are also a valuable indicator for the Commission since the completion of the Common Market is one of its main objectives. In published infringement decisions, the Commission does not always clearly describe the starting point of the procedure. In the *Cartonboard* cartel case,[97] informal complaints constituted the starting point. A British association of printed boxes manufacturers informed the Commission that cartonboard manufacturers had simultaneously and uniformly increased their prices. A French association observed the same rise on the French market and subsequently lodged an informal complaint. In other decisions, the infringements have been detected during investigations of other cases (anti-dumping cases or other complaints). The difficulty of obtaining pertinent information means it is not surprising that investigations initiated by the Commission take longer than other procedures (four years on average between 1989 and 1995, according to the evidence of the published decisions[98]). Most such cases concerned price-fixing and market-sharing agreements.

Proceedings initiated by the Commission seldom lead to infringement decisions. Between 1989 and 1995, an average of 42 proceedings were initiated by the Commission every year but only 2 infringement decisions were taken per year following such proceedings (a marginal share of terminated cases). In fact, as in the case of complaints, most of these cases are settled. Once again, the two main reasons are the following:

- Firms modify or remove the relevant clauses of their agreements. For example, in 1990, the Irish Association of Tropical Wood Importers removed a clause in its statutes that had the object of deterring its members from buying wood from suppliers that were selling to non-members.[99]
- No evidence of an infringement is found. For example, the Commission settled a file concerning some oil companies. They were refusing to purchase a new product (bio-ethanol) and the Commission suspected a concerted practice. The results of its investigations did not bring the evidence of such a practice. It appeared that there was a sound commercial and technical basis for a common refusal.[100]

5.6 Regulatory Capture and the Contacts Between Firms and the Commission

In this section, we use the findings of the survey to analyse the way in which firms seek to use their contacts with the Commission to increase their chances of success. As Neven *et al.* (1993) have emphasized, there is nothing inherently wrong with their doing so: what matters is whether the various influences exerted by firms lead to significantly distorted decision-making. It is nevertheless worth noting that some firms appeared reluctant to answer some of the questions in the survey that concerned contacts with the Commission. This shows that such activities still have a flavour of secrecy, although their existence in general terms has become common knowledge. Firms do not feel at ease about the influence they try to exert on the political and administrative world.

In order to increase the probability of a favourable outcome in a competition case, firms use a variety of means: professional advice, personal meetings with officials from the Commission and external support. The extent of these practices is described in this section. The main findings of the survey are presented in Tables 5.7 and 5.8 and in Figures 5.4 to 5.6. It is important to emphasize once more that the sample mainly reflects big European firms and that formal procedures are over-represented.

Firms whose cases were opened by a complaint or on the initiative of the Commission will hereafter be called 'suspected firms'. Notifying firms are those whose case has been opened by a notification.

Table 5.7 Activities by firms to influence the outcome of their case (according to the outcome of the case)

	Settlements (%)	Comfort letters (%)	Formal decision (%)	Total survey (%)	Informal (%)
% of firms having obtained advice from					
B1a: a law firm	85.0	79.2	93.0	87.4	81.8
B1b: a public relations firm	5.9	0.0	8.6	5.4	2.6
B1c: economic consultants	11.8	0.0	22.2	13.3	5.1
B1d: professional lobbyists	5.9	0.0	5.7	4.1	2.6
% of firms having obtained support from					
B2a: political representatives	26.3	13.6	20.6	20.0	19.5
B2b: officials from Member States	30.0	27.3	31.4	29.9	28.6
B2c: Trade Unions	10.5	0.0	3.0	4.1	4.9
B2d: professional organizations	25.0	9.1	23.5	19.7	16.7
B2e: press and media	10.0	0.0	0.0	2.7	4.8
B3a: Did you actively seek that support? (% yes)	80.0	83.3	66.7	74.2	81.3
B3b: Was it helpful to the case? (% yes)	44.4	83.3	40.0	50.0	60.0
% of firms having met with					
B4a: a rapporteur	53.3	40.0	48.5	47.1	45.7
B4b: a Head of Unit	88.2	63.6	82.9	78.4	74.4
B4c: a Director	61.1	38.1	62.9	55.4	48.7
B4d: the Director General	41.2	15.0	40.6	33.3	27.0
B4e: the Competition Commissioner	29.4	5.0	29.0	22.1	16.2
B4f: another Commissioner	29.4	5.0	10.0	13.4	16.2

5.6.1 The Sources of Advice

When engaged in a competition case, firms will usually seek professional advice. Not surprisingly, this is usually legal advice (sought by 87% of firms). Suspected firms do so slightly more frequently, but the difference is not statistically significant.

The main difference between notifying and suspected firms is that the latter have more recourse to the other sources of professional advice (see Figure 5.4). These other sources are professional lobbyists, public relations firms and economic consultants. The practice is nevertheless limited: public relations firms were used by only 5% of firms and professional lobbyists by 4%. However, 11.5% of suspected firms engaged public relations advice as against only 2% of notifying firms.

Economic consultants are another source of professional advice. It may seem surprising that only a minority of firms in the sample have had recourse to economic consultancy for their competition case (13.3%). A significant difference also appears between notifying and suspected firms: only 2% of the former engaged economic advice as compared to 35% of the latter. A closer look to the sample reveals that economic advice was sought by more than half (53%) of firms subject to prohibition decisions. None of the firms that obtained exemptions or negative clearances used economic consultancy. This observation suggests that economic argumentation acts as a form of last resort defence.

Firms receiving a comfort letter used only legal advice.

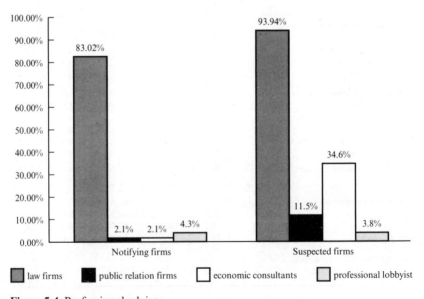

Figure 5.4 Professional advice

5.6.2 Contacts with Commission Officials

There is significant variation in the number of meetings reported in the survey. The answers vary from 0 to 25 meetings during a procedure. A minority of firms in the sample (13%) had only written and phone contacts (most of these are notifying firms). Not surprisingly, most contacts occur when the Commission moves towards a formal decision (an average of 5.2 meetings). Firms obtaining an informal settlement met with officials in DG-IV somewhat less (4.3 meetings on average). This figure illustrates the fact that the settlement practice often involves negotiations. Firms obtaining a comfort letter met less often with officials from DG-IV (only 2.6 times on average, with a maximum of 6).

An important difference is observed between the average number of meetings under the exemption procedure (an average of 6.8) and the formal negative clearance procedure (an average of 3.4). Exemption decisions need more bargaining and negotiation between the Commission and the parties. Exempted agreements are controversial by nature and, therefore, firms keep close contacts with officials in order to negotiate the exemption decision.

The survey also enquired about the level in the Commission at which contacts occur. More than half of firms meet with the Head of Units

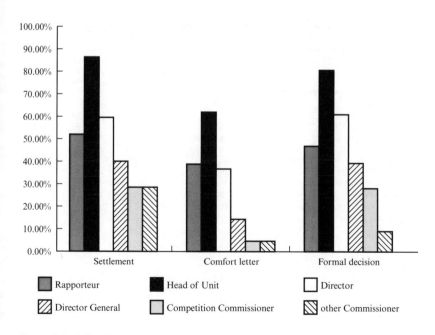

Figure 5.5 Officials met by firms

(78.4%) and the Directors (55.4%) of the different units of DG-IV. These are the persons in charge of most informal decisions, that is, of the majority of files.

The survey reveals that contacts occur at a high level in the Commission, though firms are somewhat more reluctant to give information about these contacts, especially firms that had undergone a formal decision procedure (the response rate for these firms was the lowest on this question). 27% of firms in the sample had met with at least one Commissioner. More precisely, 22% of them had held discussions with the Competition Commissioner and 13% had had discussions about the case with another Commissioner. It is worth noting that 9% of firms had met with more than one Commissioner for their case, and two-thirds of these firms saw their case settled. Of course, most firms in the sample are among the biggest companies in Europe; their opportunities to meet officials at the head of the Commission are certainly greater than those available to smaller firms.

Although these figures could seem low, they are important enough to show that firms try to influence the procedure. The firms holding discussions with the Competition Commissioner are mainly those whose cases are settled under the informal settlement practice (29% of firms whose case has been settled) and the formal procedure (29% of firms). There is a significant difference between these procedures and the procedure leading to

Table 5.8 Activities by firms to influence the outcome of their case (according to the way the case was opened)

	Notification (%)	Complaint initiative (%)	Own- Survey (%)	Total (%)	Suspected (%)
% of firms having obtained advice from					
B1a: a law firm	83.3	94.1	93.8	87.4	93.9
B1b: a public relations firm	2.1	7.7	15.4	5.4	11.5
B1c: economic consultants	2.0	30.8	38.5	13.3	34.6
B1d: professional lobbyists	4.2	7.7	0.0	4.1	3.8
% of firms having obtained support from					
B2a: political representatives	16.7	23.1	28.6	20.0	25.9
B2b: officials from Member States	25.0	37.5	38.5	29.9	37.9
B2c: Trade Unions	2.1	7.1	8.3	4.1	7.7
B2d: professional organizations	12.5	40.0	23.1	19.7	32.1
B2e: press and media	2.1	7.1	0.0	2.7	4.0
B3a: Did you actively seek that support? (% yes)	85.7	63.6	66.7	74.2	64.7
B3b: Was it helpful to the case? (% yes)	69.2	36.4	33.3	50.0	35.3
% of firms having met with					
B4a: a rapporteur	44.2	66.7	38.5	47.1	52.0
B4b: a Head of Unit	73.9	93.3	76.9	78.4	85.7
B4c: a Director	52.2	66.7	53.8	55.4	60.7
B4d: the Director General	29.5	53.8	25.0	33.3	40.0
B4e: the Competition Commissioner	18.2	33.3	25.0	22.1	29.2
B4f: another Commissioner	9.3	25.0	16.7	13.4	20.8

the issue of a comfort letter. An even more striking finding concerns contacts with other Commissioners, which took place in 29% of the cases settled informally compared with only 10% under a formal decision. It is perhaps no surprise that intense bargaining should take place for the settlement procedure, which is the least transparent part of the whole process.

5.6.3 External Sources of Support

Firms also report having obtained support in their case from external sources. These consist mainly of officials from Member States (30% of firms), political representatives (20%) and professional organizations (20%). The objectives of these agents sometimes converge with those of firms, and they are therefore willing to help in influencing the decision-making process. Officials from Member States and political representatives are sensitive to the interests of national firms for various reasons: the achievement of national industrial policy objectives, the protection of national firms in a particular industry, and so on. The main purpose of professional organizations is to defend the interests of a particular industrial sector.

There do not appear to be significant differences between notifying and suspected firms in the degree of external support (see Figure 5.6). Half of the firms who received such support considered it had been helpful to their case (though this proportion was, perhaps unsurprisingly, only 30% among firms who received prohibitions).

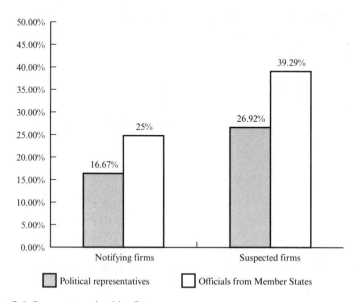

Figure 5.6 Support received by firms

5.7   Firms' Opinions about the Procedure

The survey also asked firms for opinions about the effectiveness and fairness of the procedure. The results are presented in Table 5.9 and Figures 5.7 to 5.12. As one might expect, the comments who received prohibition decisions are in general the least favourable. The views of these firms, however, do not significantly alter the general conclusions (except in one case).

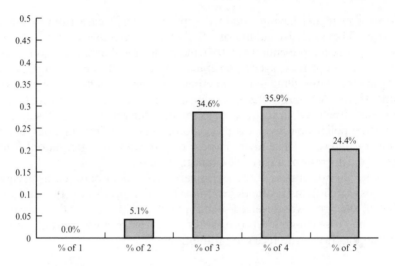

Figure 5.7 Powers of investigation (1 = inadequate to 5 = excessive)

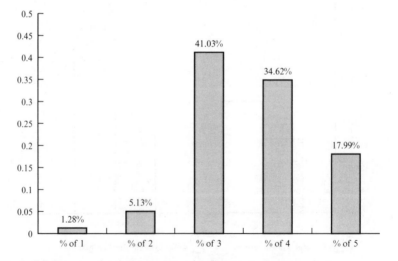

Figure 5.8 Powers of enforcement (1 = inadequate to 5 = excessive)

The first two questions concerned the powers of investigation (see Figure 5.7) and the powers of enforcement (see Figure 5.8) of the Commission for competition cases. Firms had to evaluate these powers on a scale ranging from 1 (inadequate power) to 5 (excessive power).

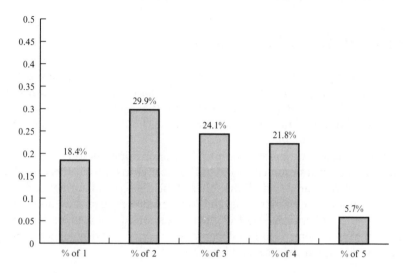

Figure 5.9 Are the Commission's procedures administratively effective? (1 = not at all to 5 = very much so)

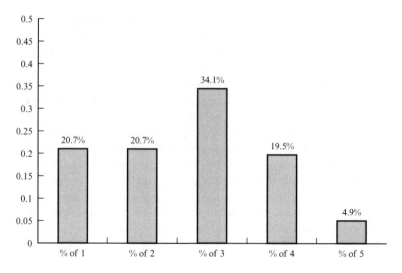

Figure 5.10 Are the Commission's procedures likely to deliver a fair judgement? (1 = not at all to 5 = very much so)

In two other questions, firms were asked first, if the procedures had been administratively effective (see Figure 5.9) and second, if the procedures demonstrated likely to deliver fair judgements (see Figure 5.10). Once again, the scale was ranging from 1 (not at all effective or not at all likely to deliver fair judgements) to 5 (very much so).

5.7.1 The Powers of the Commission

The majority of firms consider the powers of the Commission to be excessive.[101] The powers of investigation are naturally felt as excessive by most condemned firms (some firms in the sample had undergone Commission inspections). However, even without these firms the same clear conclusion emerged.[102]

There was less strong objection to the Commission's powers of enforcement. A significant difference emerges between firms whose agreement has been *formally* cleared and all the others. Only 30% of the former consider that the powers of enforcement tend to be excessive, against an average of 59.3% for all other firms. Half of the former considered the Commission's powers of enforcement to be adequate. This is not surprising since formal exemptions confer the strongest legal protection.

5.7.2 The Effectiveness of the Procedures

Most firms appear to be quite satisfied about the effectiveness of procedures (see Figure 5.11). A significant difference appears, however, between firms that have gone through a formal procedures and others. After a formal procedure, the majority of firms do not consider the procedures to be administratively effective. This result certainly reflects the costs associated with formal procedures (length of procedure, renegotiations, uncertainties, etc.). Some of them protest vehemently about the complexity and the time-consuming nature of the whole procedure.[103]

As far as the fairness of outcomes is concerned, condemned firms naturally have a very unfavourable view. Most other firms, however, consider that the Commission's procedures are quite likely to deliver fair judgements (see Figure 5.12). Many of the qualitative comments in the questionnaires, however, raised doubts about the objectivity of the Commission and voiced suspicions about its tendency to 'prejudge' cases.

Table 5.9 Firms' opinions about the Commission's powers and procedures (according to the outcome of the case)

Powers of investigation	1: inadequate % of 1	% of 2	% of 3	% of 4	5: excessive % of 5
Settlement	0.0	12.5	31.3	37.5	18.8
		12.5		56.3	
Comfort letter	0.0	4.5	36.4	45.5	13.6
		4.5		59.1	
Formal clearance decision	0.0	0.0	50.0	30.0	20.0
		0.0		50.0	
Formal prohibition decision	0.0	5.3	21.1	31.6	42.1
		5.3		73.7	
Total Survey	0.0	5.1	34.6	35.9	24.4
		5.1		60.3	

Powers of enforcement	1: inadequate % of 1	% of 2	% of 3	% of 4	5: excessive % of 5
Settlement	0.0	0.0	40.0	53.5	6.7
		0.0		60.0	
Comfort letter	0.0	0.0	40.9	45.5	13.6
		0.0		59.1	
Formal clearance decision	5.0	15.0	50.0	15.0	15.0
		20.0		30.0	
Formal prohibition decision	0.0	5.0	35.0	25.0	35.0
		5.0		60.0	
Total Survey	1.3	5.1	41.0	34.6	17.9
		6.4		52.6	

Administrative effectiveness	1: not at all % of 1	% of 2	% of 3	% of 4	5: very much so % of 5
Settlement	5.6	22.2	44.4	22.2	5.6
		27.8		27.8	
Comfort letter	9.1	27.3	27.3	27.3	9.1%
		36.4		36.4	
Formal clearance decision	12.5	41.7	16.7	25.0	4.2
		54.2		29.2	
Formal prohibition decision	45.0	20.0	15.0	15.0	5.0
		65.0		20.0	
Total Survey	18.4	29.9	24.1	21.8	5.7
		48.3		27.6	

Fairness of judgements	1: not at all % of 1	% of 2	% of 3	% of 4	5: very much so % of 5
Settlement	5.6	16.7	61.1	11.1	5.6
		22.2		16.7	
Comfort letter	4.5	22.7	31.8	31.8	9.1
		27.3		40.9	
Formal clearance decision	14.3	14.3	42.9	23.8	4.8
		28.6		28.6	
Formal prohibition decision	60.0	25.0	5.0	10.0	0.0
		85.0		10.0	
Total Survey	20.7	20.7	34.1	19.5	4.9
		41.5		24.4	

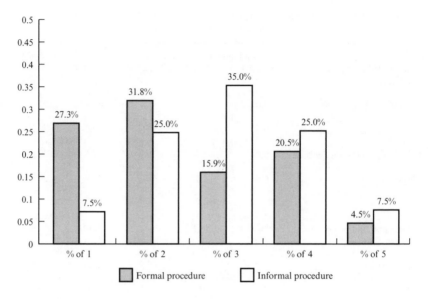

Figure 5.11 Administrative effectiveness (formal/informal procedures)

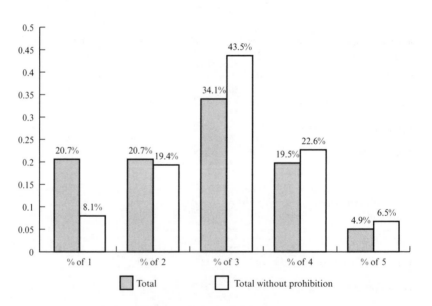

Figure 5.12 Fairness of judgement (clearance/prohibition)

5.7.3 The Quality of the Economic Analysis

Table 5.10 presents the opinion of firms about the economic analysis performed by the officials from DG-IV. Two main observations emerge from the survey: first, firms consider that the officials are in general willing to listen to their point of view; second, the Commission's analysis does not satisfy the majority of firms (only half of them agree with the most of the analysis performed for their case). When condemned firms are excluded, the picture is somewhat more favourable. More than two-thirds of firms consider that the evidence used by the Commission is of sufficient quality but only only 54.2% think that the Commission's analysis of the relevant market made sense in the light of commercial and industrial realities.

The most satisfied firms are those having received a formal *exemption* of their agreement. The great majority of them agree with most parts of the analysis (definition of relevant market, analysis of barriers to entry, and so on). This high level of satisfaction is not really surprising since these firms succeeded in obtaining the formal clearance of agreements that are by definition restrictive. The level of satisfaction is low for firms whose case has been informally settled.

In fact, one important conclusion is that firms consider the evidence in the hands of the Commission to be in general of good quality, but they are quite unsatisfied with the use made of it, for a variety of reasons. First, as already said, some claim that the Commission prejudges the cases. Second, some firms consider that the Commission does not take into account some of the evidence (two firms accuse the Commission of overlooking evidence contrary to the thesis it defends). Finally, the analysis is said to be superficial in some cases.

Following the procedure in Neven *et al.* (1993), we have computed a dissatisfaction index by adding the answers to the questions B5, B6, B8 and B9.[104] Question B7 has been excluded because of the high number of missing answers which significantly reduced the sample. The sample consists of 65 firms. Equations [1] and [2] report the results for the most statistically significant parameters:

Equation 1

DISSAT = 8.8 – 1.29 (FOR) – 1.09 (JV) + 1.12 (FPRO) – 1.47 (FCL) – 1.41 (CL)

       (19.6)   (–2.29)   (–2.28)   (1.91)   (–2.52)   (–2.38)

R^2 (adjusted) = 0.459   (t-statistics in brackets)

Equation 2

DISSAT = 8.2 – 1.4 (FOR) – 0.78 (JV) – 0.78 (FPRO) – 1.79 (FCL) – 1.6(CL) + 0.03 (TIME)

     (17.25) (–2.65)   (–1.7)   (–0.256)   (–3.21) (–2.89)   (3.01)

R^2 (adjusted) = 0.5243

Table 5.10 The opinion of firms about the Commission's analysis

		Total survey % of yes	Total survey(*) % of yes
B5	Were the officials willing to listen to their point of view?	65	76.7
B6	Does the firm consider that DG-IV's officials appreciated adequately commercial and industrial realities ...?	51.2	64.1
B7	Did the firm agree with the Commission's:		
(a)	– definition of relevant market	53.3	63.6
(b)	– analysis of barriers to entry	53.1	64.4
(c)	– assessment of competitive relationships between firms on the market	44.3	57.1
B8	Did the Commission's analysis of the relevant market made sense in the light of commercial realities ...?	45.7	54.2
B9	Was the evidence used of sufficient quality?	50.7	67.9

(*) Condemned firms excluded

According to the outcome of the case

		Settlement % of yes	Comfort letter % of yes	Formal decision of which		
				Neg.clear. % of yes	Exemption % of yes	Prohibition % of yes
B5	Were the officials willing to listen to their point of view?	66.7	81	77.7	83.3	30
B6	Does the firm consider that DG-IV's officials appreciated adequately commercial and industrial realities ...?	52.6	69.6	13	64	10
B7	Did the firm agree with the Commission's:					
(a)	– definition of relevant market	50	60	67	85	25
(b)	– analysis of barriers to entry	53.8	68.8	80	64	26.3
(c)	– assessment of competitive relationships between firms on the market	25	61.1	71	75	14.3
B8	Did the Commission's analysis of the relevant market made sense in the light of commercial realities ...?	22.2	61.9	63	83	22.7
B9	Was the evidence used of sufficient quality?	40	81	71	80	9.1

According to the way the case was opened

		Notification % of yes	Complaint % of yes	Own initiated % of yes
B5	Were the officials willing to listen to their point of view?	79.6	62.6	20
B6	Does the firm consider that DG-IV's officials appreciated adequately commercial and industrial realities ...?	67.3	40	12.6
B7	Did the firm agree with the Commission's:			
(a)	– definition of relevant market	65.2	26.7	40
(b)	– analysis of barriers to entry	64.1	50	23.1
(c)	– assessment of competitive relationships between firms on the market	64.3	16.7	12.5
B8	Did the Commission's analysis of the relevant market made sense in the light of commercial realities ...?	63.8	12.5	29.4
B9	Was the evidence used of sufficient quality?	76.7	25	5.9

Table 5.11 Explanatory variables for the dissatisfaction equations

Variable name	Definition
FOR	1 if the firm is from outside the European Union 0 otherwise
JV	1 if the agreement creates a joint venture 0 otherwise
FPRO	1 if the final decision is a formal prohibition 0 otherwise
FCL	1 if the final decision is a formal clearance 0 otherwise
CL	1 if the final decision is a comfort letter 0 otherwise
TIME	Measures the number of months between the start of the case and the final decision

The only significant nationality dummy was the foreign firm dummy (FOR). Foreign firms (mainly American firms) seem more prone to be satisfied than others with the EU procedure.

The main criticism voiced against the procedure clearly appears here. The length of the procedure (TIME) is an important factor of dissatisfaction. This variable is strongly related to prohibition decisions (FPRO). When there is no control for the length of the procedure (Equation [1]), condemned firms strongly tend to be dissatisfied. However, when the length of the procedure is introduced in the regression (Equation [2]), the fact that the firm was condemned has no impact on the dissatisfaction level. Various specifications have been tested and it appears that the length of the procedure *is* a factor of dissatisfaction even under informal procedures.

One interesting result confirms the observations presented in previous paragraphs. Firms that have gone through a formal procedure leading to an exemption (FCL) are clearly satisfied with the procedure despite the length of time and despite the changes sometimes requested. Apparently, the costs identified for a formal exemption procedure are overweighed by the benefits of the strong legal protection.

Firms that are granted a comfort letter (CL) are also more satisfied than others.

Finally, the positive and significant impact of joint-venture cases (JV) on satisfaction may reflect recent developments of the procedure concerning cooperative joint ventures.[105]

5.8 Lessons for the Future

Finally, we wanted to find out if the experience of a European competition procedure has an impact on the behaviour of firms. Table 5.12 suggests that experiencing a European competition procedure has only a minor impact on the behaviour of firms. According to the answers, such a procedure mainly allows firms to get more familiar with the atmosphere and personnel of DG-IV.

Table 5.12 Lessons drawn by firms for future strategy

	No significant lessons (%)	More familiarity but no difference (%)	Yes, some difference (%)	Yes, major difference (%)
Total survey	11.4	51.1	28.4	9.1
	62.5		37.5	

According to the case outcome	No significant lessons (%)	More familiarity but no difference (%)	Yes, some difference (%)	Yes, major difference (%)
Settlement	5.3	57.9	26.3	10.5
	63.2		36.8	
Comfort letter	16.7	62.5	12.5	8.3
	79.2		20.8	
Formal decision of which	11.1	42.2	37.8	8.9
	53.3		46.7	
Formal clearance	4.5	45.5	40.9	9.1
	50.0		50.0	
Prohibition	17.4	39.1	34.8	8.7
	56.5		43.5	

According to the way case opened	No significant lessons (%)	More familiarity but no difference (%)	Yes, some difference (%)	Yes, major difference (%)
Notification	9.4	58.5	24.5	7.5
	67.9		32.0	
Complaint	11.8	47.1	29.4	11.8
	58.9		41.2	
Own-initiative	16.7	33.3	38.9	11.1
	50.0		50.0	

37.5% of firms report that the experience acquired during the case will make a difference for the firm's future competitive strategy (but this is reported as a major difference for only 9% of firms). A formal procedure is apparently the most influential. After a formal procedure, 46.7% of firms admit that the experience will make a difference in the future behaviour against 27% of firms after an informal procedure. This result is not surprising since formal procedures are long and they often concern controversial cases. It could be expected that prohibition decisions will have the most important impact on a firm's future strategic behaviour. Some condemned firms say they have instituted a compliance programme towards European Union competition rules, but they are only a minority. For one firm, the change consists in refraining from providing information to others about sales figures and production. It would be interesting to understand why the majority of condemned firms claim that nothing will change in their future competitive strategy. Unfortunately, no comments were provided by these firms.

An analysis of these answers can be summarized in equation [3]: what type of firms are the most influenced by the procedure? The sample consists of 83 firms and the dependent variable (CHANGE) is a binary variable taking the value 1 when firms answered that the lessons from the procedure will make a difference (some or major) in its future competitive strategy, and taking the value 0 otherwise. In the probit model, the value of the estimated parameters does not necessarily represent the marginal effect of the variables. especially if the explanatory variables are binary. The method is explained in detail in Chapter 6 (pp. 159–60).

Equation 3

$$\text{CHANGE} = -0.55 - 1.28\,(\text{GR}) + 0.96\,(\text{CHEM}) + 0.42\,(\text{FORMAL})$$
$$\qquad\quad (-2.41) \qquad (-2.4) \qquad\quad (2.26) \qquad\qquad (1.46)$$

Percentage of correct prediction = 71%   (t-statistics in brackets)

As the descriptive statistics suggested, a formal procedure has some positive impact on the probability to see a firm change its behaviour (but the variable is only significant at a 0.15 level). If the firm has experienced a formal procedure, the probability that a change in future strategy is acknowledged increases by 0.16. If the firm mainly operates in the chemical sector, this probability increases by 0.23.

Finally, a European competition procedure does not have an impact on the future strategic behaviour of German firms. If the firm is German, the probability of a change decreases by 0.36.

Table 5.13 Explanatory variables for the change equation

Variable name	Definition
GR	1 if the firm is German 0 otherwise
CHEM	1 if the firm mainly operates in the chemical sector 0 otherwise
FORMAL	1 if the firm has gone through a formal procedure 0 otherwise

5.9   Concluding Remarks

The results of the survey have tended to confirm the impression gained at the outset that the Commission's procedure is not only lengthy and costly, but grants large discretionary powers to the Commission, with regard both to the choice of formal or informal procedures and also such matters as the level of fines. In the circumstances it is only to be expected that firms will make considerable efforts to influence the outcomes of cases in their own favour, and it is perhaps surprising that such efforts are not more widespread than our survey has revealed them to be.

Interesting questions therefore arise about the factors that determine the tendency of firms to influence the decision-making process, and about the effectiveness of such influence. These will be investigated more systematically in Chapter 6.

6

The Determinants of Lobbying: an Econometric Analysis

6.1 Introduction

In the previous chapter, the procedure of application of the European competition rules was analysed in the light of the information provided by firms. In this chapter we investigate more systematically the factors determining how firms seek to influence the outcome of this procedure. To do so we have confined our attention to a sub-sample of 71 firms (covering 63 cases), consisting of those firms that answered all the questions in the survey concerning the contacts they had had within the Commission and the support they have received from external sources.

Tables 6.1 to 6.3 give some insight into the representativeness of this sub-sample.

In brief, the problems are the same as those pointed out for the total sample, that is:

- The sub-sample covers only a marginal share of the informal decisions taken between 1989 and 1994, but formal decisions are reasonably represented.
- The sub-sample reflects correctly the division of cases according to the manner in which they were opened, but formal procedures are over-represented in the total of final decisions.

In terms of sectors, the sub-sample also reflects reasonably faithfully the structure of the Commission's workload: in the sample, most agreements were concluded in the chemical sector (18.3%), transport services (13.3%) and electrical machines (8.3%). It can be seen in Table 6.2 that for Article 85 formal decisions, these sectors also have the most important shares.

Table 6.1 The Commission's activity and the survey

	Commission's workload (1989–94)	Sample	Representative (%)
No. of cases	4720	63	1.3
No. of formal decisions	126	25	19.8
No. of informal decisions	4594	38	0.8

	Commission's activity (1989–94) (%)	Sample (%)
Cases opened by notification	61.7	65.1
Cases opened by complaint	27.1	20.6
Cases opened by own procedure	11.1	14.3
Cases closed by settlement	76.2	28.6
Cases closed by comfort letter	21.0	31.7
Cases closed by formal decision	2.8	39.7

Source: Survey and *XXIVth Annual Report on Competition Policy* (Commission, 1994)

Table 6.2 The share of economic sectors in sample and Article 85 decisions

	Formal 85 decisions (1989–94) (%)	Sample (%)
Chemical products	14.8	18.3
Transport services	14.8	13.3
Electrical machines	11.1	8.3

Source: Survey and formal 85 decisions published between 1989 and 1994

Table 6.3 The share of nationalities in the sample and in the Commission's workload

	Commission's workload (1989–94) (%)	Sample (%)
British	28.9	25.4
French	13.6	15.5
German	10.7	14.1
Other European Union	36.2	28.2
Non-European Union of which	10.5	16.9
American	5.6	9.9
Japanese	1.5	4.2

Source: Survey and list of cases having led to some publication between 1989 and 1994

As far as nationalities are concerned, the classification of countries in the sample also appears to fit well to reality (see Table 6.3). However, non-European Union firms (mainly American and Japanese) have a greater share in our sample.

As was stated in Chapter 5, one of our objectives was to gather information about the informal procedure which is the least transparent part of DG-IV's work. Despite the fact that formal procedures are over-represented, the majority of cases in the sub-sample are cases settled with an informal decision (60.3%).

6.2   The Determinants of Lobbying

Lobbying has been divided into two types: private lobbying performed by firms themselves and 'political' lobbying, taking the form of external support.

6.2.1   Private lobbying

Dependent Variables

In order to determine the factors explaining private lobbying, a probit model will be used. The dependent variable ($LOBBY$) takes the value 1 if, during the case, the firm has met with the Director General, the Competition Commissioner or another Commissioner. It takes the value 0 otherwise. These persons are the most highly-ranked officials within the Commission; holding discussions with them about the case clearly goes beyond what is provided for by the normal procedural rules.

Explanatory Variables

Lobbying can be determined by the characteristics of the case and also by the characteristics of the firm. Case-specific variables should normally explain why firms would want to influence the decision. The lobbying behaviour may, however, differ across firms for the same type of case. Our aim is to find out which variables appear to be the most relevant in determining when lobbying will be done. All variables have been constructed according to the information available in the survey.

Case-Specific Variables

1. The first variable ($OPEN$) takes the value 1 if the case was opened following a complaint or on the Commission's own initiative, and the value 0 otherwise. This variable is expected to have a positive effect on lobbying. Most notified agreements have a high probability of being

cleared and, therefore, notifying firms are expected to lobby less at a high level in the Commission. In a case opened by a third party there is, however, more initial reason to suspect an infringement. In such cases, firms may have more incentives to lobby in order to obtain a favourable settlement.

2. A second variable (*DIFF*) was constructed in order to characterize the 'difficulty' of the case. A difficult case is to be understood as a case for which the outcome is not obvious. Such cases should lead to more lobbying. The construction of this difficulty indicator was not easy because of the lack of information concerning the cases, and the results should be treated with caution because of the unavoidable element of subjectivity they embody. *DIFF* takes three values. The value 0 corresponds to very easy cases, the value 1 corresponds to cases presenting some difficulty and the value 2 is attributed to very controversial cases. The evaluation of difficulty is made by means of an *ex-post* judgement relying on various indicators. The evaluating rule worked as follows: we assume that there are strong presumptions that a case was difficult at the outset if firms have disagreed with the Commission's analysis, if they had to bring important changes to the agreement, if the case had a political dimension (often mentioned in questionnaires) and if the procedure has been very long. Despite the shortcomings of the adopted methodology, the indicator should be a reasonable proxy of the difficulty of the case. Nevertheless, to check for robustness we report equation specifications both with and without this variable.

3. The variable *JV* takes the value 1 if the agreement concerns the creation of a joint venture and the value 0 otherwise. The Commission has always been favourable to the creation of joint ventures especially if they included the creation or exchange of technology. An important number of horizontal joint ventures have been exempted over the years (most of them included technological cooperation but did not fall within the scope of block exemptions). This tendency to favour joint ventures may derive from intensive lobbying. On the other hand, one can expect firms to lobby less for such operations since the Commission is known to have a lenient attitude.

4. Finally, the variable *RD* is a dummy variable taking the value 1 if the firm mainly operates in an R&D intensive sector and the value 0 otherwise. Like the joint-venture dummy, this variable can be expected to be negatively correlated to the dependent variable. Since the Commission has always declared its willingness to promote innovation (competition policy being one of its tools to promote this goal), DG-IV has appeared to be more lenient on agreements taking place in high technology industries and therefore one could expect firms to lobby less.

Firm specific variables

1. The 'experience' of firms in competition matters as well as the relations they have established with DG-IV's officials across the years can appear to be helpful for a particular case. In the survey, firms were asked in how many competition cases they had been involved since 1989. Unfortunately, we have only one part of the information since our question relates to the period after 1988. However, the impact of frequent relations between the Commission and firms is more likely to have a sense if these contacts are recent. The occurrence of frequent contacts with DG-IV allows firms to acquire a better knowledge of competition rules and also allows them to build privileged relationships with officials from DG-IV. Therefore, two opposite effects can be expected: first, a lot of experience of competition rules (i.e. a high number of cases) will influence the design of agreements in the sense that firms will write them in compliance with competition law. In such cases, the uncertainties about the decision are minimized and there is no need to seek contacts at a high level in the Commission; second, frequent contacts can facilitate meetings at a high level in order to influence the procedure. Due to the presence of outliers in the sample, we have taken the logarithm of the number of competition cases *LOGNUM*.

2. It is also interesting to see if the nationality of the firm has an impact on its tendency to lobby. Do European firms resort more frequently to lobbying than others? If this appears to be the case, the explanation would probably lie in a greater proximity between European firms and the European institutions. What if, on the contrary, foreign firms appear to lobby at higher levels than European firms? It may suggest that they need more lobbying because of a less lenient attitude of the Commission towards foreign firms. If they sign an important agreement in the European Union, they want to maximize their chance of getting a positive decision. Four nationality dummies have been constructed in order to determine if a nationality effect can be detected. These variables are the following: *GR* takes the value 1 if the firm is German, and 0 otherwise. *UK* takes the value 1 if the firm is British, and 0 otherwise. *FR* takes the value 1 if the firm is French, and 0 otherwise. The variable *FOR* takes the value 1 if the firm is from outside the European Union and 0 otherwise.

3. The size of the firm is also expected to have an impact on its tendency to lobby. Bigger firms can be expected to have a frequent recourse to lobbying. First, bigger firms have more bargaining power because of their position and their 'weight' in national economies. The Commission's officials may be more willing to listen to their representatives. Second,

bigger firms have more important interests to protect. Small firms are more likely to sign agreements that do not infringe European competition rules and, therefore, they do not need to lobby for their case within the Commission. They can also be part of cartels including big firms and in such cases, the latter will probably manage to lobby in their favour. The value of the firm's annual turnover was computed in billions of ECU. Once more, we were confronted by the presence of outliers. The variance of this variable being enormous, the size of the firms is reflected by the logarithm of the turnover (*LOGTURN*).

4. The sector of activity in which the firm mainly operates can also have an impact on lobbying activities. In the Commission's decisions it appears that there are two main sectors in which agreements take place: the chemical sector and transport services. Two dummy variables represent the economic sector in which the firm operates: (*CHEM*) for the chemical industry and (*TRANSP*) for transports. These variables take the value 1 if the firm is mainly operating in the sector and the value 0 otherwise. Is there a higher propension to lobby in one of these sectors? Some conjectures can be made about the behaviour of transport firms who have for long been regulated. Despite the process of deregulation in some areas, the transport sector is still characterized by dominant firms. Such firms can be expected to have significant bargaining power, a long tradition of close contacts with regulators but mainly a strong willingness to perpetuate their protection from competitive forces. Due to their position in their country's economy and their close relation with governments, we expect transport firms to have recourse to lobbying more easily.

The specifications for the lobbying equations are the following:

Equation L1

LOBBY = f (*OPEN, DIFF, JV, RD, LOGNUM, FOR, GR, UK, FR, LOGTURN, TRANSP, CHEM*)

Equation L2

LOBBY = f (*OPEN, JV, RD, LOGNUM, FOR, GR, UK, FR, LOGTURN, TRANSP, CHEM*)

They differ in that L1 includes but L2 excludes the variable *DIFF* capturing the difficulty of the case.

6.2.2 Political Support

The Dependent Variable

As has already been said, private lobbying and political support are aimed at influencing the outcome of a competition case, but the motives explaining the willingness to influence the outcome may be different.

In this model, the dependent variable (*SUP*) takes the value 1 if political representatives and/or officials from Member States were reported as supportive of the case and 0 otherwise.

Explanatory Variables

If public agents are supposed to defend national interests whereas firms defend private interests, it can be expected that support will be brought when private interests converge with national interests. For example, when a joint venture is set up (with restrictive clauses), the parent companies will lobby to obtain a clearance in order to benefit from the expected profits produced by the joint venture. A political representative will be willing to bring its support if, for example, employment is created in his country thanks to the joint venture.

Case-specific variables should have an impact on the willingness to bring support for a particular case. The case-specific variables introduced in the lobby equation are used as explanatory variables for the support equation. Difficult cases should normally receive more support than easy cases. The *OPEN* variable will allow us to check whether suspected firms have more chances to receive support than others. The conjectures about the joint venture (*JV*) and high technology (*RD*) dummies are not straightforward. One might expect support to be brought in cases involving joint ventures or agreements in high-technology sectors because of the benefits that such agreements can create at a national level. As in the case of private lobbying, however, support may also be useless because of the known disposition of the Commission to treat such cases sympathetically.

The following hypothesis will also be tested:

1. Political support is a country specific phenomenon.
2. Political support is a sectoral phenomenon.
3. Political support depends on the size of the firm.

Some conjectures can be made about expected signs for the second and the third hypothesis. *TRANSP* is expected to have a positive impact on the probability that support is brought for the same reasons as those presented for lobbying. *LOGTURN* is also expected to increase the probability of support. It seems reasonable to conjecture that officials from Member States as well as political representatives are more sensitive to the interests of big firms with an important weight in national economies.

This regression will also allow us to compare our results to those obtained by Neven *et al.* (1993). They performed a simple probit regression in order to test the factors explaining the support received by firms for merger cases.

Two specifications are tested for the support equation:

Equation S1

SUP = f ($OPEN$, $DIFF$, JV, RD, FOR, GR, UK, FR, $LOGTURN$, $TRANSP$, $CHEM$)

Equation S2

SUP = f ($OPEN$, JV, RD, FOR, GR, UK, FR, $LOGTURN$, $TRANSP$, $CHEM$)

Table 6.4. summarizes all the variables used for the econometric analysis.

Table 6.4 Dependent and explanatory variables

	Description	Mean	Percentage
DEPENDENT VARIABLES			
Lobby equation			
LOBBY	One if the firm has met with a Director General, the Competition Commissioner and/or a Commissioner from another DG		
	Zero if the firm has met with no official from DG-IV, or if it has met with a rapporteur or a Head of Unit	0.408	40.8
Support equation			
SUP	One if the firm has sought support from an external source (political representatives and/or officials from Member States)		
	Zero otherwise	0.352	35.2
EXPLANATORY VARIABLES			
Case specific variables			
OPEN	One if the file has been opened by a complaint or a Commission's own-initiated proceeding, zero otherwise	0.394	39.4
DIFF	Zero if the case is easy (clearly no impact on competition, rapid settlement)		32.4
	One if the case presented some difficulty (rapid settlement but negotiations were needed)		28.2
	Two if the case was difficult (negotiations, firm disagreed with the Commission's analysis, political content, long procedure)	1.070	39.4

Table 6.4 Continued

	Description	Mean	Percentage
JV	One if the agreement concerned the creation of a joint venture, zero otherwise	0.296	29.6
RD (*)	One if the firm mainly operates in a high-tech sector, zero otherwise	0.141	14.1
Firm specific variables			
LOGNUM	The logarithm of the number of competition cases the firm has had since 1989	0.843	
FOR	One if the firm is from outside the European Union, zero otherwise	0.169	16.9
GR	One if the firm is German, zero otherwise	0.141	14.1
UK	One if the firm is British, zero otherwise	0.254	25.4
FR	One if the firm is French, zero otherwise	0.155	15.5
LOGTURN (**)	the logarithm of the annual turnover of the firm (ECUs millions)	7.789	
TRANSP	One if the firm mainly operates in the transport sector, zero otherwise	0.128	12.8
CHEM	One if the firm mainly operates in the chemical sector, zero otherwise	0.155	15.5

(*) The following sectors are considered as R&D intensive: Aerospace, Office & Computing Equipment, Radio, TV & Communications and Pharmaceuticals.
(**) In the questionnaire, most firms gave their 1994 world-wide turnover. This variable gives the annual turnover in millions of ECU (computing using the 1994 yearly average exchange rate of the ECU).

We now report the results of the estimation.

6.3 Empirical Results

6.3.1 The Lobbying Equation

Both specifications perform well since 81.7% of the occurrence of lobbying is successfully predicted by the model under specification L1[106] and 80.3% under specification L2. Likelihood Ratio tests suggest that case-specific variables and firm-specific variables are both important in determining private lobbying.

As can be seen in Table 6.5, all nationality dummies are significant and have a positive sign. They show that German, French, British and foreign firms are more prone to lobby than other European firms. This is especially true for German and French firms (if a firm is German, the probability of lobbying increases by 0.79 and by 0.7 if the firm is French). The dummy for foreign firms is significant only when the difficulty variable is introduced in the regression.

Table 6.5 Coefficient estimates and marginal effects in the lobbying equation

Variables	Specification L1	Marginal effect	Specification L2	Marginal effect
C	**–2.393** *(–1.997)***		–0.787 *(–0.813)*	
OPEN	0.473 *(0.836)*	**0.181**	**0.933** *(1.79)**	**0.350**
DIFF	**1.100** *(2.648)***	**0.417**	–	–
JV	0.390 *(0.726)*	0.150	0.227 *(0.469)*	0.087
RD	**1.483** *(1.973)***	**0.531**	0.844 *(1.328)*	0.372
LOGNUM	–0.100 *(–0.438)*	–0.038	–0.142 *(–0.639)*	–0.054
FOR	**1.260** *(1.725)**	**0.469**	0.66 *(1.04)*	0.257
GR	**3.496** *(3.302)***	**0.787**	**2.216** *(2.705)***	**0.682**
UK	**1.801** *(2.834)***	**0.627**	**1.67** *(2.781)***	**0.595**
FR	**2.350** *(3.107)***	**0.704**	**2.099** *(3.205)***	**0.670**
LOGTURN	–0.172 *(–1.552)*	–0.065	**–0.182** *(–1.602)**	**–0.069**
TRANSP	**1.967** *(2.384)***	**0.633**	**1.449** *(2.182)***	**0.522**
CHEM	0.299 *(0.434)*	0.088	0.524 *(1.023)*	0.204
Log L	–28.42432		–33.1108	
% correct predictions	81.69%		80.28%	

t-statistics in brackets
Significant parameters are in bold.
*90% significance
**95% significance

In order to analyse the impact of dummies, the estimated probability that LOBBY = 1 is computed for both values of the dummies (0 and 1) at the sample mean of all the other variables. The effect of the dummy on the probability is then given by the difference between these two estimated probabilities.

Two other firm-specific variables have an impact on the probability of lobbying: the turnover and the transport-sector dummies. The turnover variable is only significant in specification L2 (without the difficulty variable) and it does not have the expected sign.[107] This result was unexpected since a positive sign was predicted. This result could suggest that important firms in Europe (in terms of annual turnover) do not feel the need to lobby at a high level in the Commission. The reason may be that their weight in national (or European) economies is a factor taken into account by officials in the Commission. This result should, however, be taken cautiously since the variable is only significant at a 10% level. Moreover, the majority of firms in the sample are already important firms and hence, the expected size effect is not captured by the sample.

Finally, as expected, if a firm operates in transport services, the probability that it will lobby at a high level increases (by 0.63).

As far as case-specific variables are concerned, the difficulty dummy has a clear positive impact on the probability to lobby at a high level. Firms will lobby more for difficult cases.[108] When a case is easy, the probability that firms lobby at a high level is extremely low. The results suggest that the difficulty is linked to the way the case was opened. When regressions are performed without the difficulty proxy, the (*OPEN*) variable becomes significant and it has the expected sign – that is, suspected firms will lobby more than notifying firms. This result suggests that for private lobbying, difficulty is associated to the suspicion of infringement. When we do not control for difficulty, the probability of lobbying increases by 0.35 if the file has been opened by a third party.

Firms also appear to lobby more for agreements occuring in a high-technology sector (an increase of 0.53 in the probability). As is the case for the foreign dummy, this variable is only significant in specification L1.

6.3.2 The Support Equation

In the political support regression, there are only two significant variables and they are both firm-specific variables (see Table 6.6.)

First, the French nationality dummy is significant and has a positive sign. If a firm is French, the probability that it will receive support increases (by 0.41). This result suggests that French officials and political representatives have a strong tendency to defend national interests within the Commission. Concerning German firms, it can be seen that the sign of the dummy has changed and is negative. Although the variable is not significant, we would like to note that in their analysis of mergers, Neven *et al.* (1993, p. 143) had found that German firms were less likely to receive support for their case. Second, firms operating in the transport sector are also more likely to receive political support than others (the probability increases by 0.42).

Table 6.6 Coefficient estimates and marginal effects in the support equation

Variables	Specification S1	Marginal effect	Specification S2	Marginal effect
C	−1.072 (−1.255)		−0.739 (−0.913)	
OPEN	0.194 (0.454)	0.070	0.367 (0.922)	0.133
DIFF	0.293 (1.147)	0.105	−	−
JV	0.250 (0.557)	0.091	0.203 (0.459)	0.074
RD	0.150 (0.186)	0.038	0.019 (0.034)	0.007
FOR	0.184 (0.339)	0.067	0.022 (0.042)	0.008
GR	−0.617 (−0.781)	−0.190	−0.766 (−1.033)	−0.231
UK	0.471 (1.062)	0.175	0.455 (1.025)	0.170
FR	**1.085** **(1.962)****	**0.411**	**1.074** **(1.983)****	**0.407**
LOGTURN	−0.029 (−0.346)	−0.010	−0.030 (−0.348)	−0.011
TRANSP	**1.099** **(2.188)****	**0.417**	**1.036** **(2.122)****	**0.394**
CHEM	−0.092 (−0.184)	−0.032	−0.017 (−0.034)	−0.006
Log L	−38.04956		−38.7216	
% correct predictions	69.01%		70.42%	

t-statistics in brackets
significant parameters are in bold
*90% significance
**95% significance

The characteristics of a case have no impact on the probability of receiving political support.

The support equation clearly performs more poorly than the lobby equation. It successfully predicts 69% of the support brought to firms in specification S1 and 70.4% in specification S2. The LR test for the joint hypothesis that all coefficients are zero is only rejected at confidence level of 0,15 suggesting that the explanatory power of the variables in the model is very weak. The dominance of firm-specific variables is, however, confirmed.

The results of this model show that the offering of support is a country specific phenomenon (showing that the French have a strong tendency to offer political support) and also a sectoral phenomenon in the sense that transport firms are more likely to receive support than others. The weak performance of this model suggest the support offered by officials from Member States and political representatives is determined by many factors that do not appear in the model. Some relevant factors are indeed missing from the analysis: for example, the lobbying occurring at a national level in order to get support or the existence of relationships between firms and officials or political representatives.

Box 6.1 Main findings

1. The characteristics of a case will determine only private lobbying. The probability of private lobbying increases for difficult cases and high-technology agreements. Firms associate difficulty with the suspicion of infringement.
2. The characteristics of a firm determine both private and political lobbying.
3. French firms appear to maximize all sources of potential influences (private lobbying and political support) whereas British, German and foreign firms mainly act themselves in order to influence decisions.
4. In the transport sector, lobbying (private and political) is more intense than in other sectors

---

6.4 Does Lobbying Work?

One question it would naturally be interesting to investigate is whether lobbying in fact succeeds in influencing the outcome of a case. Assessing the impact of lobbying is, however, very hard. The reason is that, as the previous equations have demonstrated, the choice of lobbying behaviour is itself influenced by features of the case and the firms involved. 'Difficult' cases will tend both to involve more lobbying and to have less favourable outcomes. Without controlling for the endogeneity of lobbying any estimates of its effects will be biased, tending to associate lobbying with unfavourable outcomes and, therefore, underestimating its benefits to the firms involved.

Unfortunately our sample is too small (given the discontinuous nature of the variables) to perform simultaneous equation estimation with any degree of reliability. We have attempted to estimate the factors influencing the outcome of a case without controlling for the endogeneity of lobbying, but the equations perform very poorly, and the impact of lobbying is insignificant; which is unsurprising given its association with cases that are likely to be settled in an unfavourable way for the firm. Further investigation would therefore have to await a better set of data or other forms of evidence (such as detailed studies of particular cases).

7

Conclusions

This book has reviewed European Union policy towards agreements between firms from the point of view of modern industrial and institutional economics. It has considered both the legal framework and the application of this policy in practice. The book highlights the main strengths and weaknesses of the current approach and formulates specific proposals for improvement.

Our diagnosis comes in three parts. We first consider notified agreements and start from the observation that the Commission and the Court apply a very narrow definition of what constitutes a restriction of competition under Article 85§1. This has been noted by a number of legal commentators and we confirm, from a economic perspective, that there are many instances where agreements have been unlawful even though they have had negligible effects on third parties. As a consequence of such a narrow approach, firms seeking legal security have a strong incentive to notify their agreements. The need for legal security is itself enhanced by the provision of Article 85§2 according to which agreements that fall under the prohibition of Article 85§1 are legally void. As a consequence, firms have an incentive to obtain clearance of their agreement to avoid the risk of challenge, possibly by a partner in the agreement in case of dispute. Such challenges can be particularly costly where irrecoverable investments have been undertaken as a result of the agreement in question. A large number of agreements are therefore notified, and the Commission labours under a very heavy case load. Rather than seeking to reduce the flow of cases, however, the Commission has merely increased its exercise of discretion in ignoring or settling cases informally. This may speed up the process but at significant costs in terms of the opacity of the procedure and the difficulty for firms in predicting its outcome. The majority of cases are thus cleared or negotiated away from public scrutiny. As our study of the determinants of lobbying indicates, the opacity of the procedure also increases the tendency for firms to seek to influence the process to their own advantage.

Second, we observe that exemptions granted under Article 85§3 follow a rigid legal structure and often fail to consider efficiency benefits in any depth. The range of efficiency benefits that are referred to is large, but hardly any of them is given a serious hearing. Some of the arguments refer to genuine externalities which might enhance efficiency. Others refer in vague terms to general objectives which have a remote and unspecified link with economic efficiency. In all cases, the arguments are simply stated and there is no attempt to evaluate their significance, let alone to quantify their importance.

Turning to explicit or implicit 'cartel' agreements that are concealed by the firms involved, we observe that Commission practice has a great deal to recommend it. In particular, the Commission (and the Court) seems, rightly in our view, to look tolerantly on implicit agreements between firms which do not involve explicit coordination. Our main concern in this area relates to the requirements imposed by the Court on the material evidence required to convict firms. Such requirements appear excessive in light of the small cost that wrongful conviction may entail in this area, and also explain the apparent lack of deterrent effect that the current policy has on cartels. We also formulate a number of detailed proposals in the area which may help improve the Commission's analysis.

Our main proposal for improvement relates to notified agreements. We recognize that there is need for a more systematic basis for distinguishing between horizontal and vertical agreements. It would also be desirable to find ways of applying Article 85§1 less restrictively, so that many agreements are not obliged to pass through the legal process at all unless there is a real likelihood of their damaging competition. Finally there is need for a more systematic treatment of efficiency benefits.

Regarding the distinction between horizontal and vertical agreements, we suggest a simple test, namely whether parties to the contract operate in the same product market in respect of the goods or services specified in the contract, or in markets for sufficiently close substitutes. If not, the agreement should be seen as vertical and there should be a *prima facie* presumption that it is legal. If products are substitutes, the agreement is horizontal and there should be a presumption of illegality.

For evaluating vertical agreements, we propose a two-step procedure. The first would evaluate whether in the case of a full vertical integration, the parties would together possess substantial market power for their combined final product. The answer to this question will hinge on the extent of inter-brand competition. If it is sufficiently strong, the contract should be seen as legal, unless it can be shown that the parties are seriously likely to exert more market power without vertical integration. If full integration would lead to substantial market power, a further investigation would take place in a second step; this investigation would focus on external effects exerted by the contract on third parties. If consumers, competitors and potential entrants are not likely to be damaged by the contract, it should be deemed legal. If these effects are, however, significant, the agreement should be seen as unlawful under Article 85§1.

Regarding horizontal agreements, we focus on those involving the creation of a joint venture (which account for a large proportion of cases). We suggest, once again, that it is useful to begin by comparing the joint venture with the benchmark case of full integration between the activities of the parents. If a merger of these activities would be allowed, then a joint venture should also be allowed. Conversely, if a merger would not be allowed, then there should a presumption that the joint venture also involves serious restrictions of competition. In those circumstances, it should be deemed illegal unless it can be shown that the parents are unlikely to be able to use the joint venture as a coordination mechanism. We suggest that two conditions will be essential for this assessment: the extent to which the joint venture can appropriate the benefits from the pricing decisions of the parents, and the extent to which the parents will be able to capture the average profit made by the joint venture.

Regarding the evaluation of efficiency benefits, we focus again on joint ventures where this consideration is most important. We suggest that the Commission should focus on the benefits that are specific to joint ventures. These benefits arise from the various strategic commitment mechanisms that joint ventures can implement, regarding the management of specific assets and outputs from the joint venture.

There is some scope for argument as to whether the proposals that we put forward could be implemented without major changes to Community legislation. These proposals can certainly be considered without changes in the Treaty itself, but they might require important changes in secondary legislation, in particular block exemptions and Commission notices. In our view, the need for a change is urgent, and current Commission proposals, which in any case relate only to vertical restraints, go nowhere near far enough. A sharp change in policy could be implemented through a set of published guidelines which clearly laid out the principles of the Commission's intended new practice, and recognized officially a degree of departure from some of the earlier case law. A set of published guidelines would both help firms to predict the likelihood of their agreements' being found to infringe competition law, and provide the Commission itself with an incentive for consistency in its application of that law.

Notes

1. Articles 85 and 86 are reproduced in Appendix 2.
2. In practice, this condition has been reformulated: an agreement should have an 'appreciable' effect on trade before it is caught by Article 85§1.
3. Council Regulation of 6 February 1962 in OJL 13/204 of 21 February 1962.
4. The main regulations are the following:
   Regulation No. 1017/68 for transport by land and inland waterways in OJL 175/1 of 23 July 1968.
   Regulation No. 4056/86 for maritime transports in OJL 378/4 of 31 December 1986.
   Regulation No. 3975/87 for air transports in OJL 374/1 of 31 December 1987.
5. One for Directorates C and D, and one for Directorates E and F.
6. Directorate B is in charge of mergers.
7. Competitiveness has been defined by De Woot (1990) as the capacity of a firm, under free and fair market conditions, to produce goods and services that meet the test of international markets while, at the same time, maintaining or expanding its real income. For a country, competitiveness can be defined as the capacity to raise market shares on export markets or to sustain a higher growth rate without deteriorating its current balance (*European Economy* 54 (1993), p. 176). The Commission in its report on 'The Competitiveness of European Industry' (Commission, 1997) defines a competitive economy as one that achieves high levels of productivity and employment.
8. See the ***Toys'R'Us*** case, in which the Federal Trade Commission charged that the firm employed its 'market power over manufacturers . . . illegally to compel the manufacturers to go along with its efforts to keep the warehouse clubs from competing effectively with it' (*FTC News*, Federal Trade Commission, May 22 1996). Comanor and Rey (1997) use the case to illustrate some important issues that arise when distributors have market power.
9. Excellent empirical and theoretical accounts of the issues involved are given by Lyons (1996) and Vickers (1996).
10. For those who find acronyms helpful as mnemonics, this policy rule, dependent as it is on identifying a Substantial Adverse Negative Externality, can be described as SANE.
11. Rey and Tirole (1996) claim that the direction of the vertical relation matters, but their reasons for saying so do not challenge the argument made here. Their point is that the market structure faced by final consumers matters, a point with which we agree.
12. In a fuller model, it might be thought appropriate to make it endogenous which components were contractible and which not, but nothing of importance turns on this point.
13. It might be thought that, since the firm itself is not a single entity but a hierarchy characterized by agency problems, the firm as such has no more privileged access to or

control over its non-contractible strategies than its contracting partners do. Firm 1, it might be argued, cannot contractually control the actions of the employees of Firm 2; but neither can Firm 2; understood as the legal entity rather than the collection of individuals. However, this overlooks a crucial difference between Firm 1 and Firm 2 with respect to the actions of Firm 2's employees: since Firm 2 owns the assets with which they work, it can institute much more thorough and invasive mechanisms of monitoring than Firm 1 can. The owners of Firm 2 can and do send supervisors into the buildings in which the employees work; Firm 1 can send representatives to the buildings of Firm 2 to inspect the work that is being carried out, but they have the right of admission only if the owners of Firm 2 or their representatives choose to allow them in. To put the matter another way: ownership of a firm's assets allows the owners access to a range of strategies that would not be possible under any other contractual relationship than ownership, because it allows physical access to the place in which those strategies must be implemented, and it carries with it the right to deny such access to any parties who are not owners. Ownership preserves privacy, one might say.

14. For an excellent analytical survey of vertical restraints, see also OECD (1994).
15. If the problem is concave it is straightforward to show also that social welfare is higher at the joint profit-maximizing equilibrium than at the non-cooperative outcome.
16. This argument highlights the importance of establishing that the *net* externality is negative and not just that there exists a negative externality of some kind.
17. This is particularly true if the scarcity of the resource varies significantly according to unforeseen events. Bolton and Whinston (1993) develop a model in which the desire for security of supply promotes vertical integration which is sometimes socially harmful.
18. The law often uses the term 'foreclosure' more generally, when competitors' market presence is diminished rather than prevented altogether. Analytically such a case is best understood as an instance of raising rivals' costs.
19. Ironically, efforts by the authorities to prevent discrimination between customers, by making such renegotiation more difficult, may act as a commitment device helping the owner of the bottleneck facility to maintain its market power, as Rey and Tirole point out (1996, pp. 22–4).
20. See, for example, Freeman (1997), which argues that other Court decisions allow more scope for the systematic application of a rule of reason than is evident from a consideration of *Consten & Grundig* and *Technique Minière* alone.
21. Commission decisions are not classified according to whether they concern primarily vertical or primarily horizontal arrangements, and it is clear that a number of horizontal agreements raise significant vertical issues (for instance the 1992 *Astra* case, in which the Commission decided that a joint venture between British Telecom and the Societe Européenne des Satellites infringed Article 85§1, involved considerable examination of the possibility of foreclosure). So the classification here is potentially subjective; nevertheless, the broad features of EU policy are well illustrated by the cases in the list we have compiled.
22. Regulation 123/85 on motor vehicles defined an 'authorised intermediary' (with whom a manufacturer might not lawfully refuse to deal) as one that had 'prior written authority' from the final consumer. See the decision of the Court of First Instance in *Peugeot* (case T-9/92), where the Court had to clarify that a commercial concern could qualify. It is clearly absurd that the lawfulness of territorial exclusivity should depend on such arcane distinctions.
23. See for instance Guerrin and Kyriazis (1992).
24. See also Rotemberg and Saloner (1986) and Rees (1985). Abreu *et al.* (1986) extend the Green and Porter (1984) model by allowing for more severe punishments. They show that a global optimum can be supported as perfect equilibrium when such punishments are allowed for. See also Kandori and Matsushima (1994) and Compte (1994) which allow for private information about demand.
25. See Kuhn and Vives (1994) on this topic.
26. See Harrington (1989) who considers firms with different discount factors.
27. See Compte *et al.* (1996). It is unclear, however, whether product differentiation is a favourable circumstance. On the one hand, product differentiation reduces the benefits from short-term deviation. On the other, it enhances the magnitude of the punishment. See Ross (1992), Häckner (1994), Levy and Reitzes (1993).

28. See Bernheim and Whinston (1990).
29. See Martin (1990).
30. Harrington (1989) has combined a non-cooperative repeated game with a cooperative selection of a particular outcome (modelled as a Nash bargaining game). Sugden (1995) develops a theory of focal-point selection.
31. Slade (1992) proposes a model to uncover supergame strategies during price wars. In this model, she does not test whether collusion is taking place. Rather, she focuses on trying to distinguish between alternative strategies that can support collusion. She considers strategies that are only dependent on the prices chosen in the previous period. She finds that rather simple strategies support the equilibrium and that these strategies do not change during price wars.
32. See Neven and Röller (1996) who endogenize wages and Ng and Seabright (1997) who allow for endogenous wages and labour productivity, both with applications to the European airlines industry.
33. One can also wonder whether quantitative methods are suitable for use on a routine basis in anti-trust investigations. The robustness of the results may be a concern as indicated for instance by the study of Porter (1985) which was subsequently revised by Ellison (1994), who shows that the conclusions of Porter are very sensitive to the specification of demand. So far, if references to theoretical models are increasingly frequent in Commission and Court decisions (see for instance *Soda Ash*, *Wood Pulp* and *Polypropylène*), econometric evidence is still rare. Interestingly, the Commission used a structural estimation in its defence on *Wood Pulp*, attempting to show that margins in the industry were unusually high. The Court expressed interest in the method and wished that the Commission has used such evidence earlier in the proceedings (CMLR 407 (1993), p. 519).
34. CMLR 295 (1976).
35. Indeed, the US anti-trust authorities have not also shown the same wisdom; the US case law regarding the application of Paragraph 1 of the Sherman Act tends to draw a distinction between independent behaviour and a joint action. Independent behaviour is defined in a very strict fashion and excludes the type of strategic interdependence envisaged by the *Zuiker Unie* decision (see for instance Yao and DeSanti, 1993). By contrast, a joint action is supposed to entail a conscious commitment to a common scheme. The problem with this distinction is of course that it does allow for a complete typology to the extent that an action that is not independent is not necessarily a joint action. By including some strategic interactions as legitimate behaviour, the *Zuiker Unie* decision avoids this pitfall.
36. See for instance, *Chemiefarma* case, *European Community Report* 661.
37. Indeed, prohibited agreements are legally void under the second paragraph of Article 85.
38. The particular distinction between agreement and concerted practices referred to here, which was established early on in the case law, has certainly meant that the Commission and the Court did not have to extend to concept of an agreement beyond common usage. The wisdom of this approach is apparent if it is compared with the US approach in which agreements are supposed to catch all forms of coordination. As a consequence, the US case law had to extend the meaning of an agreement as far as considering that indirect means of communications may constitute an agreement (see for example Kovacic, 1993).
39. CMLR 60 (1972), p. 571.
40. CMLR 295 (1976).
41. The same attitude can be found in the United States, where the requirement of the Sherman Act that an agreement should be proved has never been stretched to the point that evidence on outcomes was sufficient to deduce the existence of an agreement. Even under article 5 of the FTC act, which does not require proof that an agreement exists, evidence on outcomes has not so far been considered sufficient (see Kovacic, 1993).
42. Indeed, the very notion of an agreement under US law, defined as a conscious commitment to a common scheme requires some intent (see Kovacic, 1993).
43. CMLR 84 (1992).

44. CMLR 84 (1992) and OJL 230/1 (1986).
45. OJL L 33/44 (1989).
46. OJL L 74/21 (1989).
47. CMLR 295 (1976).
48. A similar incident occurred a couple of years later where, in line with the principles discussed above, there is also evidence of prices creeping up to their original level (rather than adjusting abruptly).
49. However, the combination of pre-announcements with most-favoured-customer clauses can act as a facilitating practice (see Holt and Scheffman, 1987). In the present case, there is evidence of contracts using most favoured customer clauses.
50. See for instance, Neven and Phlips (1985) and Smith and Venables (1988).
51. See Bernheim and Whinston (1990). Admittedly, the Commission decision was published less than two years after the relevant academic paper was published.
52. Interestingly, the Advocate General explicitly took this view in the *Flat Glass* decision. In Paragraph 159 (CMLR 302, 1992), the Advocate General states: 'The Court considers . . . that the appropriate definition of the market in question is a necessary precondition of any judgement concerning allegedly anti-competitive behaviour'.
53. See Neven *et al.* (1993) for a discussion of these methods.
54. *European Economy* 59 (1995).
55. The Commission statement is somewhat puzzling in other respects: in October 1995, the Commission imposed anti-dumping duties of 13.5% on US producers (see *Financial Times*, 11 October 1995). At that time, the dollar was however stronger than at the time of the decision (the exchange rate was about $1.18 per ECU). Accordingly, it seems that according to the Commission, US producers are dumping even though they are competitive (without dumping).
56. This figure was however disputed by the Commission who claims that transport cost would not exceed half of the estimate suggested by the defendants.
57. Accordingly to debates in Court. Interestingly, the Commission classified overall production in Italy as a business secret!
58. CMLR 302 (1992) p. 309.
59. Kühn and Vives (1994) suggest that information exchange could be seen an independent violation of Article 85§1, which could however be exempted under Article 85§3. Their proposal would thus require a change of Regulation 17. By contrast, the proposal that information exchanges shift the burden of proof, while leaving firms with the possibility of arguing against the presumption, does not require such a change.
60. Note the importance of specifying real returns. Two factories producing identical products are not complementary assets merely in virtue of the fact that their joint operation, by lowering output and raising prices, would raise joint profits. For assets to be complementary requires that the production frontier when they are separately operated lies strictly inside the frontier when they are jointly operated.
61. This would imply that the parent companies are risk averse with respect to profits, since they will presumably also have difficulty claiming full credit if the venture succeeds.
62. A similar point is made in by Whish and Suffrin (1988). They argue that the evaluation of whether parents could have undertaken the activity on their own under Article 85§1 is similar to the analysis of whether restrictions were necessary (or 'ancilliary' under Article 85§3).
63. The real rate is 12% but some of the questionnaires cannot be used because they concern merger cases or cases that are not yet settled.
64. This problem became evident in the work undertaken for the Commission's own study of the effectiveness of the Single Market (Commission, 1997).
65. See the XXIIIrd Annual Report (Commission, 1993, point 208): 'The reduction (in the backlog) is due to DG-IV's continual efforts to clear the backlog'. The Commission closed an important number of files concerning cases that were no longer in force.
66. This observation relies on the information available in published decisions.
67. Negative clearance also but these are extremely rare.

68. Immunity from fines is granted by Article 15§5(a) for the time elapsed between the notification and the decision taken by the Commission (exemption or not). Since the comfort letter is not a decision, the notification continues to produce its effects.
69. See the **Langnese-Igloo GmbH** and the **Schöller Lebensmittel GmbH & Co. KG** decisions – OJL 183/1. SLG had received a comfort letter for its standard-form supply contract but after a complaint lodged by Mars, it finally was condemned for an infringement of Article 85§1.
70. In its 'Notice on Cooperation Between National Courts and the Commission in Applying Articles 85 and 86 of the EC Treaty' – OJC 39/6 (1993).
71. **Scottish Salmon Board** decision – OJL 246/37, 17 August 1992.
72. **Bayer Dental** decision – OJL 351/46, 15 December 1990.
73. All references for these cases are given in footnotes 10 and 11 of Van Bael's article.
74. **Selective distribution system of Givenchy perfumes** decision – OJL 236/11, 19 August 1992.
75. **International Private Satellite Partners** – OJL 354/75, 31 December 1994.
    Elopak/Metal Box Odin – OJL 209/15, 8 August 1990.
    Konsortium ECR 900 – OJL 228/31, 22 August 1990.
76. **ACI** decision – OJL 224/29, 30 August 1994.
77. **Bayer/BP Chemical** decision – OJL 174/34, 8 July 1994.
78. **Warner Lambert/Gillette and others – BIC/Gillette and others** decision – OJL 116/21, 12 May 1992.
79. **Eurocheque** decision – OJL 95/50, 9 April 1992.
80. 'Guidelines on the method of setting fines imposed pursuant to Article 15§2 of Regulation No. 17 and Article 16 of The ECSC Treaty', published in OJC 9, 14 January 1998.
81. In the **Cartonboard** decision – OJL 243/1, 19 September 1994, some producers received substantial reductions of their fines (66% and 33%) for their cooperative attitude.
82. Van Bael (1995) suggests the application of the US system of tariffs. In the United States, an independent Commission determines guidelines for fines in anti-trust cases. This idea has been rejected by the European Commission on the basis that predictable fines achieve less deterrence. However, the same reasoning could be applied to plea bargaining. If firms know that the fine is significantly reduced when they do not contest the infringement and offer some evidence of it, the deterrent effect of fines is reduced (the only remaining uncertainty being the amount of the reduction). The aim here is not to start a long discussion about the problems associated with the wide discretionary power in the hands of the Commission about fines but rather to point out an additional uncertainty associated with the procedure.
83. **Newitt vs. Dunlop Slazenger Int.** decision – OJL 131/32, 16 May 1992.
84. **Cement** decision – OJL 343/1, 30 December 1994.
85. **SCK-FNK** decision – OJL 117/30, 7 May 1994 and **Vichy** decision – OJL 75/57, 21 March 1991.
86. **Film purchase by German television** decision – OJL 284/36, 3 October 1989; **EBU/Eurovision system** decision – OJL 179/23, 22 July 1993 and **PMI-DSV** decision – OJL 221/34, 19 September 1995.
87. In reality, this figure is higher because some cases have been opened by informal complaints and finally investigated following a Commission's own-initiated proceeding. The real figure is at least 64%.
88. See the **B&I/Sealink** case (page XX)
89. In 1992, MTV lodged a complaint against Video Performance Ltd, the International Federation of the Phonographic Industry and the five major record companies in the world. MTV had signed an agreement with VPL and IFPI for the licensing of music videos. This agreement expired and MTV was concerned that it would not be renewed. Following the Commission's intervention in response to the complaint, MTV managed to obtain the extension of the agreement.
90. **Ford/Volkswagen** decision – OJL 20/14, 28 January 1993.
91. Annual Report (Commission, 1994) p. 412, Annex II.

92. A third motive for settlement is that the complaint does not fulfill the conditions presented in the 'Notice on cooperation . . . .' There may be an infringement but the case has no 'political, economic or legal significance for the Community'.
93. Press Release, 21 June 1990 (cited in *European Competition Law Review* 5 (1990), p. 146).
94. Printed in the OJC 39, 13 February 1993, p. 6.
95. *French-West African shipowners' committees* decision – OJL 18 May 1992.
96. *Screensport/EBU Members* decision – OJL 63/32, 9 March 1991.
97. *Cartonboard* decision – OJL 234/1, 19 September 1994.
98. This may be an under-estimate because not all decisions give the starting-date of the investigation.
99. XXth Annual Report (Commission, 1990), point 98.
100. XXIIIrd Annual Report (Commission, 1993) point 3 (Annex III).
101. The share of firms having answered with a 4 or a 5 is 60.3% (see Table 5.9).
102. If condemned firms are excluded, the share of firms having answered with a 4 or a 5 is 56%.
103. '. . . *complex and obscure* . . .' are the words used by one of them.
104. For questions B5 and B6, answer (a) scores 1 point, answer (b) scores 2 points and so on. For question B8, answer (a) scores 1 point and answers (b) and (c) score 2 points. Finally, for question B9, a 'yes' scores 1 point and a 'no' scores 2 points. The index can, therefore, range from 4 (completely satisfied) to 12 (completely unsatisfied).
105. In 1993, the Commission adopted a new internal procedure for cooperative joint ventures. The decision-making process has been accelerated through the setting of deadlines.
106. The likelihood ratio test rejects the hypothesis that all coefficients are nil.
107. We have also tested this hypothesis by replacing the variable *LOGTURN* by a variable taking the value one when the firm appeared in the TOP 5000 undertakings in Europe and zero otherwise. This variable also had a negative effect on the probability of lobbying.
108. Alternative specifications were tested for the difficulty variable. Three dummy variables were constructed in order to characterise each level of difficulty: *EASY* taking the value 1 for easy cases, and so on. The same conclusion is drawn: the probability of lobbying decreases significantly for easy cases and increases significantly for very difficult cases.

Appendix 1
List of the Commission's formal decisions under Article 85 (1989–95)

List of formal decisions published in the Official Journal

Reference	Name of the case/concerned firms	Description of agreement	Type	Economic sector	Relevant market	Geographic market	Non EU firms	Starting point	Length of procedure	Crt	Taken decision	Nationalities
1 30-Jan-95 IV/33.686 OJL 122/37 of 02.06.95	Coapi (colegio oficial de Agentes de la Propriedad Industrial)	Price-fixing agreement	Horizontal	Intellectual property rights	1 Market for services connected with the enjoyment of industrial property rights in Spain [...] sought by non-residents 2 Market for services connected with the enjoyment of industrial property rights in Spain or abroad sought by clients resident in Spain		No	Informal complaint	Informal complaint on 29.08.90 Co.'s decision to start procedure on 06.07.93 (2 years+ 11 months) Decision on 30.01.95 **4 years+5 months**		Infringement	
2 31-Jan-95 IV/33.375 OJL 221/34 of 19.09.95	PMI-DSV	Horse-racing licensing agreement	Horizontal	Betting services	The market in relaying televized pictures and news of horse races for the customers of betting shops	Each national market is separate	No	Complaint by Ladbroke Deutschland GmbH (competitor)	Complaint on 24.11.89 Notification on 15.02.91 Communication on 24.09.92 (1 year+7 months) Decision on 31.01.95 **5 years+2months**		Negative clearance	
3 12-Jul-95 IV/33.802 OJL 272/16 of 15.11.95	BASF Lacke+ Farben AG and Accinauto SA	Export ban	Vertical	Chemical	Motor vehicle refinishing paints	United Kingdom	No	Complaint by IMF and Calbrook (customer/distributor)	Complaint on 28.01.91 Decision on 12.07.95 **4 years+6 months**		Infringement + fines	
4 29-Nov-95 IV/34.179 IV/34.202 IV/34.216 OJL 312/79 of 23.12.95	SCK/FNK	Erection of barriers to entry	Horizontal	Building	Building		No	Complaint by M.W.C.W. van Marwijk and 10 other firms (competitors)	Complaint on 13.01.92 Notification in February 1992 Immunity from fines relaxed in 1994. Decision on 29.11.95 **3 years+10 months**		Infringement + fines	

Reference	Name of the case/concerned firms	Description of agreement	Type	Economic sector	Relevant market	Geographic market	Non EU firms	Starting point	Length of procedure	Crt	Taken decision	Nationalities
5 21-Feb-94 IV/30.525 OJL 68/35 of 11.03.94	International Energy Agency (18 oil companies and one association of oil companies)	Agreement between OECD members in order to respond to oil supply distortions	Horizontal	Energy	Oil market	World	Yes	Application for renewal of exemption	Application on 12.10.93 Communication on 06.11.93 (1 month) Decision on 21.02.94 (3 months) **4 months**		Renewal of exemption from 01.01.94 to 31.12.2003	International (OECD)
6 29-Mar-94 IV/33.941 OJL 104/34 of 23.04.94	HOV-SVZ/MCN	Agreement for the joint exploitation of transport services associated to common tariffs (discriminatory pricing)	Horizontal	Rail transport	Inland carriage of sea-borne containers to or from Germany through a Belgian, Dutch or German port	Germany, Belgium and Netherlands	No	Complaint lodged by HOV (customer)	Application according to Article 10 of Regulation 1017/68 on 16.05.94 Decision on 29.03.94 **2 years+10 months**		Infringement	German, Belgian and Dutch
7 29-Apr-94 IV/34.456 OJL 131/15 of 25.05.94	Stichting Baksteen	Rationalization agreement (reduction of capacity)	Horizontal	Brick industry	Brick	Netherlands	No	Notification	Notification on 19.08.91 Co.'s decision to start procedure on 28.01.92 (5 months) New notification on 10.09.92 Communication on 06.02.93 (5 months) Decision on 5.04.94 (1 year+ 2 months) **2 years+8 months**		Exemption from 10.09.92 to 30.10.97	Dutch
8 18-May-94 IV/33.640 OJL 144/20 of 09.06.94	Exxon/Shell	Establishment of a joint venture	Horizontal	Chemical	Combined market for LLDPE and LDPE	Whole community		Application for negative clearance	Applications on 21.11.91 and on 29.05.92 by Exxon Applications on 02.12.91 and on 10.06.92 by Shell Publication on 02.04.93 (more or less 1 year) Decision on 18.05.94 (1 year+1 month) **2 years+1 month**		Exemption contingent to some obligations	

Reference	Name of the case/concerned firms	Description of agreement	Type	Economic sector	Relevant market	Geographic market	Non EU firms	Starting point	Length of procedure	Crt	Taken decision	Nationalities
9 06-Jun-94 IV/32.075 OJL 174/34 of 08.07.94	Bayer BP, BP Chemicals International and Erdölchemie	Technical cooperation	Horizontal	Chemical	Polyethylene		No	Application for change of the decision 88/330/CEE and mainly of one condition imposed in the decision of exemption	Application for changes 1991 (unknown date) Communication on 19.02.92 decision on 06.06.94 (2 years +4 months) **At least 2 years and a half**		Change of two conditions: The closure of the plant is postponed to the end of 1994 and the dates at which the reports have to be sent to the Co. are also changed	German
10 13-Jul-94 IV/33.833 OJL 243/1 of 19.09.94	Carton board	Price-fixing and market-sharing cartel	Horizontal	Cardboard industry				Co.'s decision to start procedure	Informal complaint by BPIF on 22.10.90 and later by other Co.'s Decision to start procedure on 21.12.92 Decision on 13.07.94. **3 years+8 months**		Infringement + fines going from 100,000 ECUs to 22,750,000 ECUs	
11 27-Jul-94 IV/34.857 OJL 223/36 of 27.08.94	British Telecommunications and MCI	Setting of a joint venture and BT acquires 20% stake in MCI	Horizontal	Telecommunications	Market for value-added and enhanced services to large multinational corporations and other intensive users of telecommunication services	EEC + world	Yes	Notification under Regulation 4064/89 but converted into an application for negative clearance and notification for exemption	Conversion of the original notification on 18.09.93 Communication on 30.03.94 (6 months) Decision on 27.07.94 (4 months) **At least 10 months**		1. Negative clearance for: acquisition by BT of 20% of MCI. MCI becoming the exclusive distributor of Newco in the Americas, BT as exclusive distributor of Newco in the rest of the world, MCI's and BT's loss of rights 2. Negative clearance for the duration of the exemption granted to the JV in respect to some provisions	English and American

Reference	Name of the case/concerned firms	Description of agreement	Type	Economic sector	Relevant market	Geographic market	Non EU firms	Starting point	Length of procedure	Crt	Taken decision	Nationalities
											3. Exemption from 16.11.93 to 15.11.2000 to the JV and BT as exclusive distributors in the EEA 4. Exemption for five years from the date of adoption of the decision to one article of the investment agreement	
12 27-Jul-94 *IV/34.518* OJL 224/28 of 30.08.94	ACI (Allied Continental Intermodal Services Ltd)	Setting of a cooperative joint venture	Horizontal	Rail transport	International transport of goods between the United Kingdom and the continent		No	Notification under Article 2 of Regulation 1017/68	Notification on 13.11.92 Publication on 27.02.93 (3 months) Co.'s decision to raise doubts on 27.05.93 (3 months) Publication on 26.04.94 (11 months) Decision on 27.07.94 (3 months) **1 year + 8 months**		Five year Exemption under conditions	French, British. ACI is a co-operative society, common subsidiary of 24 railway companies
13 27-Jul-94 *IV/31.865* OJL 239/14 of 14.09.94	PVC	Price-fixing and market-sharing cartel	Horizontal	Petrochemical (chemical)				Commission's own procedure	Decision to initiate proceedings on 24.03.88 Decision on 27.07.94 **6 years + 4 months**		Infringement + fines	
14 21-Sept-94 *IV/34.600* OJL 259/20 of 07.10.94	Night Services	Cooperative joint-venture	Horizontal	Rail transport	Two service markets 1. transport of business travellers 2. transport of leisure travellers.	Routes served by ENS: London-Amsterdam; London-Frankfurt/Dortmund; Paris-Glasgow/Swansea; Brussels-Glasgow/Plymouth	No	Notification under 1017/68	Notification on 29.01.93 Publication on 29.05.93 (4 months) Co.'s decision to raise doubts on 23.08.93 (3 months) Publication on 04.06.94 (10 months) **1 year+5 months**		Exemption	French, Dutch, German, Belgian.

Reference	Name of the case/ concerned firms	Description of agreement	Type	Economic sector	Relevant market	Geographic market	Non EU firms	Starting point	Length of procedure	Crt	Taken decision	Nationalities
15 06-Oct-94 IV/34.776 OJL 309/1 of 02.12.94	Pasteur Mérieux-Merck	Setting of a joint venture + one exclusive distribution agreement	Horizontal + vertical	Pharmaceutical (chemical)	Human vaccination specific immunoglobulines, diagnostics in vivo and serums	National markets are all specific and constitute separate relevant markets	Yes	Notification under 4064/89 which became Notification under Article 2 or Article 4 of Regulation 17	Notification on 04.06.93 Publication on 31.03.94 (8 months) Decision on 06.10.94 (7 months) **1 year+3 months**		Exemption	French and American
16 19-Oct-94 IV/34.446 OJL 376/1 of 31.12.94	Transatlantic agreement (TAA)	Agreement on tariffs, capacities and transport conditions	Horizontal	Maritime transport	Liner shipping services between Europe and the US and inland container transport services, in Europe and the US	Catchment areas of Northern Europe (Ireland,UK. DK. NL. Northern and central F. B. L. D)	Yes	Notification and complaints later	Notification on 28.08.92 Decision on 19.10.94 **2 years+2 months**		Infringement	Dutch, German. British. Swiss. Polish. American. Japanese. Korean and Mexican
17 11-Nov-94 IV/34.410 OJL 309/24 of 02.12.94	Olivetti-Digital	Cooperation agreement (technological agreement)	Horizontal	Computers (office machinery)	The market for the RISC technology	World	Yes	Application for negative clearance	Application on 30.07.92 Communication on 14.10.93 (1 year + 3 months) Decision on 11.11.94 (1 year + 1 month) **2 years+4 months**		Negative clearance + exemption	Italian and American
18 30-Nov-94 IV/33.126 IV/33.322 OJL 343/1 of 30.12.94	Cement Industry	Market-sharing cartel	Horizontal	Cement				Commission's own proceeding	Inspections started in April 1989 Co.'s decision to start proceedings on 12.11.91 Decision on 30.11.94 **5 years+8 months**	YES	Infringement + fines	
19 12-Dec-94 IV/34.891 OJL 341/66 of 30.12.94	Fujitsu AMD Semiconductor	Setting of a joint venture	Horizontal	Semi-conductor (telecommunications)	NVM composites	World	Yes	Notification and application for negative clearance	Notification and application on 21.10.93 Publication on 04.06.94 (8 months) Decision on 12.12.94 (6 months) **1 year+2 months**		Negative clearance and exemption	Japanese and American

Reference	Name of the case/ concerned firms	Description of agreement	Type	Economic sector	Relevant market	Geographic market	Non EU firms	Starting point	Length of procedure	Crt	Taken decision	Nationalities
20 13-Dec-94 *IV/32.490* OJL 354/66 of 31.12.94	Eurotunnel, British Rail and SNCF	Agreement for the joint exploitation of international trains	Horizontal	Rail transport				Application for renewal of exemption	Exemption expired 15.11.91 Publication on 30.07.94 (2 years + 8months) Decision on 13.12.94 (5 months) **3 years + 1 month**		Renewal of exemption	
21 15-Dec-94 *IV/34.768* OJL 354/75 of 31.12.94	International Private Satellite Partners	Creation of a limited partnership firm	Horizontal	Telecommun- ications	Two relevant markets: Market of international telecommunication services for private affairs. Market for the supply of capacity of satellite transmission	North America, Eastern Europe and major part of EEE (at least)	Yes	Notification	Notification and application on 28.06.93 Communication on 11.11.93 and 10.06.94 (5 months) (7 months) Decision on 15.12.94 (6 months) **1 year + 6 months**		Negative clearance	American, Canadian and Italian
22 16-Dec-94 *IV/33.863* OJL 354/87 of 31.12.94	Asahi – Saint Gobain	Setting of a joint venture	Horizontal	Glass (mineral and non-metal)			Yes	Notification	Notification on 03.01.91 Communication on 21.04.93 (2 years and 3 months) Decision on 16.12.94 (1 year + 8 months) **3 years + 11 months**		Exemption	Japanese and French
23 21-Dec-94 *IV/34.252* OJL 378/37 of 31.12.94	Philips International- Osram GmbH	Setting of a joint venture	Horizontal	Glass (mineral non-metal)	Lead glass tubing			Notification	Notification on 03.03.92 Communication on 26.01.94 (1 year + 10 months) Decision on 21.12.94 (11 months) **2 years + 9 months**		Exemption	
24 21-Dec-94 *IV/32.498* *IV/34.590* OJL 378/45 of 31.12.94	Tretorn and others	Export ban	Vertical	Rubber	Tennis balls			Commission's own initiative	Co.'s decision to start procedure on 14.05.93 Decision on 21.12.94 **1 year + 7 months**		Infringement + fines	

Reference	Name of the case/ concerned firms	Description of agreement	Type	Economic sector	Relevant market	Geographic market	Non EU firms	Starting point	Length of procedure	Crt	Taken decision	Nationalities
25 21-Dec-94 IV/33.218 OJL 378/17 of 31.12.94	Far Eastern Freight conference	Price-fixing agreement	Horizontal	Maritime transport				Complaint (customer)	Complaint on 28.04.89 Decision on 21.12.94 **5 years + 8 months**		Infringement + fines	
26 24-Feb-93 IV/34.494 OJL 73/38 of 26.03.93	The 12 European national railway companies	Agreement fixing the tariff structure	Horizontal	Combined transport industry	Rail transport services provided by railway companies to combined transport operators	Community as a whole	No	Notification	First agreement in 1990, statement of objections New agreement notified on 21.01.92 Communication on 01.08.92 (7 months) Decision on 24.04.93 (6 months) **3 years**		Exemption for five years under conditions	European
27 26-May-93	British Railways and Coras Iompair			Combined transport industry	Rail transport services provided by railway companies to combined transport operators	Community as a whole	No	The two railway companies informed the Commission			Two railway companies excluded from the decision of the 24.02.93	European
28 11-Jun-93 IV/32.150 OJL 179/23 of 22.07.93	EBU (European Broadcasting Union)/ Eurovision system	Agreement concerning the acquisition of television rights to sport events (refusal of the EBU and its members to grant Screen-sport sub-licences to sport events)	Horizontal	TV Broadcasting	Market for acquisition of television sports programmes	Community as a whole	No	Complaint by Screensport (competitor) Second complaint by Still Moving films (production of sport programmes)	Complaint on 17.12.87 Co.'s decision to start procedure on 05.12.88 (1 year) Notification on 03.04.89 (5 months) Communication on 05.10.90 (1 year + 6 months) Decision on 11.06.93 (2 year + 8 months) **5 years+7 months**		Exemption for five years under conditions	European

Reference	Name of the case/concerned firms	Description of agreement	Type	Economic sector	Relevant market	Geographic market	Non EU firms	Starting point	Length of procedure	Crt	Taken decision	Nationalities
29 22-Jun-93 IV/31.550 IV/31.898 OJL 272/28 of 04.11.93	Zera/Montedison and Hinkens/Stähler	Export ban	Vertical	Chemical industry	Trifuraline used in the product named Digermin which is a herbicide (used in the culture of colza)	Germany	No	Application by Zera and Hinkens according to Article 3§2 of Regulation 17 (competitors)	Complaint on 20.05.85 Co.'s decision to start procedure on 27.09.89 Decision on 22.06.93 **8 years**		Infringement of Article 85§1	German and Italian
30 30-Jun-93 IV/33.407 OJL 203/27 of 13.08.93	CNSD (Consiglio nazionale degli spedizionieri doganali) and AICAI (Associazione italiana dei corrieri aerei)	Agreement on tariff structure	Horizontal	Customs	Services provided by customs agents	Imports from and exports to Italy	No	Complaint lodged by the AICAI (customer)	Complaint on 16.06.90 Co.'s decision to start procedure on 25.09.91 (1 year+3 months) Decision on 30.06.93 **3 years**		Infringement of Article 85§1	Italian
31 24-Nov-93 IV/32.031 IV/32.366 IV/32.404 OJL 306/50 of 11.12.93	Auditel	Agreement between Auditel's shareholders	Horizontal	Broadcasting	Market for the data concerning the audience of television broadcast	Mainly Italy but also other European countries	No	Notification and request for negative clearance or exemption + application by two firms according to Article 3§2 of Regulation 17 (Competitors)	Notification on 15.09.86 Complaints on 11.06.87 and on 07.08.89 (10 months) Co.'s decision to start procedure on 07.10.91 (2 years+2 months) Decision 24.11.93 (2 years+1 month) **5 years+1 month**		Infringement of 85§1 by a clause that has been removed + negative clearance for the agreements	Italian
32 21-Dec-93 IV/29.420 OJL 20/15 of 25.01.94	Grundig's EEC selective distribution system	Standard selective distribution agreement	Vertical	Electronics (Electrical machines)	Consumer electronics equipment	Community as a whole	No	Application by Grundig for the extension of exemption	Application for extension of exemption on 12.01.89 Communication on 17.07.92 (3 years+6 months) Decision on 21.12.93 (1 year+5 months) **4 years+11 months**		Renewal of exemption until 28.09.99 (but conditions)	German

Reference	Name of the case/concerned firms	Description of agreement	Type	Economic sector	Relevant market	Geographic market	Non EU firms	Starting point	Length of procedure	Crt	Taken decision	Nationalities
33 14-Jan-92 IV/33.100 OJL 37/16 of 14.02.92	A large number of Insurance companies (Assurpol)	Rules of the reinsurance pool	Horizontal	Insurance	Contracts for the covering of environmental risks	France, DOM-TOM and Monaco	No	Notification of agreement by Assurpol	Notification on 17.02.89 Communication on 19.07.91 (2 years + 5 months) Decision on 14.01.92 (6 months) **2 years+11 months**		Exemption condition	Mostly French
34 18-Mar-92 IV/32.290 OJL 131/32 of 16.05.92	Newitt vs. Dunlop Slazenger Int., All weather sports and Pinguin	Export ban	Vertical Exclusive distribution	Sports goods (rubber)	Mainly tennis and squash balls	Netherlands	No	Complaint from Newitt (distributor/competitor)	Complaint on 18.03.87 Decision on 18.03.92 **5 years**	Appeal for annulment Case T-43/92 Action dismissed	Infringement + fine 5 million ECU for DSI and 150,000 ECU for AWS. Infringement for Pinguin	English and Dutch
35 05-Feb-92 IV/31.571 IV/32.572 IV/32.571 OJL 92/1 of 07.04.92	SPO (association of undertakings in the building and construction industry)	Price-fixing agreement and coordination of behaviour	Horizontal	Building and construction		Mostly Netherlands	No	Notification by SPO Complaints by municipality of Rotterdam (customer)	Co.'s own initiated proceeding Notification on 13.01.88 Complaint lodged on 26.07.89 Decision on 05.02.92 **4 years+1 month**		Infringement + fines	Dutch
36 17-Feb-92 IV/31.446 IV/31.370 OJL 68/19 of 13.03.92	UK Agricultural Tractor Registration Exchange 8 manufacturers and importers of agricultural machinery (Ford, Massey-Ferguson Case. John. Renault, Watveare, Fiat, Same-Lamborghini)	Information exchange agreement	Horizontal	Agricultural machinery	The market for tractor	United Kingdom	No	Notification by the Agricultural engineers association Ltd.	Co.'s own initiated proceeding on 28.10.84 after complaints Notification on 04.01.88 Decision on 17.02.92 **7 years+4 months (notification: 4 years+1 month)**	Appeal for annulment Cases T-34/92 and T-35/92 Action dismissed	Infringement	Mostly European

Reference	Name of the case/concerned firms	Description of agreement	Type	Economic sector	Relevant market	Geographic market	Non EU firms	Starting point	Length of procedure	Crt	Taken decision	Nationalities
37 26-Feb-92 *IV/33.544* OJL 96/34 of 10.04.92	British Midland vs. Aer Lingus	One condition of an agreement on tariff consultation was not respected by Aer Lingus	Horizontal	Air transport	Provision and sales of air transport between Dublin and London (Heathrow)	Dublin-Heathrow route	No	Complaint lodged by British Midland (competitor)	Complaint on 26.04.90 Decision on 26.02.92 **1 year+10 months**		Infringement	British and Irish
38 25-Mar-92 *IV/30.717/4* OJL 95/50 of 09.04.92	Helsinki agreement between the groupement français des cartes bancaires (CB) and Eurochèque int.	Price-fixing agreement	Horizontal	Banking	Foreign Eurochèques drawn in the retail sector in France	France	No	Notification by the groupement français des cartes bancaires	Notification on 16.07.90 Decision on 25.03.92 **4 years** (it really started in 1988 following some complaints)	Banks asked for annulment Cases T-39/92 and T-40/92 Articles 1 and 3 cancelled for Eurochèque. Fine lowered for CB	Infringement + fine for CB and Eurochèque	French
39 01-Apr-92 *IV/32.450* OJL 134/1 of 18.05.92	French-West African shipowner's committees	Erection of barriers to entry	Horizontal	Maritime transport	Services provided by liner vessels for the transport of general cargo			Complaint under Article 10 of Regulation 4056/86 (competitor)	Complaint on 10.07.87 and 20.07.87 Decision 01.04.92 **4 years+9 months**		Infringement + fines	
40 15-Jul-92 *IV/32.725* OJL 233/27 of 15.08.92	Viho vs. Parker Pen	Export ban	Vertical: Exclusive distribution	Office equipment	Writing utensils manufactured and distributed by Parker (except pencils and technical drawing instruments)	Netherlands	No	Complaint lodged by Viho (distributor/competitor)	Complaint on 19.05.88 Decision on 15.07.92 **4 years+2 months**	Appeal for annulment Case T-77/92 Action dismissed	Infringement + fine to Herlitz and Parker	British, Italian, German and Dutch
41 24-Jul-92 *IV/33.542* OJL 236/11 of 19.08.92	Givenchy	Standard selective distribution agreement	Vertical distribution	Cosmetics (Chemical)	Luxury cosmetic products EEC		No	Notification by Givenchy in order to obtain an exemption	Notification on 19.03.90 Communication on 08.10.91 (1 year+5 months) Decision on 24.07.92 (9 months) **2 years+2 months**	YES by Kruidvat	Exemption until 31.05.97	French

Reference	Name of the case/ concerned firms	Description of agreement	Type	Economic sector	Relevant market	Geographic market	Non EU firms	Starting point	Length of procedure	Crt	Taken decision	Nationalities
42 27-Jul-92 IV/32.800 IV/33.335 OJL 235/9 of 18.08.92	Quantel international continuum vs. Quantel SA	Market-sharing agreement	Horizontal	Laser products (Electrical products)	Pulsed solid-state and dye lasers for scientific research	EEC	Yes	Complaint lodged by Quantel International (subsidiary)	Complaint on 20.07.88 Notification on 17.10.89 Decision on 27.07.92 **4 years**		Infringement by QSA	French and American
43 30-Jul-92 IV/33.494 OJL 246/37 of 27.08.92	Scottish Salmon Board	Price-fixing agreement	Horizontal	Pisciculture (Food and beverage)	Farmed salmon		Yes	Decision of the Commission to start a procedure (anti-dumping procedure)	Co.'s own procedure on 20.03.90 Decision on 30.07.92 **2 years+4 months**		Infringement	British and Norwegian
44 27-Oct-92 IV/33.378 IV/33.384 OJL 326/31 of 12.11.92	Distribution of package tours during the 1990 world cup	Exclusive distribution agreement	Vertical	Distribution of tickets for a sporting event	Package tours to World Cup 90 in Italy	Stadia in Italy	No	Application made by Pauwels Travel (distributor/ competitor)	Complaint on 28.11.89 Decision on 27.10.92 **3 years+1 month**		Infringement	Italian and Belgian
45 10-Nov-92 IV/33.440 IV/33.486 OJL 116/21 of 12.05.93	Warner Lambert, Gillette and others BIC, Gillette and others	Commercial cooperation	Horizontal	Metal products	Wet-shaving market			Complaints by Warner Lambert and BIC (competitors)	Complaint on 12.02.90 and 14.03.90 Notification on 23.02.90 Decision on 10.11.92 **2 years + 9 months**		Infringement	
46 25-Nov-92 IV/33.585 OJL 366/47 of 15.12.92	Distribution of railways tickets by travel agents	Agreement between railway companies to set conditions for the appointment of travel agents selling train tickets + joint fixing of the commission rates	Horizontal	Distribution of railway tickets by travel agents	Railway tickets		EEC	Co.'s own initiated proceedings	Co.'s own initiated proceeding opened on 05.06.90 Statement of objections sent on 10.10.91 Decision on 25.11.92 **2 years+5 years**		Infringement + fine	All Member States

Reference	Name of the case/concerned firms	Description of agreement	Type	Economic sector	Relevant market	Geographic market	Non EU firms	Starting point	Length of procedure	Crt	Taken decision	Nationalities
47 04-Dec-92 IV/32.797 IV/32.798 OJL 4/26 08.01.93	Lloyd's underwriters' association (LUA) and the Institute of London Underwriters (ILU)	Agreement on technical modalities for the renewal of insurance policies (mainly)	Horizontal	Insurance	Marine hull insurance	World	No	Notification of the agreement	Notification on 07.06.89 Communication on 08.04.92 (2 years + 10 months) Decision on 04.12.92 (8 months) **3 years+6 months**		Negative clearance	United Kingdom
48 15-Dec-92 IV/31.400 OJL 20/1 of 28.01.93	Ford Agricultural	Export ban	Vertical	Agricultural machinery	Tractors for agricultural use	EEC	Yes	The Commission received several complaints (competitors/ distribution)	Statement of objection sent on 17.05.90 Decision on 15.12.92 **2 years+7 months**		Infringement	American
49 21-Dec-92 IV/33.031 OJL 20/10 of 28.01.93	Fiat-Hitachi	Setting of a joint venture	Horizontal	Earth-moving machinery	Hydraulic excavators of between 10.5 and 45 tonnes	Western Europe, Mediterranean basin and Africa	Yes	Notification of the agreement	Notification on 23.12.88 Communication on 07.08.91 (2 years + 9 months) Decision on 21.12.92 (1 year+4 months) **3 years +1 month**		Exemption until 31.12.2001	Italian and Japanese
50 22-Dec-92 IV/33.151 IV/33.997 OJL 50/14 of 02.03.93	Jahrhundert-Vertrag General Association of the coalmining industry (GVSt), Association of German Public Electricity supply industry (VDEW) and the Association of industrial producers of electricity (VIK)	Supply agreement	Vertical	Coal-mining and electricity production	Electricity generation and distribution	Germany	No	Notification of the agreements	Notification on 01.06.89 Communication on 29.06.90 (1 year) Communication on 30.04.91 (8 months) Decision on 22.12.92 (1 year+8 months) **3 years+4 months**		Exemption on conditions	German

Reference	Name of the case/ concerned firms	Description of agreement	Type	Economic sector	Relevant market	Geographic market	Non EU firms	Starting point	Length of procedure	Crt	Taken decision	Nationalities
51 23-Dec-92 IV/32.745 OJL 20/23 of 28.01.93	British Telecommunications plc. Société européenne des satellites and BT Astra SA	Setting of a joint venture	Horizontal	Telecommunications	2 markets: Provision of satellite transponder capacity for the distribution of television channels and uplink services	EEC	No	Notifications of agreements	Notification on 03.06.88 Decision on 23.12.92 **4 years+6 months**		Infringement	Luxembourg British
52 23-Dec-92 IV/33.814 OJL 20/14 of 28.01.93	Ford/Volkswagen	Setting of a joint venture	Horizontal	Car market	Multi-purpose vehicle	EEC	Yes	Notification of the agreement	Notification on 04.02.91 Communication on 13.07.91 (5 months) Decision on 23.12.92 (1 year+5 months) **1 year+10 months**		Exemption on conditions	American and German
53 23-Dec-92 IV/31.533 IV/34.072 OJL 183/1 of 26.07.93	Schöller Lebensmittel GmbH & Co. KG (SLG)	Exclusive distribution agreement	Vertical	Food market	Impulse and catering ice-cream	Germany	No	Complaint lodged by Mars GmbH (competitor)	Notification by Schöller on 07.05.85 Comfort letter on 20.09.85 Complaint lodged on 18.09.91 Decision on 23.12.92 **1 year+3 months**		Infringement	German
54 23-Dec-92 IV/34.072 OJL 183/19 of 26.07.93	Langnese-Iglo GmbH	Exclusive distribution agreement	Vertical	Food market	Impulse and catering ice-cream	Germany	No	Complaint lodged by Mars GmbH (competitor)	Complaint lodged on 18.09.91 Decision on 23.12.92 **1 year+3 months**	Langnese and Iglo applied for annulment Cases T-7/93R and T-9/93R Action dismissed	Infringement	German
55 23-Dec-92 IV/32.448 IV/32.450 OJL 34/20 of 10.02.93	CEWAL	Erection of barriers to entry	Horizontal	Maritime transport				Complaint lodged by the Danish Shipowners Association and the Danish Government	Complaint on 10.07.87 and 20.07.87 Decision 23.12.92 **5 years+5 months**		Infringement + fines	

Reference	Name of the case/concerned firms	Description of agreement	Type	Economic sector	Relevant market	Geographic market	Non EU firms	Starting point	Length of procedure	Crt	Taken decision	Nationalities
56 16-Jan-91 IV/32.732 OJL 28/32 of 02.02.91	Ijsselcentrale and others	Export and import ban	Horizontal	Electricity generation	Electricity generation and distribution	Netherlands	No	Application made by some firms pursuant to Article 3 of Regulation 17 (Complaint) (customer)	Complaint on 25.05.88 Decision on 16.01.91 **2 years+8 months**	Case T-16/91	Infringement of 85§1	Dutch
57 15-Feb-91 IV/31.559 OJL 60/19 of 07.03.91	SIPPA (association in the paper industry in connection with trade events)	General regulation of SIPPA	Horizontal	Trade events in the paper industry	Paper products presented in exhibitions	France	No	Notification and application for negative clearance	Notification on 12.06.85 Communication on 11.09.90 (5 years+3 months) Decision on 15.02.91 (5 months) **5 years+8 months**		85§1 inapplicable from 19.04.90 to 18.04.00	French
58 19-Feb-91 IV/32.524 OJL 63/32 of 09.03.91	Screensport vs. EBU	Setting of the Eurosport joint venture (signed between 16 members of the EBU)	Horizontal	Broadcasting	Commercial transnational satellite television sport channel services	Community as a whole	No	Complaint lodged by Screensport (competitor)	Complaint on 17.12.87 Co.'s decision to start procedure on 05.12.88 (1 year) Notification on 17.01.89 (1 month) Decision on 19.02.91 (2 years+1 month) **3 years+2 months**		Infringement of 85§1	European
59 30-Apr-91 IV/33.473 OJL 178/31 of 06.07.91	Scottish Nuclear, Nuclear Energy Agreement	Supply agreement	Vertical	Electricity	Production, supply and distribution of electricity	United Kingdom	No	Notification	Notification on 27.02.90 Communication on 27.09.90 (7 months) Decision on 30.04.91 (7 months) **1 year+2 months**		Exemption from 27.02.90 to 31.03.05	Scottish

Reference	Name of the case/concerned firms	Description of agreement	Type	Economic sector	Relevant market	Geographic market	Non EU firms	Starting point	Length of procedure	Crt	Taken decision	Nationalities
60 15-May-91 IV/32.186 OJL.185/23 of 11.07.91	Gosme/Martell-DMP	Export ban	Vertical	Wines and spirits	Martell Cognac	France and Italy	No	Application by Gosme pursuant to Article 3§1 of Regulation 17 (distributor/competitor)	Complaint on 25.11.86 Co.'s decision to start procedure on 26.04.89 (2 years+5 months) Decision on 15.05.91 (2 years+1 months) **4 years+6 months**		Infringement + fine for Martell and DMP	French
61 05-Jun-91 IV/32.879 OJL.287/39 of 17.10.91	Viho/Toshiba	Export ban	Vertical	Office equipment	Electrostatic and plain paper copying machines distributed by Toshiba	EEC	Yes	Application by Viho pursuant to Article 3§1 of Regulation 17 (distributor/competitor)	Complaint on 06.05.88 Co.'s decision to start procedure on 21.03.90 (1 year+10 months) Decision on 05.06.91 (1 year+3 months) **3 years+1 month**		Infringement + fines for Toshiba	Japanese and Dutch
62 30-Jul-91 IV/32.659 OJL.258/18 of 16.09.91	IATA Passenger Agency Programme	IATA's resolutions concerning travel agencies	Horizontal	Air transport	Air travel agency services	EEC		Application for negative clearance and notification for exemption pursuant to Articles 2 and 4 of Regulation 17	Notification on 21.03.88 Communication on 23.10.90 (2 years+7 months) Decision on 30.07.91 (9 months) **3 years+4 months**		Exemption from 21.03.88 to 20.03.98	
63 30-Jul-91 IV/32.792 OJL.258/29 of 16.09.91	IATA Cargo Agency Programme	IATA's resolutions concerning cargo agencies	Horizontal	Air transport	Air freight cargo agency services	EEC		Application for negative clearance and notification for exemption pursuant to Articles 2 and 4 of Regulation 17	Notification on 07.07.88 Communication on 20.12.90 (2 years+5 months) Decision on 30.07.91 (8 months) **3 years+1 month**		Exemption from 07.07.88 to 06.07.98	

Reference	Name of the case/ concerned firms	Description of agreement	Type	Economic sector	Relevant market	Geographic market	Non EU firms	Starting point	Length of procedure	Crt	Taken decision	Nationalities
64 18-Oct-91 *IV/32.737* OJ L 306/22 of 07.11.91	Eirpage	Setting of a joint venture	Horizontal	Telecommunications	Interconnected paging service	Ireland	No	Application for negative clearance and notification pursuant to Articles 2 and 4 of Regulation 17	Notification on 17.05.88 Communication on 24.11.90 (2 years+6 months) Decision on 18.10.91 (11 months) **3 years+5 months**		Exemption from 26.03.90 to 31.07.01 (but under some conditions)	Irish
65 04-Dec-91 *IV/33.157* OJ L 66/1 of 11.03.92	ECO System/Peugeot	Refusal of supply	Vertical	Motor industry	Peugeot Talbot cars	France	No	Complaint lodged by ECO System (application pursuant to Article 3 of Regulation 17) (distributor/ competitor)	Complaint on 19.04.89 Co.'s decision to start procedure on 27.11.89 (7 months) Decision on 04.12.91 (2 years+1 month) **2 years+8 months**	Peugeot applied for annulment Case T-9/92 Action dismissed	Infringement of 85§1 and of Regulation 123/85 Removal of benefit of exemption under 123/85 if Peugeot does not withdraw the circular within two months (Article 10§2 of Regulation 123/85)	French, Belgian and Luxembourgese
66 16-Dec-91 *IV/33.142* OJ L 12/24 of 18.01.92	Yves Saint Laurent perfumes	Standard selective distribution agreement	Vertical	Cosmetics	Luxury cosmetic products	EEC	No	Application for negative clearance and notification pursuant to Articles 2 and 4 of Regulation 17	Notification on 06.07.89 Communication on 20.12.90 (1 year+5 months) Decision on 16.12.91 (1 year) **2 years+5 months**		85§1 inapplicable from 01.06.91 to 31.05.97 (but under some conditions)	French
67 12-Jan-90 *IV/32.006* OJ L 32/19 of 03.02.90	Alcatel Espace/ANT Nachrichtentechnik	Cooperation agreement	Horizontal	Telecommunications	Satellites and components	EEC	No	Application for negative clearance and notification for exemption	Notification on 28.07.86 Communication on 15.07.89 (3 years) Decision on 12.01.90 (6 months) **3 years+6 months**		Exemption from 28.07.86 to 31.12.96	French and German

Reference	Name of the case/concerned firms	Description of agreement	Type	Economic sector	Relevant market	Geographic market	Non EU firms	Starting point	Length of procedure	Crt	Taken decision	Nationalities
68 23-Mar-90 IV/32.736 OJL 100/32 of 20.04.90	Moosehead/Whitbread	Exclusive licensing agreement	Vertical	Beverage brewing sector	Moosehead beer	United Kingdom	Yes	Notification according to Article 4 of Regulation 17	Notification on 02.06.88 Communication on 15.07.89 (1 year) Decision on 23.03.90 (8 months) **1 year+8 months**		Exemption from 03.06.88 to 02.06.98	Canadian and British
69 13-Jul-90 IV/32.009 OJL 209/15 of 08.08.90	Elopak/Metal Box – Odin	Setting of a joint venture	Horizontal	Packages (paper industry)	Product is not yet developed but the project concerns a container with a carton base and a separate closure that can be filled by an aseptic process with UHT processed food	EEC	Yes	Notification and application for negative clearance	Notification on 01.08.86 Communication on 13.08.89 (3 years) Decision on 13.07.90 (11 months) **3 years+11 months**		Negative clearance	Norwegian and British
70 27-Jul-90 IV/32.688 OJL 228/31 of 22.08.90	Konsortium ECR 900 – AEG/Alcatel/ Oy Nokia	Cooperation agreement	Horizontal	Telecommunications	Digital cellular mobile telephone system	EEC	No	Notification of the agreement	Notification on 07.04.88 Communication on 07.12.89 (1 year+8 months) Decision on 27.07.90 (7 months) **2 years+3months**		Negative clearance	French, German and Finnish
71 15-Oct-90 IV/32.681 OJL 299/64 of 30.10.90	Cekacan – Akerlund & Rausing (A&R)/ Europa Carton Aktiengesellschaft (ECA)	Setting of a joint venture	Horizontal	Packages	All packaging for dry oxygen sensitive food stuffs	Germany, France, Italy, Netherlands, Belgium, Luxemburg, Greece. Spain, Portugal, Austria and Switzerland	No	Notification and application for negative clearance	Notification on 28.03.88 Communication on 21.11.89 (1 year+8 months) Decision on 15.10.90 (11 months) **2 years+7 months**		Exemption from 27.04.89 to 26.04.99	Swedish and German
72 28-Nov-90 IV/32.877 OJL 351/46 of 15.12.90	Bayer Dental	Export ban	Vertical	Dental products	Dental products	Germany	No	Decision of the Commission to initiate proceeding upon its own initiative	Request for information on 15.09.88 Co.'s decision to start proceedings on 06.03.89 Decision on 28.11.90 **2 years+2 months**		Infringement (in the past)	German

Reference	Name of the case/concerned firms	Description of agreement	Type	Economic sector	Relevant market	Geographic market	Non EU firms	Starting point	Length of procedure	Crt	Taken decision	Nationalities
73 12-Dec-90 IV/32.363 OJL 19/25 of 25.01.91	KSB/Goulds/Lowarra/ITT	R&D and production cooperation agreement	Horizontal	Pumps (machine building)	Water pumps, more precisely single stage, single flow radial centrifugal pump made from chrome nickel steel	EEC	Yes	Notification and application for negative clearance	Notification on 05.06.87 Communication on 12.10.89 (2 years+4 months) Decision on 12.12.90 (1 year+2 months) **3 years+6 months**		Exemption from 22.07.87 to 31.05.93 but under condition and the joint exploitation of results won't be considered as needed after end of exemption	German, Italian and American
74 19-Dec-90 IV/32.595 OJL 20/42 of 26.01.91	D'Ieteren motor oils	Standard form agreement with dealers	Vertical			Belgium	No	Notification and application for negative clearance	Notification on 12.02.88 Communication on 13.05.89 (1 year+3 months) Decision on 19.12.90 (1 year+7 months) **2 years+10 months**		Negative clearance does not fulfil the conditions for application of 85§1	Belgian
75 19-Dec-90 IV/33.133A OJL 152/1 of 15.06.91	Soda-ash – Solvay/ICI	Market-sharing agreement	Horizontal	Chemical	Synthetic soda-ash	EEC	No	Commission decision to open procedure under Article 3 of Regulation 17	Inspections carried out in March 1989 Co.'s decision to initiate proceeding on 19.02.90 Decision on 19.12.90 **1 year+9 months**		Infringement + fine	Belgian and British
76 19-Dec-90 IV/33.133B OJL 152/16 of 15.06.91	Soda-ash – Solvay/CFK	Market-sharing agreement	Horizontal	Chemical	Synthetic soda-ash	Germany	No	Commission decision to open procedure under Article 3 of Regulation 17	**1 year+9 months**		Infringement + fine	Belgian and German
77 19-Dec-90 IV/33.106 OJL 152/54 of 15.06.91	ANSAC (American Natural Soda-ash Corporation)	Arrangements between ANSAC members for selling natural dense soda-ash in the Community	Horizontal	Chemical	Natural dense soda-ash	EEC	Yes	Notification and application for negative clearance	Notification on 09.12.88 Co.'s decision to initiate proceeding on 03.07.89 (8 months) Decision on 19.12.90 (1 year+5 months) **2 years+1 month**		Infringement	American

Reference	Name of the case/concerned firms	Description of agreement	Type	Economic sector	Relevant market	Geographic market	Non EU firms	Starting point	Length of procedure	Crt	Taken decision	Nationalities
78 09-Jun-89 IV/27.958 OJL 190/22 of 05.07.89	National Sulphuric Acid Association	Rules of the joint buying pool	Horizontal	Chemical	Sulphur	United Kingdom	No	Application pursuant to Article 8§2 of Regulation 17 for the renewal of exemption	Communication on 23.06.88 Decision on 05.07.89 **1 year+1 month**		Exemption extended until 31.12.98 under the same conditions of the previous decision	British
79 12-Jul-89 IV/30.566 OJL 226/25 of 03.08.89	UIP – United International Pictures	Setting of a joint venture	Horizontal	Film production and distribution	Primarily the market in which distributors compete with each other to obtain the best terms and viewing slots from exhibitors of these films	EEC	Yes	Notification and application for negative clearance	Notification on 11.02.82 Communication from Co.'s on 20.06.85 to parties in order to change some clauses Audition on 29 and 30.01.86 in Dec. 87 and July 88 some modifications described Communication on 10.11.88 Decision on 12.07.88 **7 years+5 months**		Exemption from 27.07.88 to 26.07.93 under some obligations	American and Dutch
80 19-Jul-89 IV/31.499 OJL 253/1 of 30.08.89	Dutch banks	Regulations issued by Dutch banking associations	Horizontal	Banking		EEC	No	Notification and application for negative clearance	Notification on 19.03.85, on 22.10.86, on 27.11.86 and on 04.12.87 Communication on 05.11.88 (3 years+8 months) Decision on 19.07.89 (8 months) **4 years+4 months**		Negative clearance for some regulations, circulars and agreements Exemption for some circulars from 10.05.88 to 09.05.98 and obligation	Dutch
81 02-Aug-89 IV/31.553 OJL 260/1 of 06.09.89	Welded steel mesh	Price-fixing and market-sharing cartel	Horizontal	Steel industry	Welded steel mesh	Benelux, France, Netherlands and Germany	No	Proceeding initiated by Commission	Verifications on 06.11.85 Co.'s decision to initiate proceedings on 26.01.87 Decision on 02.08.89 **3 years+9 months**		Infringement + fines From 13.000 ECU to 4.500.000 ECU	French, German, Italian, Luxembourg and Belgian

Reference	Name of the case/ concerned firms	Description of agreement	Type	Economic sector	Relevant market	Geographic market	Non EU firms	Starting point	Length of procedure	Crt	Taken decision	Nationalities
82 15-May-89 *IV/31.734* OJL 284/36 of 03.10.89	Film purchases by German television stations	Exclusive right to broadcast	Vertical	Broadcasting	Feature films, television films and series (owned by MGM/UA)	Germany, Austria, Lichtenstein, Luxembourg and two other regions	Yes	Proceeding initiated by Commission Notification and application later	Commission's decision to initiate proceeding on 15.12.86 Notification on 02.12.88 Communication on 03.03.89 (4 months) Decision on 15.09.89 (6 months) **2 years+9 months**		Exemption from 03.02.89 until 02.02.99 Conditions	German, Dutch and American
83 13-Dec-89 *IV/32.026* OJL 21/71 of 26.01.90	Bayo-n-ox	Purchasing conditions (resell ban)	Vertical	Animal food industry	Feedingstuff additives 'Bayo-n-ox'	EEC	No	Proceeding initiated by Commission	Request for information in December 1987 Co.'s decision to initiate proceedings on 22.11.88 Decision on 13.12.89 **2 years**	Bayer lodged an appeal Case T-12/90	Infringement + fine of 500,000 ECU	German
84 14-Dec-89 *IV/32.202* OJL 18/35 of 23.01.90	APB (Association pharmaceutique belge)	Standard agreement for a quality label	Vertical	Pharmaceutical	Parapharmaceutical products	Belgium	No	Notification and application for negative clearance	Notification on 01.12.86 Communication on 16.08.89 (2 years+9 months) Decision on 14.12.89 (4 months) **3 years+1 month**		Negative clearance	Belgian
85 19-Dec-89 *IV/32.414* OJL 31/35 of 02.02.90	Sugar beet (Confédération des betteraviers belges. Société Générale de fabricants de sucre de Belgique et la Raffinerie Tirlemontoise)	Exclusivity agreement	Vertical	Agriculture and Food industry	Sugar beet	Belgium	No	Complaint lodged by 30 French sugar beet planters (suppliers)	Complaint in August 1986 Commission's decisions to initiate proceeding on 22.11.88 Decision on 19.12.89 (1 year+1 month) **3 years+4 months**		Infringement	Belgian and French

Reference	Name of the case/ concerned firms	Description of agreement	Type	Economic sector	Relevant market	Geographic market	Non EU firms	Starting point	Length of procedure	Crt	Taken decision	Nationalities
86 20-Dec-89 *IV/32.408* OJL 13/34 of 17.01.90	Technische Kontor für die Maschinen-B-U-Versicherung (TEKO)	Cooperation agreement	Horizontal	Insurance	Insurance against the operating losses due to machine breakings and satellite insurance	Mainly Germany	No	Notification and application for negative clearance	Notification on 11.08.87 Communication 08.08.89 (2 years) Decision on 20.12.89 (4 months) **2 years+4 months**		Exemption from 11.08.87 to 11.08.97	German
87 20-Dec-89 *IV/32.265* OJL 15/25 of 19.01.90	Concordato Italiano Incendio Rischi Industrial	Convention about the activities of the association	Horizontal	Insurance	Fire insurance for industrial risks	Italy	No	Notification and application for negative clearance	Notification on 04.02.88 Communication on 12.10.89 (1 year+8 months) Decision on 20.12.89 (2 months) **1 year+8 months**		Exemption from 04.02.88 to 03.02.98	Mainly Italian

Appendix 2
Legislation

Reproduced here are the full texts of Articles 85, 86 and 87 of the Treaty of Rome 1957 and Council Regulation No. 17 of 6 February 1962. For details of other relevant pieces of legislation, please see the DG-IV web site at:

http://www.europa.eu.int/en/comm/dgO4

Of most notable interest will be the pages relating to:

(a) Block exemptions of exclusive dealing agreements and franchising agreements (of particular relevance to Chapter 2).
(b) Block exemptions of specialization and research and development agreements (of particular relevance to Chapter 4).

1.   Treaty of Rome, Articles 85–87

Article 85

1. The following shall be prohibited as incompatible with the common market: all agreements between undertakings, decisions by associations of undertakings and concerted practices which may affect trade between Member States and which have as their object or effect the prevention, restriction or distortion of competition within the common market, and in particular those which:
   (a) directly or indirectly fix purchase or selling prices or any other trading conditions;
   (b) limit or control production markets, technical development or investment;

   (c) share markets or sources of supply;

   (d) apply dissimilar conditions to equivalent transactions with other trading parties, thereby placing them at a competitive disadvantage;

   (e) make the conclusion of contracts subject to acceptance by the other parties of supplementary obligations which, by their nature or according to commercial usage, have no connection with the subject of such contracts.

2. Any agreements or decisions prohibited pursuant to this Article shall be automatically void.

3. The provisions of paragraph 1 may, however, be declared inapplicable in the case of:

   – any agreement or category of agreements between undertakings;

   – any decision or category of decisions by associations of undertakings;

   – any concerted practice or category of concerted practices;

which contributes to improving the production or distribution of goods or to promoting technical or economic progress, while allowing consumers a fair share of the resulting benefit, and which does not:

   (a) impose on the undertakings concerned restrictions which are not indispensable to the attainment of these objectives;

   (b) afford such undertakings the possibility of eliminating competition in respect of a substantial part of the products in question.

Article 86

Any abuse by one or more undertakings of a dominant position within the common market or in a substantial part of it shall be prohibited as incompatible with the common market in so far as it may affect trade between Member States.

   Such abuse may, in particular, consist in:

   (a) directly or indirectly imposing unfair purchase or selling prices or other unfair trading conditions;

   (b) limiting production, markets or technical development to the prejudice of consumers;

   (c) applying dissimilar conditions to equivalent transactions with other trading parties, thereby placing them at a competitive disadvantage;

   (d) making the conclusion of contracts subject to acceptance by the other parties of supplementary obligations which, by their nature or according to commercial usage, have no connection with the subject of such contracts.

Article 87

1. Within three years of the entry into force of this Treaty the Council shall, acting unanimously on a proposal from the Commission and after consulting the European Parliament, adopt any appropriate regulations or directives to give effect to the principles set out in Articles 85 and 86.

   If such provisions have not been adopted within the period mentioned, they shall be laid down by the Council, acting by a qualified majority on a proposal from the Commission and after consulting the European Parliament.

2. The regulations or directives referred to in paragraph 1 shall be designed in particular:
   (a) to ensure compliance with the prohibitions laid down in Article 85(1) and in Article 86 by making provision for fines and periodic penalty payments;
   (b) to lay down detailed rules for the application of Article 85(3) taking into account the need to ensure effective supervision on the one hand, and to simplify administration to the greatest possible extent on the other;
   (c) to define, if need be, in the various branches of the economy, the scope of the provisions of Articles 85 and 86;
   (d) to define the respective functions of the Commission and of the Court of Justice in applying the provisions laid down in this paragraph;
   (e) to determine the relationship between national laws and the provisions contained in this section or adopted pursuant to this Article.

2. Regulation No.17 of the Council of 6 February 1962 First Regulation implementing Articles 85 and 86 of the Treaty (OJ No. 13, 21 February 1962, p. 204/162)

Amended by: Regulation No. 59 of the Council of 3 July 1962; Regulation (EEC) No. 118/63 of the Council of 5 November 1963; Regulation (EEC) No. 2822/71 of the Council of 20 December 1971: Council Regulation (EEC Euratom) No. 3308/80 of 16 December 1980.

Amended by: Act of Accession of Denmark, Ireland and the United Kingdom; Act of Accession of Greece; Act of Accession of Spain and Portugal: Act of Accession of Austria, Finland and Sweden, adapted by Decision 95/1/EC, Euratom, ECSC.

Article 1

Basic Provision

Without prejudice to Articles 6, 7 and 23 of this Regulation, agreements, decisions and concerted practices of the kind described in Article 85(1) of the Treaty and the abuse of a dominant position in the market, within the meaning of Article 86 of the Treaty, shall be prohibited no prior decision to that effect being required.

Article 2

Negative Clearance

Upon application by the undertakings or associations of undertakings concerned, the Commission may certify that, on the basis of the facts in its possession, there are no grounds under Article 85(1) or Article 86 of the Treaty for action on its part in respect of an agreement, decision or practice.

Article 3

Termination of Infringements

1. Where the Commission, upon application or upon its own initiative, finds that there is infringement of Article 85 or Article 86 of the Treaty, it may by decision require the undertakings or associations of undertakings concerned to bring such infringement to an end.

2. Those entitled to make application are:
   (a) Member States;
   (b) natural or legal persons who claim a legitimate interest.

3. Without prejudice to the other provisions of this Regulation, the Commission may, before taking a decision under paragraph 1, address to the undertakings or associations of undertakings concerned recommendations for termination of the infringement.

Article 4

Notification of New Agreements, Decisions and Practices

Agreements, decisions and concerted practices of the kind described in Article 85(1) of the Treaty which come into existence after the entry into force of this Regulation and in respect of which the parties seek application of Article 85(3) must be notified to the Commission. Until they have been notified, no decision in application of Article 85(3) may be taken.

Article 5

Notification of Existing Agreements, Decisions and Practices

1. Agreements, decisions and concerted practices of the kind described in Article 85(1) of the Treaty which are in existence at the date of entry into force of this Regulation and in respect of which the parties seek application of Article 85(3) shall be notified to the Commission before 1 November 1962. However, notwithstanding the foregoing provisions, any agreements, decisions and concerted practices to which not more than two undertakings are party shall be notified before 1 February 1963.

2. Paragraph 1 shall not apply to agreements decisions or concerted practices falling within Article 4(2); these may be notified to the Commission.

Article 6

Decisions Pursuant to Article 85(3)

1. Whenever the Commission takes a decision pursuant to Article 85(3) of the Treaty, it shall specify therein the date from which the decision shall take effect. Such a date shall not be earlier than the date of notification.

2. The second sentence of paragraph 1 shall not apply to agreements, decisions or concerted practices falling within Article 4(2) and Article 5(2), nor to those falling within Article 5(1) which have been notified within the time limit specified in Article 5(1).

Article 7

Special Provisions for Existing Agreements, Decisions and Practices

1. Where agreements, decisions and concerted practices in existence at the date of entry into force of this regulation and notified within the time limits specified in Article 5(1) do not satisfy the requirements of Article 85(3) of the Treaty and the undertakings or associations of undertakings concerned cease to give effect to them or modify them in such a manner that they no longer fall within the prohibition contained in Article 85(1) or that they satisfy the requirements of Article 85(3) the prohibition contained in Article 85(1) shall apply only for a period fixed by the Commission. A decision by the Commission pursuant to the foregoing sentence shall not apply as against undertakings and associations of undertakings which did not expressly consent to the notification.

2. Paragraph 1 shall apply to agreements, decisions and concerted practices falling within Article 4(2) which are in existence at the date of entry into force of this Regulation if they are notified before 1 January 1967.

Article 8

Duration and Revocation of Decisions under Article 85(3)

1. A decision in application of Article 85(3) of the Treaty shall be issued for a specified period and conditions and obligations may be attached thereto.

2. A decision may on application be renewed if the requirements of Article 85(3) of the Treaty continue to be satisfied.

3. The Commission may revoke or amend its decision or prohibit specified acts by the parties:
    (a) where there has been a change in any of the facts which were basic to the making of the decision;
    (b) where the parties commit a breach of any obligation attached to the decision;
    (c) where the decision is based on incorrect information or was induced by deceit;
    (d) where the parties abuse the exemption from the provisions of Article 85(1) of the Treaty granted to them by the decision.

In Cases to which subparagraphs (b), (c) or (d) apply, the decision may be revoked with retroactive effect.

Article 9

Powers

1. Subject to review of its decision by the Court of Justice, the Commission shall have sole power to declare Article 85(1) inapplicable pursuant to Article 85(3) of the Treaty.

2. The Commission shall have power to apply Article 85(1) and Article 86 of the Treaty; this power may be exercised notwithstanding that the time limits specified in Article 5(1) and in Article 7(2) relating to notification have not expired.

3. As long as the Commission has not initiated any procedure under Articles 2, 3 or 6, the authorities of the Member States shall remain competent to apply Article 85(1) and Article 86 in accordance with Article 88 of the Treaty; they shall remain competent in this respect notwithstanding that the time limits specified in Article 5(1)and in Article 7(2) relating to notification have not expired.

Article 10

Liaison with the Authorities of the Member States

1. The Commission shall forthwith transmit to the competent authorities of the Member States a copy of the applications and notifications together with copies of the most important documents lodged with the Commission for the purpose of establishing the existence of infringements of Articles 85 or 86 of the Treaty or of obtaining negative clearance or a decision in application of Article 85(3).

2. The Commission shall carry out the procedure set out in paragraph 1 in close and constant liaison with with the competent authorities of the Member States; such authorities shall have the right to express their views upon that procedure.

3. An Advisory Committee on Restrictive Practices and Monopolies shall be consulted prior to the taking of any decision following upon a procedure under paragraph 1, and of any decision concerning the renewal,

amendment or revocation of a decision pursuant to Article 85(3) of the Treaty.

4. The Advisory Committee shall be composed of officials competent in the matter of restrictive practices and monopolies. Each Member State shall appoint an official to represent it who, if prevented from attending, may be replaced by another official.

5. The consultation shall take place at a joint meeting convened by the Commission; such a meeting shall be held not earlier than fourteen days after dispatch of the notice convening it. The notice shall, in respect of each case to be examined, be accompanied by a summary of the case together with an indication of the most important documents, and a preliminary draft decision.

6. The Advisory Committee may deliver an opinion notwithstanding that some of its members or their alternates are not present. A report of the outcome of the consultative proceedings shall be annexed to the draft decision. It shall not be made public.

Article 11

Requests for Information

1. In carrying out the duties assigned to it by Article 89 and by provisions adopted under Article 87 of the Treaty, the Commission may obtain all necessary information from the Governments and competent authorities of the Member States and from undertakings and associations of undertakings.

2. When sending a request for information to an undertaking or association of undertakings, the Commission shall at the same time forward a copy of the request to the competent authority of the Member State in whose territory the seat of the undertaking or association of undertakings is situated.

3. In its request the Commission shall state the legal basis and the purpose of the request and also the penalties provided for in Article 15(1) (b) for supplying incorrect information.

4. The owners of the undertakings or their representatives and, in the case of legal persons, companies or firms, or of associations having no

legal personality, the persons authorised to represent them by law or by their constitution shall supply the information requested.

5. Where an undertaking or association of undertakings does not supply the information requested within the time limit fixed by the Commission, or supplies incomplete information, the Commission shall by decision require the information to be supplied The decision shall specify what information is required, fix an appropriate time limit within which it is to be supplied and indicate the penalties provided for in Article 15(1) (b) and Article 15(1) (c) and the right to have the decision reviewed by the Court of Justice.

6. The Commission shall at the same time forward a copy of its decision to the competent authority of the Member State in whose territory the seat of the undertaking or association of undertakings is situated.

Article 12

Inquiry into Sectors of the Economy

1. If in any sector of the economy the trend of trade between Member States, price movements, inflexibility of prices or other circumstances suggest that in the economic sector concerned competition is being restricted or distorted within the common market, the Commission may decide to conduct a general inquiry into that economic sector and in the course thereof may request undertakings in the sector concerned to supply the information necessary for giving effect to the principles formulated in Articles 85 and 86 of the Treaty and for carrying out the duties entrusted to the Commission.

2. The Commission may in particular request every undertaking or association of undertakings in the economic sector concerned to communicate to it all agreements, decisions and concerted practices which are exempt from notification by virtue of Article 4(2) and Article 5(2)

3. When making inquiries pursuant to paragraph 2, the Commission shall also request undertakings or groups of undertakings whose size suggests that they occupy a dominant position within the common market or a substantial part thereof to supply to the Commission such particulars of the structure of the undertakings and of their behaviour as are requisite to an appraisal of their position in the light of Article 86 of the Treaty.

4. Article 10(3) to (6) and Articles 11, 13 and 14 shall apply correspondingly.

Article 13

Investigations by the Authorities of the Member States

1. At the request of the Commission, the competent authorities of the Member States shall undertake the investigations which the Commission considers to be necessary under Article 14(1), or which it has ordered by decision pursuant to Article 14(3). The officials of the competent authorities of the Member States responsible for conducting these investigations shall exercise their powers upon production of an authorisation in writing issued by the competent authority of the Member State in whose territory the investigation is to be made. Such authorisation shall specify the subject matter and purpose of the investigation.

2. If so requested by the Commission or by the competent authority of the Member State in whose territory the investigation is to be made, the officials of the Commission may assist the officials of such authorities in carrying out their duties.

Article 14

Investigating Powers of the Commission

1. In carrying out the duties assigned to it by Article 89 and by provisions adopted under Article 87 of the Treaty the Commission may undertake all necessary investigations into undertakings and associations of undertakings. To this end the officials authorised by the Commission are empowered:
   (a) to examine the books and other business records;
   (b) to take copies of or extracts from the books and business records;
   (c) to ask for oral explanations on the spot;
   (d) to enter any premises; land and means of transport of undertakings.

2. The officials of the Commission authorised for the purpose of these investigations shall exercise their powers upon production of an authorisation in writing specifying the subject matter and purpose of the investigation and the penalties provided for in Article 15(1) (c) in cases where production of the required books or other business records is incomplete. In good time before the investigation, the Commission shall inform the competent authority of the Member State in whose territory the same is to be made of the investigation and of the identity of the authorised officials.

3. Undertakings and associations of undertakings shall submit to investigations ordered by decision of the Commission. The decision shall specify the subject matter and purpose of the investigation, appoint the date on which it is to begin and indicate the penalties provided for in Article 15(1) (c) and Article 16(1) (d) and the right to have the decision reviewed by the Court of Justice.

4. The Commission shall take decisions referred to in paragraph 3 after consultation with the competent authority of the Member State in whose territory the investigation is to be made.

5. Officials of the competent authority of the Member State in whose territory the investigation is to be made may, at the request of such authority or of the Commission, assist the officials of the Commission in carrying out their duties.

6. Where an undertaking opposes an investigation ordered pursuant to this Article, the Member State concerned shall afford the necessary assistance to the officials authorised by the Commission to enable them to make their investigation. Member States shall, after consultation with the Commission, take the necessary measures to this end before 1 October 1962.

Article 15

Fines

1. The Commission may by decision impose on undertakings or associations of undertakings fines of 100 to 5000 ECU where, intentionally or negligently:
   (a) they supply incorrect or misleading information in an application pursuant to Article 2 or in a notification pursuant to Articles 4 or 5; or
   (b) they supply incorrect information in response to a request made pursuant to Article 11(3) or (5) or to Article 12, or do not supply information within the time limit fixed by a decision taken under Article 11(5); or
   (c) they produce the required books or other business records in incomplete form during investigations under Article 13 or 14, or refuse to submit to an investigation ordered by decision issued in implementation of Article 14(3).

2 The Commission may by decision impose on undertakings or associations of undertakings fines of 1000 to 1,000,000 ECU or a sum in excess thereof but not exceeding 10% of the turnover in the preceding business year of each of the undertakings participating in the infringement where, either intentionally or negligently:

(a) they infringe Article 85(1) or Article 86 of the Treaty, or

(b) they commit a breach of any obligation imposed pursuant to Article 8(1).

In fixing the amount of the fine, regard shall be had both to the gravity and to the duration of the infringement.

3. Article 10(3) to (6) shall apply.

4. Decisions taken pursuant to paragraphs 1 and 2 shall not be of a criminal law nature.

5. The fines provided for in paragraph 2 (a) shall not be imposed in respect of acts taking place:

(a) after notification to the Commission and before its decision in application of Article 85(3) of the Treaty, provided they fall within the limits of the activity described in the notification;

(b) before notification and in the course of agreements, decisions or concerted practices in existence at the of entry into force of this Regulation, provided that notification was effected within the time limits specified in Article 5(1) and Article 7(2).

6. Paragraph 5 shall not have effect where the Commission has informed the undertakings concerned that after preliminary examination it is of opinion that Article 85(1) of the Treaty applies and that application of Article 85(3) is not justified.

Article 16

Periodic Penalty Payments

1. The Commission may by decision impose on undertakings or associations of undertakings periodic penalty payments of 50 to 1000 ECU per day, calculated from the date appointed by the revision, in order to compel them:

(a) to put an end to an infringement of Article 85 or 86 of the Treaty, in accordance with a decision taken pursuant to Article 3 of this Regulation;

(b) to refrain from any act prohibited under Article 8(3);

(c) to supply complete and correct information which it has requested by decision taken pursuant to Article 11(5);

(d) to submit to an investigation which it has ordered by decision taken pursuant to Article 14 (3).

2. Where the undertakings or associations of under-takings have satisfied the obligation which it was the purpose of the periodic penalty payment to enforce, the Commission may fix the total amount of the periodic penalty payment at a lower figure than that which would arise under the original decision.

3. Articles 10 (3) to (6) shall apply.

Article 17

Review by the Court of Justice

The Court of Justice shall have unlimited jurisdiction within the meaning of Article 172 of the Treaty to review decisions whereby the Commission has fixed a fine or periodic penalty payment; it may cancel, reduce or increase the fine or periodic penalty payment imposed.

Article 18

Unit of Account

For the purposes of applying Articles 15 to 17 the unit of account shall be that adopted in drawing up the budget of the Community in accordance with Articles 207 and 209 of the Treaty.

Article 19

Hearing of the Parties and of Third Persons

1. Before taking decisions as provided for in Articles 2, 3, 6, 7, 8, 15 and 16, the Commission shall give the undertakings of associations of undertakings concerned the opportunity of being heard on the matters to which the Commission has taken objection.

2. If the Commission or the competent authorities of the Member States consider it necessary they may also hear other natural or legal persons.

Applications to be heard on the part of such persons shall, where they show a sufficient interest be granted.

3. Where the Commission intends to give negative clearance pursuant to Article 2 or take a decision in application of Article 85(3) of the Treaty, it shall publish a summary of the relevant application or notification and invite all interested third parties to submit their observations within a time limit which it shall fix being not less than one month. Publication shall have regard to the legitimate interest of undertakings in the protection of their business secrets.

Article 20

Professional Secrecy

1. Information acquired as a result of the application of Articles 11, 12, 13 and 14 shall be used only for the purpose of the relevant request or investigation.

2. Without prejudice to the provisions of Articles 19 and 21, the Commission and the competent authorities of the Member States, their officials and other servants shall not disclose information acquired by them as a result of the application of this Regulation and of the kind covered by the obligation of professional secrecy.

3. The provisions of paragraphs 1 and 2 shall not prevent publication of general information or surveys which do not contain information relating to particular undertakings or associations of undertakings.

Article 21

Publication of Decisions

1. The Commission shall publish the decisions which it takes pursuant to Articles 2, 3, 6, 7 and 8.

2. The publication shall state the names of the parties and the main content of the decision; it shall have regard to the legitimate interest of undertakings in the protection of their business secrets.

Article 22

Special Provisions

1. The Commission shall submit to the Council proposals for making certain categories of agreement, decision and concerted practice falling within Article 4(2) or Article 5(2) compulsorily notifiable under Article 4 or 5.

2. Within one year from the date of entry into force of this Regulation, the Council shall examine, on a proposal from the Commission, what special provisions might be made for exempting from the provisions of this Regulation agreements, decisions and concerted practices falling within Article 4(2) or Article 5(2).

Article 23

Transitional Provisions Applicable to Decisions of Authorities of the Member State

1. Agreements, decisions and concerted practices of the kind described in Article 85(1) of the Treaty to which, before the entry into force of this Regulation, the competent authority of a Member State has declared Article 85(1) to be inapplicable pursuant to Article 85(3) shall not be subject to compulsory notification under Article 5. The decision of the competent authority of the Member State shall be deemed to be a decision within the meaning of Article 6; it shall cease to be valid upon expiration of the period fixed by such authority but in any event not more than three years after the entry into force of this Regulation Article 8(3) shall apply.

2. Applications for renewal of decisions of the kind described in paragraph 1 shall be decided upon by transmission commission in accordance with Article 8(2).

Article 24

Implementing Provisions

The Commission shall have power to adopt implementing provisions concerning the form, contents and other details of applications pursuant to Articles 2 and 3 and of notifications pursuant to Articles 4 and 5, and concerning headings pursuant to Article 19(1) and (2).

Article 25

1. As regards agreements, decisions and concerted practices to which Article 85 of the Treaty applies by virtue of accession, the date of accession shall be substituted for the date of entry into force of this Regulation in every place where reference is made in this Regulation to this latter date.

2. Agreements, decisions and concerted practices existing at the date of accession to which Article 85 of the Treaty applies by virtue of accession shall be notified pursuant to Article 5(1) or Article 7(1) and (2) within six months from the date of accession.

3 Fines under Article 15(2) (a) shall not be imposed in respect of any act prior to notification of the agreements, decisions and practices to which paragraph 2 applies and which have been notified within the period therein specified.

4. New Member States shall take the measures referred to in Article 14(6) within six months from the date of accession after consulting the Commission.

5. The provisions of paragraphs 1 to 4 above still apply in the same way in the case of the accession of the Hellenic Republic, the Kingdom of Spain and of the Portuguese Republic.

6. The provisions of paragraphs 1 to 4 still apply in the same way in the case of the accession of Austria, Finland and Sweden. However, they do not apply to agreements, decisions and concerted practices which at the date of accession already fall under Article 53 (1) of the EEA Agreement.

This Regulation shall be binding in its entirely and directly applicable in all Member States.

References

Abreu, D., Pearce, D., and Stacchetti, E. (1986), 'Optimal Cartel Equilibria with Imperfect Monitoring', *Journal of Economic Theory* 39(1), June 1986, pp. 251–69.

Abreu, D., Pearce, D., and Stacchetti, E. (1990), 'Toward a Theory of Discounted Repeated Games with Imperfect Monitoring', *Econometrica* 58(5), September 1990, pp. 1041–63.

Aghion, P. and Bolton, P. (1987), 'Contracts as a Barrier to Entry', *American Economic Review* 77(3), June 1987, pp. 388–401.

Baker, J.B. (1989), 'Identifying Cartel Policing under Uncertainty: The U.S. Steel Industry, 1933–1939', *Journal of Law and Economics* 32(2), October 1989, pp. S47–S76.

Baker, J.B. (1993), 'Two Sherman Act Section 1 Dilemmas: Parallel Pricing, the Oligopoly Problem, and Contemporary Economic Theory', *The Antitrust Bulletin* 38(1), Spring 1993, pp. 143–219.

Baker, J.B. and Bresnahan, T.F. (1992), 'Empirical Methods of Identifying and Measuring Market Power', *Antitrust Law Journal* 6, 1992, pp. 3–16.

Baumol, W.J. and Blinder, A.S. (1988), *Economics – Principles and Policy*, 4th edn, San Diego, Harcourt Brace Jovanovich.

Baumol, W.J. and Ordover, J.A. (1985), 'Use of Antitrust to Subvert Competition', *Journal of Law and Economics* 28(2), May 1985, pp. 247–65.

Baxter, W. (1990), 'Substitutes, Complements and the Contours of the Firm', in Trebilcock, M., Walker, M. & Mathewson, F. (eds.) (1990), *The Law and Economics of Competition Policy*, Vancouver, Fraser Institute, pp. 27–41.

Becker, G. (1968) 'Crime and Punishment: an Economic Approach', *Journal of Political Economy* 76(2), March 1968, pp. 169–217.

Bernheim, B.D. and Whinston, M.D. (1985), 'Common Marketing Agency as a Device for Facilitating Collusion', *Rand Journal of Economics* 16(2), Summer 1985, pp. 269–81.

Bernheim, B.D. and Whinston, M.D. (1986), 'Common Agency', *Econometrica* 54(4), July 1986, pp. 923–42.

Bernheim, B.D. and Whinston, M.D. (1990), 'Multimarket Contact and Collusive Behaviour', *Rand Journal of Economics* 21(1), Spring 1990, pp. 1–26.

Besanko, D. and Spulber, D.F. (1989a), 'Delegated Law Enforcement and Non-cooperative Behaviour', *Journal of Law, Economics and Organisation* 5(1), Spring 1989, pp. 25–52.

Besanko, D. and Spulber, D.F. (1989b), 'Antitrust Enforcement under Asymmetric Information', *Economic Journal* 99(396), June 1989, pp. 408–25.

Bolton, P. and Whinston, M.D. (1993), 'Incomplete Contracts, Vertical Integration and Supply Assurance', *Review of Economic Studies* 60(1), January 1993, pp. 121–48.

Bresnahan, T.F. (1989), 'Empirical Studies of Industries with Market Power', in Schmalensee, R. and Willig, R. (eds.), *Handbook of Industrial Organization*, vol. 2, New York, Elsevier Science Publishers, pp. 1011–57.

Brown, A. (1993), 'Notification of Agreements to the EC Commission: Whether to submit to a flawed system', *European Law Review* 17, pp. 323–42.

Cassiman, B. (1996), 'The Organization of Research Corporations snf Researcher Ability', Barcelona, Universitat Pompeu Fabra, mimeo.

Chang, M.H. (1992), 'Intertemporal Product Choice and Its Effect on Collusive Firm Behaviour', *International Economic Review* 33(4), November 1992, pp. 773–93.

Coase, R.H. (1972), 'Durability and Monopoly', *Journal of Law and Economics* 15(1), April 1972, pp. 143–9.

Comanor, W.S. (1985) 'Vertical Price Fixing, Vertical Market Restrictions and the New Antitrust Policy', *Harvard Law Review* 98, pp. 983–1002.

Comanor, W.S. (1990) 'The Two Economics of Vertical Restraints', *Review of Industrial Organisation* 5(2), Summer 1990, pp. 99–126.

Comanor, W.S. and Rey, P. (1997), 'Vertical Restraints and the Market Power of Large Distributors', Los Angeles, University of California, mimeo.

Commission des Communautés Européennes, (1972 to 1995), *Annual Report on Competition Policy*, Office des publications Officielles des Communautés Européennes.

Commission des Communautés Européennes (1990), *Droit de la Concurrence dans les Communautés Européennes – Volume I: règles applicables aux entreprises*, Office des publications Officielles des Communautés Européennes.

Commission des Communautés Européennes (1996), *Survey of the Member State National Laws Governing Vertical Distribution Agreements*, Office des publications Officielles des Communautés Européennes.

Commission des Communautés Européennes (1997) *Green Paper on Vertical Restraints in EC Competition Policy*, Office des publications Officielles des Communautés Européennes, January 1997.

Common Market Law Review (MLR), 1972, 1976, 1992, 1993.

Compte, O. (1994), 'Private Observations, Communication and Coordination in Repeated Games', Stanford University, Ph.D. Dissertation, 1994.

Compte, O., Jenny, F. and Rey, P. (1996), 'Capacity constraints, mergers and collusion', mimeo.

Crampin, L. (1997), 'Empty Core Theory and its Relevance to Real-World Industries', University of Cambridge, BA Dissertation.

Cramton, P.C. and Palfrey, T.R. (1990), 'Cartel Enforcement with Uncertainty about Costs', *International Economic Review* 31(1), February 1990, pp. 17–47.

Crocker, K.J. and Lyon, T.P. (1994) 'What do Facilitating Practices Facilitate? An Empirical Investigation of Most Favoured Nation Clauses in Natural Gas Contracts', *Journal of Law and Economics* 37(2), October 1994, pp. 297–322.

d'Aspremont C. and Jacquemin, A. (1988), 'Cooperative and Non-cooperative R&D in Duopoly with Spillovers', *American Economic Review* 78(5), December 1988, pp. 1133–7.

De Bondt, R. (1997), 'Spillovers and Innovative Activities', *International Journal of Industrial Organization* 5(1), February 1997, pp. 1–28.

Deneckere, R. (1983), 'Duopoly Supergames with Product Differentiation', *Economics Letters* 11, 1983, pp. 37–42.

De Woot, P. (ed.) (1990), *High Technology Europe: Strategic Issues for Global Competitiveness*, Oxford, Basil Blackwell, 1990.

Diamond, P.A., (1971), 'A Model of Price Adjustment', *Journal of Economic Theory* 3(2), June 1971, pp 156–68.

Dobson, P. and Waterson, M. (1996a), 'Vertical Restraints and Competition Policy', *OFT Research Paper*, December 1996.

Dobson, P. and Waterson, M. (1996b), 'The Competition Effects of Resale Price Maintenance', University of Nottingham, mimeo.

Ellison, G. (1994), 'Theories of Cartel Stability and the Joint Executive Committee', *Rand Journal of Economics* 25(1), Spring 1994, pp. 37–57.

Farrell, J. and Maskin, E. (1989), 'Renegotiation-Proof Equilibrium: Reply', *Journal of Economic Theory* 49(2), December 1989, pp. 376–8.

Feinberg, R.M. (1989), 'Imports as a Threat to Cartel Stability', *International Journal of Industrial Organization* 7(2), 1989, pp. 281–8.

Forrester, N. (1998), 'The Current Goals of EC Competition Policy', forthcoming in Amato, G. and Ehlermann, C.-D *Proceedings of the Florence Annual Workshop on Competition Law*, Florence, European University Institute, 1998.

Freeman, P. (1997) 'New Developments in Vertical Restraints', Simmons & Simmons, mimeo.

Friedman, J. (1971) 'A non-cooperative equilibrium for supergames', *Review of Economic Studies* 38(1), pp. 1–12.

Ginsburg, D.H. (1993), 'Nonprice Competition', *Antitrust Bulletin* 38(1), Spring 1993, pp. 83–111.

Green, E.J., and Porter, R.H. (1984), 'Non-cooperative Collusion under Imperfect Price Information', *Econometrica* 52(1), January 1984, pp. 87–100.

Greene W. (1993), *Econometric Analysis*, 2nd edn, New York, Macmillan.

Grossman, S.J. and Hart, O.D. (1986), 'The Costs and Benefits of Ownership: A Theory of Vertical and Lateral Integration', *Journal of Political Economy* 94(4), August 1986, pp. 691–719.

Grossman, G. and Shapiro, C. (1986), 'Research Joint Ventures: An Antitrust Analysis', *Journal of Law, Economics and Organisation* 2(2), pp. 315–37.

Guerrin, M. and Kyriazis, G. (1992), 'Cartels: Proofs and Procedural Issues', *1992 Fordham Corporate Law Institute*.

Häckner, J. (1994), 'Collusive Pricing in Markets for Vertically Differentiated Products', *International Journal of Industrial Organization* 12(2), June 1994, pp. 155–77.

Harrington, J.E. Jr. (1987), 'Collusion in Multiproduct Oligopoly Games under a Finite Horizon', *International Economic Review* 28(1), February 1987, pp. 1–14.

Harrington, J.E. Jr. (1989), 'Collusion among Asymmetric Firms: The Case of Different Discount Factors', *International Journal of Industrial Organization* 7(2), 1989, pp. 289–307.

Harrington, J.E. Jr. (1991), 'The Determination of Price and Output Quotas in a Heterogeneous Cartel', *International Economic Review* 32(4), November 1991, pp. 767–92.

Hart, O. and Tirole, J. (1990), 'Vertical Integration and Market Foreclosure', *Brookings Papers on Economic Activity*, Special Issue, 1990, pp. 205–85.

Holt, C. and Scheffman, D. (1987), 'Facilitating Practices: the Effects of Advance Notice and Best-Price Policies', *Rand Journal of Economics* 18(2), Summer 1987, pp. 187–97.

Hörnig, S., Lofaro, A., and Phlips, L. (1996), 'How Much to Collude without Being Detected', discussion paper.

Jacquemin, A., and Slade, M.E. (1989), 'Cartels, Collusion, and Horizontal Merger', in Schmalensee & Willig (eds.) (1989), *Handbook of Industrial Organisation*, vol. 2, New York, Elsevier Science Publishers, pp. 415–73.

Johnsen, D. B. (1991), 'Property Rights to Cartel Rents: The Socony-Vacuum Story', *Journal of Law and Economics* 34(1), April 1991, pp. 177–203.

Jullien, B., Rey, P. and Vergé, T. (1997), 'Pratique des prix imposés et collusion', *IDEI*, University of Toulouse, mimeo.

Kandori, M. and Matsushima, H. (1994), 'Private Observation and Communication in Implicit Collusion', *Woodrow Wilson School Discussion Paper in Economics* 168, Princeton University, January 1994, 39 pages.

Kay, J.A. (1990), 'Vertical Restraints in European Competition Policy', *European Economic Review* 34(2–3), May 1990, pp. 551–61.

Kay, J., Manning, A. and Szymanski, S. (1989), 'The Economic Benefits of the Channel Tunnel', *Economic Policy* 8, April 1989, pp. 211–34.

Kihlstrom, R. and Vives, X. (1992), 'Collusion by Asymmetrically Informed Firms', *Journal of Economics and Management Strategy* 1(2), Summer 1992, pp. 371–96.

Klemperer, P. (1987), 'Markets with Consumer Switching Costs', *Quarterly Journal of Economics* 102(2), May 1987, pp. 375–94.

Klemperer, P. (1995), 'Competition When Consumers Have Switching Costs: An Overview with Applications to Industrial Organisation, Macroeconomics and International Trade', *Review of Economic Studies* 62(4), October 1995, pp. 515–39.

Korah, V., (1990), 'From Legal Form towards Economic Efficiency – Article 85(1) of the EEC Treaty in Contrast to US Antitrust,' *Antitrust Bulletin* 35(4), Winter 1990, pp. 1009–36.

Kovacic, W. E. (1993), 'The Identification and Proof of Horizontal Agreements under the Antitrust Laws', *The Antitrust Bulletin* 38(1), Spring 1993, pp. 5–81.

Krattenmaker, T. and Salop, S. (1986), 'Anticompetitive Exclusion: Raising Rivals' Costs to Achieve Power over Price', *Yale Law Journal* 96, pp. 209–93.

Kühn, K.-U., Seabright, P. and Smith, A. (1992), 'Competition Policy Research: Where Do We Stand?', *CEPR Occasional Paper No. 8*, July 1992, 30 pages.

Kühn, K.-U. and Vives, X., (1994), *Information exchange among firms and their impact on competition*, Report to DG-IV.

Langenfeld, J. (1989), '"Identifying Cartel Policing under Uncertainty: The U.S. Steel Industry, 1933-1939": Comment.', *Journal of Law and Economics* 32(2), October 1989, pp. S77–S82.

Lanning, S.G. (1987), 'Costs of Maintaining a Cartel', *The Journal of Industrial Economics* 36(2), December 1987, pp. 157–74.

Levy, D.T. and Reitzes, J.D. (1993), 'Product Differentiation and the Ability to Collude: Where Being Different Can Be an Advantage', *Antitrust Bulletin* 38(2), Summer 1993, pp. 349–68.

Lyons, B. (1996), 'The Empirical Relevance of Efficient Contract Theory: Inter-Firm Contracts', *Oxford Review of Economic Policy* 12(4), Winter 1996, pp. 27–52.

McAfee, R.P. and Schwartz, M. (1993), 'Opportunism in Multilateral Vertical Contracting: Nondiscrimination, Exclusivity and Uniformity', *American Economic Review* 84(1), March 1994, pp. 210–30.

McChesney, F. S. and Shughart, W. F. II (eds.) (1995), *The Causes and Consequences of Antitrust: the Public-Choice Perspective*, Chicago and London, University of Chicago Press.

Martin, S. (1990), Fringe Size and Cartel Stability, Working Paper 90/16, Florence, European University Institute.

Martin, S. (1993), *Advanced Industrial Economics*, Oxford, Blackwell.

Myer, M., Milgrom, P. and Roberts, J. (1992) 'Organizational Prospects, Influence Costs and Ownership Changes', *CEPR Discussion Paper* 665, June 1992, 25 pages.

Neven, D.J., Nuttall, R. and Seabright, P. (1993), *Merger in Daylight: The Economics and Politics of European Merger Control*, London, CEPR.

Neven, D.J. and Phlips, L. (1985), 'Discriminating Oligopolists and Common Markets', *Journal of Industrial Economics* 34(2), December 1985, pp. 133–49.

Neven, D.J. and Röller, L.H. (1996), 'Rent Sharing in the European Airline Industry', *European Economic Review* 40(3–5), April 1996, pp. 933–40.

Neven, D.J. and Seabright, P. (1997), 'Trade Liberalisation and the Co-ordination of Competition Policy', in Waverman, L. (ed.), *Competition Policy in a Global Economy*, London, Routledge.

Ng, C.K. and Seabright, P. (1997) 'Competition, Privatisation and Productive Efficiency: Evidence from the Airline Industry.' University of Cambridge, mimeo.

Nye, W. (1992), 'Can a joint venture lessen competition more than a merger?', *Economics Letters* 40(4), December 1992, pp. 487–9.

Ordover, J. and Willig, R. (1985), 'Antitrust for High-Technology Industries: Assessing Research Joint Ventures and Mergers', *Journal of Law and Economics* 27(2), May 1985, pp. 311–33.

Organisation for Economic Cooperation & Development (1994), *Competition Policy and Vertical Restraints: Franchising Agreements*.

Phlips, L. (1996), 'On the Detection of Collusion and Predation', *European Economic Review* 40(3–5), April 1996, pp. 495–510.

Porter, M.E. (1985), *Competitive Advantage: Creating and Sustaining Superior Performance*, New York, Free Press.

Porter, M.E. (1990), *The Competitive Advantage of Nations*, London, Macmillan.

Porter, R.H. (1983), 'Optimal Cartel Trigger Price Strategies', *Journal of Economic Theory* 29(2), April 1983, pp. 313–28.

Rees, R. (1985), 'Cheating in a duopoly supergame', *Journal of Industrial Economics* 33(4), June 1985, pp. 387–400.

Rey, P. and Stiglitz, J. E. (1988), 'Vertical Restraints and Producers' Competition', *National Bureau of Economic Research Working Paper* 2601, May 1988.

Rey, P. and Tirole, J. (1986), 'The Logic of Vertical Restraints', *American Economic Review* 76(5), December 1986, pp. 921–39.

Rey, P. and Tirole, J. (1996), 'A Primer on Foreclosure', *IDEI*, University of Toulouse, mimeo.

Riley, A.J. (1993), 'More Radicalism, Please: the Notice on Cooperation Between National Courts and the Commission in Applying Articles 85 and 86 of the EEC Treaty', *European Competition Law Review* 3, pp. 91–6

Robb, G. (1994), *Balzac: A Biography*, London, Picador.

Ross, T.W. (1992), 'Cartel Stability and Product Differentiation', *International Journal of Industrial Organisation* 10(1), 1992, pp. 1–13.

Rotemberg, J. and Saloner, G. (1986), A Supergame-Theoretic Model of Price Wars during Booms, *American Economic Review* 76, pp. 390–407.

Salop, S. and Sheffman, D. (1983), 'Raising Rivals' Costs', *American Economic Review* 73(2), May 1983, pp. 267–71.

Schelling, T.C. (1960), *The Strategy of Conflict*, Cambridge Mass, Harvard University Press.

Scherer, (1980) *Industrial Market Structure and Performance*, Chicago Ill., Rand McNally.

Segerstrom, P.S. (1988), 'Demons and Repentance', *Journal of Economic Theory* 45(1), June 1988, pp. 32–52.

Sjostrom, W. (1989), 'Collusion in Ocean Shipping: A Test of Monopoly and Empty Core Models', *Journal of Political Economy* 97(5), October 1989, pp. 1160–79.

Slade, M.E. (1992), 'Vancouver's Gasoline-Price Wars: An Empirical Exercise in Uncovering Supergame Strategies', *Review of Economic Studies* 59(2), April 1992, pp. 257–76.

Sleuwaegen, L. (1986), 'On the Nature and Significance of Collusive Price Leadership', *International Journal of Industrial Organization* 4(2), June 1986, pp. 177–88.

Smith, A. and Venables, A. (1988), 'Completing the Internal Market in the European Community: Some Industry Simulations', *European Economic Review* 32(7), September 1988, pp. 1501–25.

Stevens D. (1994), 'The 'Comfort Letter': Old Problems, New Developments', *European Competition Law Review* 2, pp. 81–8.

Stigler, G. (1965) 'A theory of Oligopoly', *Journal of Political Economy* 72(1), pp. 44–61.

Sugden, R. (1995), 'A Theory of Focal Points', *Economic Journal* 105(430), May 1995, pp. 535–50.

Suzumura, K. (1992), 'Cooperative and Non-cooperative R&D in an Oligopoly with Spillovers', *American Economic Review* 82(5), December 1992, pp. 1307–20.

Telser, L.G. (1985), 'Cooperation, Competition and Efficiency', *Journal of Law and Economics* 28(2), May 1985, pp. 271–95.

Temple Lang, J. (1981), 'The Powers of the Commission to Order Interim Measures in Competition Cases', *Common Market Law Review* 18, pp. 49–61.

Temple Lang, J. (1981), 'Community Antitrust Law: Compliance and Enforcement', *Common Market Law Review* 18, pp. 335–62.

Tirole, J. (1988), *The Theory of Industrial Organization*, Cambridge, Massachusetts and London, England, MIT Press.

Van Bael, I. (1986), 'The Antitrust Settlement Practice of the EC Commission', *Common Market Law Review* 23, pp. 61–90.

Van Bael, I. (1995), 'Fining à la Carte: the Lottery of EU Competition Law', *European Competition Law Review* 4, pp. 237–43.

Vickers, J. (1996), 'Market Power and Inefficiency: a Contracts Perspective', *Oxford Review of Economic Policy* 12(4), Winter 1996, pp. 11–26.

Von Weizsäcker, C.C. (1980), 'A Welfare Analysis of Barriers to Entry', *Bell Journal of Economics* 11(2), Autumn 1980, pp. 399–420.

Walbroeck, D. (1986), 'New Forms of Settlements of Antitrust Cases and Procedural Safeguards: Is Regulation 17 Falling Into Abeyance?', *European Law Review*. 11 (August) pp. 268–80.

Walbroeck, M. (1990–1991, 4th edn), *Droit Economique des Communautés Européennes*, Presses Universitaires de Bruxelles, Université Libre de Bruxelles.

Whish R. (1993), *Competition Law*, 3rd edn, London, Butterworths.

Whish, R. and Suffrin, B. (1988), 'Article 85 and the Rule of Reason', *Oxford Yearbook of European Law* pp. 1–38.

Winter, R. (1997), 'Colluding on relative prices', *Rand Journal of Economics* 28(2), Summer 1997, pp. 359–71.

Yao, D.A. and DeSanti, S. S. (1993), 'Game Theory and the Legal Analysis of Tacit Collusion', *The Antitrust Bulletin*, Spring 1993, pp. 113–41.

Index

List of Cases